D0960166

Gene Selleck
10/4/84

BRIDGE STRATEGY
AT TRICK ONE

Fred L. Karpin

DOVER PUBLICATIONS, INC.

NEW YORK

Published in Canada by General Publishing Company, Ltd., 30 Lesmill Road, Don Mills, Toronto,
Ontario.
Published in the United Kingdom by Constable
and Company, Ltd., 10 Orange Street, London WC 2.

This Dover edition, first published in 1976, is
an unabridged and corrected republication of the
work originally published by Dell Publishing Co.,
Inc., New York, in 1964 under the title *Winning
Play in Contract Bridge: Strategy at Trick One.*

International Standard Book Number: 0-486-23296-4
Library of Congress Catalog Card Number: 75-30256

Manufactured in the United States of America
Dover Publications, Inc.
180 Varick Street
New York, N.Y. 10014

contents

♠ introduction

Fred Karpin has established himself as the most prolific writer of bridge books in America. Not only students of the game in his own country but bridge experts throughout the world read and admire his work. He can be proud of this; he should be prouder still of the fact that he has made a unique contribution to the voluminous literature of bridge by singling out and exhaustively analyzing some aspects of the game that previously had been neglected.

In this, the latest of Fred Karpin's books, the subject is both illuminating and appealing. I am proud to introduce the book, not only because of its subject but also because I think it is a great book.

End positions are dramatic and several worthy books have been written about them. It seldom occurs to students of the game that valid end positions would not have occurred if the foundation, the play to the first trick, had been inadequate.

The first trick is not merely the play of four cards, one by each player. There is a background in the bidding. There is a consequence in the result of the remaining twelve tricks. Mr. Karpin's modestly titled book is actually a treatise on everything that is important in bridge. I have learned much from it and I trust that you, the reader, will consider yourself equally rewarded by reading it.

—ALBERT H. MOREHEAD
New York, 1964

♠ foreword

During the past decade, as a direct consequence of the introduction, development, and refinement of the point-count method of bidding, there was a tremendous over-emphasis on bidding technique, per se. Under the circumstances, it was rather natural that the study and mastery of the technique of play became de-emphasized and relegated to a secondary role—the forgotten man of bridge, as it were.

As a result of this inordinate stress on bidding technique, the general standard of play declined appreciably; and through either lack of time to devote to a more thorough understanding of the play, or just plain lethargy, an unhealthy atmosphere of unbalance was created. To borrow a phrase from our psychologists, the majority of our players lapsed into a condition of "arrested development": as their bidding ability spiralled upward to greater heights, their playing ability simultaneously descended to lower depths. In my opinion, the disparity between proper bidding and proper play has currently become so pronounced that the plane of average bridge living has retrogressed to a mere survival level.

That this inverse state of affairs should exist is most lamentable and, actually, paradoxical, for surely bidding should be subordinate to the play of the hand. After all, when one stops to consider it, bidding is nothing more than a contractual estimate of the number of tricks that one hopes to win in the play. This prevailing state of affairs—of the cart's being put before the horse—is doubly unfortunate for the new generation of bridge players who were attracted to the game as an avocation because it was sold to them as the most fascinating and mentally-stimulating of all the card games. Through expert guidance, they learned how to bid authoritatively, to arrive at the optimum contract—and were then abandoned and left to their own resources (mainly trial and error) to fulfill their contracts.

Viewing the situation from a pedagogic point of view, there is nothing more frustrating to aspiring bridge players, and nothing more conducive to the shattering of their confidence, than the too-frequent arrival at a game or slam contract that goes down in defeat through incorrect play of the cards. Unless these neglected ones can be made to see that they have played the hand incorrectly, the cumulative impact of their defeats must ultimately make them feel that they have bid too optimistically. And, psychologically, from having been burned so often, they will tend to tread too cautiously in the future and approach their bidding in unduly pessimistic fashion; they will now embark on the path of underbidding, with the desired effect being to obtain at least a little profit, instead of showing a loss. The inevitable result will be that instead of trying to elevate their standard of play to their higher standard of bidding, they will lower their standard of bidding to the level of necessary survival. All of which can be summed up in one word: degeneration.

The *general* purpose of this book is to assist in re-establishing the correct relationship between bidding and play: to bring the play of the cards to the fore, where it properly belongs. It is the hope of the author that in the not too distant future, there will come about a resurgence of interest in the *play* of the cards, leading to a renaissance of playing ability. Only then will the healthy and normal balance between bidding and play become restored, and accurate bidding will achieve its just reward—the fulfillment of the contract.

The *specific* purpose of this book is to get the reader off on the right foot: to enable him to observe and understand *how all-important the play at trick one can be, and how it can determine his destiny*. As an undisputed fact of life at the bridge table, continuing victories are not achieved by some fortuitous fall of the cards at tricks 10, 11, 12, or 13. They are won early in the game, when the requisite "long-range" strategy and tactics of the specific deal are formulated and promptly put into action. Far more often than one imagines, bridge victories are won (or lost) right at the opening lead, when the defenders launch their initial attack. What happens at trick one often leads, inexorably, to victory or defeat: the correct play (or lead) is made, and victory becomes guaranteed; the incorrect play (or defense) is made, and defeat becomes unavoidable, for there now can be no recovery and no escape.

In my opinion, the history of most deals is the history of trick one, and is written in indelible ink. As to whether my opinion is valid or not, the reader can determine for himself by (1) recalling how many unnecessary tragedies *he* has experienced by playing hurriedly and/or thoughtlessly at trick one, and by (2) observing the evidence as it unfolds in this book.

And now the curtain rises. Or, to pervert Shakespeare and Hamlet, his spokesman of the moment: "The play's the thing." Enter Act I.

—F.L.K.

chapter 1 To Finesse or Not To Finesse

♠ It is an undisputed fact that the most recurring type of play in bridge is the finesse.* Although no official statistics have been compiled regarding the frequency of occurrence of finesses, reliable sources estimate that the opportunities for the employment of a finesse arise on the average about once per deal. Sometimes, in a particular deal, there will be no finesses in existence; but, in other deals, the opportunities for finessing may arise two, three, or even four times.

Generally speaking—and perhaps at the risk of appearing to be naive—the primary objective of a finesse is to gain a vitally needed trick by creating a winner that wasn't there before. In the hands of the expert player, the finesse has become a most powerful tool, for he has learned how to wield it selectively and not promiscuously. In the hands of the non-expert player, who repeatedly applies the finesse in indiscriminate and automatic fashion, it develops into a play that often results in destruction (or depletion of the financial resources) of the user. Far too frequently the non-expert plays out a hand as though it were ordained that finesses are compulsory whenever a finessing position exists. As a consequence, he loses many contracts that would have been fulfilled had a little judgment—instead of wishful thinking—been applied.

And thus we arrive at the crux of the matter: *the finesse*

*Defined formally, a "finesse" might be described as *an attempt to win a trick with a specific card when there is a higher card (or cards) outstanding.* In effect the finesse is really "wishful thinking" put into action. That is, you figuratively put a card, which is possessed by one of your two enemies, into the hand of the one specific enemy you would desire to have it—and then proceed to ambush it by surrounding and trapping it. In other words, you create the condition that must exist if your finesse is to succeed—and then attack as though your creation were a reality.

is not an all-purpose tool. It is a "special-occasion" tool, to be used only when observation, reinforced by judgment, indicates that it is the most logical one for tackling the situation at hand.

The deals in this chapter—To Finesse or Not To Finesse —are devoted to a presentation of finessing situations that occurred AT TRICK ONE. Each of these deals arose in actual competition. If my publisher had insisted on my adding a subtitle to this chapter heading, I would have added: "He who lives by the finesse will perish by the finesse."

Deal 1:

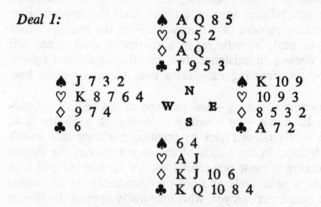

```
              ♠ A Q 8 5
              ♡ Q 5 2
              ◇ A Q
              ♣ J 9 5 3
♠ J 7 3 2              ♠ K 10 9
♡ K 8 7 6 4     N      ♡ 10 9 3
◇ 9 7 4      W    E    ◇ 8 5 3 2
♣ 6             S      ♣ A 7 2
              ♠ 6 4
              ♡ A J
              ◇ K J 10 6
              ♣ K Q 10 8 4
```

With no adverse bidding, South arrived at a *five-club* contract. West opened the two of spades.

South, not one to spurn a finesse, put up dummy's queen, East's king winning. East returned the ten of hearts, and now having little choice, declarer finessed again, losing to West's king. Since no one has as yet invented a way to avoid the loss of a trick to an adversely held ace of trumps, South went down a trick.

Let's you and I play this hand together. West opens the two of spades. We take inventory: we have a potential loser in spades; we have no losers in hearts, since two of dummy's hearts can be discarded on two of our high diamonds after trumps are drawn (our heart ace will take care of dummy's queen, after which we can ruff out our jack of hearts); we have no losers in diamonds; and a trump trick will be lost to the defenders' ace. Just two losers is all we have.

So we win the opening lead with the ace of spades and lead a trump. East will take his ace on the first or second lead of trumps. He then returns a heart, which we win with our ace. Making sure that the opponents' trumps have all been removed from circulation, we then play a diamond to the board's ace, after which we overtake the queen with our king. Now come the jack and ten of diamonds, upon which we discard dummy's two and five of hearts. Next we trump out the jack of hearts, graciously concede a spade trick to the outstanding king of spades—and chalk up the score for a game bid and made. And we take no credit for playing the hand well. Anybody could have done as well.

Deal 2:

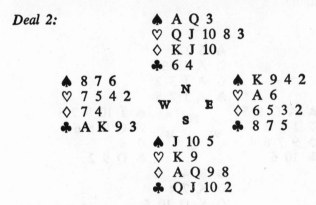

Both sides vulnerable. South dealer.

South	West	North	East
1 ♣	Pass	1 ♡	Pass
1 NT	Pass	3 NT	Pass
Pass	Pass		

West chose to open the eight of spades, and South, feeling that no harm could come from taking the finesse, played dummy's three-spot. East took the trick with the king and shifted to the eight of clubs. South covered this with the ten, West's king winning. West then played back the three of clubs, and East's seven forced declarer's jack.

Declarer now plunked down the king of hearts, which East won. East then produced the five of clubs, and declarer's Q 2 was entrapped by West's K 9. All in all, the defenders took one spade, one heart, and three clubs.

Shall you and I play this one also? Let's go.

We count our tricks and perceive that we have one spade, four diamonds, and four hearts as soon as we drive out the defenders' ace of hearts. Hence, why risk the finesse in spades?

So we win the opening lead with dummy's ace of spades and lead a heart to our king. It wins, let's assume. Then the heart nine is overtaken by dummy's ten, East taking his ace. No matter what East returns, our contract is now there for the taking.

Deal 3:

```
                    ♠ 6 2
                    ♡ A 10 3
                    ◇ A J 3 2
                    ♣ A J 7 5
    ♠ A Q 8 5            N        ♠ J 10 9 7 3
    ♡ J 5 2                       ♡ Q 9 8 6
    ◇ 9 7 6 4     W        E      ◇ 8
    ♣ 10 6            S           ♣ Q 9 2
                    ♠ K 4
                    ♡ K 7 4
                    ◇ K Q 10 5
                    ♣ K 8 4 3
```

Both sides vulnerable. North dealer.

North	East	South	West
1 ◇	Pass	2 NT	Pass
3 NT	Pass	Pass	Pass

Against South's *three–no–trump* contract, West selected the opening lead of the ten of clubs. Had he chosen to lead his best suit, spades, declarer would have made his ninth trick then and there.

The proper play to make at trick one is much easier when you're looking at all four hands instead of just the North-South hands. At the table, when the club ten is opened, you speculate about the significance of the lead: West could have the 10 9 x x; or perhaps the Q 10 9 x; or, perhaps, he's leading from the doubleton 10 9; or perhaps from the 10 x, the top of a worthless doubleton. It could be any of these or even some other combination.

Your worry on the hand is (or *should be*) that East might obtain the lead, to play a spade through your K x. And, if *West* happens to possess the spade ace, your goose will be cooked. So, consciously or subconsciously, you realize that you must do everything in your power to keep East out of the lead. Of course, all along you are aware of the fact that you have just eight tricks.

When this deal arose in actual play, my partner, Dr. Joseph Henry, professor of dentistry at Howard University, made the winning play after about 10 seconds of observation and thought. He permitted the ten of clubs to win! It mattered not what West led next for the contract was now assured. Actually, West returned another club, and Joe made three club tricks, plus four diamonds and two hearts.

In retrospect, allowing West's ten of clubs to win the opening lead was such a logical, simple play. If the five adversely held clubs were divided 3-2 originally, the ace and king of clubs would then fell the outstanding clubs, thereby promoting dummy's jack of clubs into declarer's ninth trick. And, if West had started with the Q 10 9 x x or the Q 10 9 x of clubs, the situation would be revealed on either the opening lead (East failing to follow suit) or on the second club lead, taken by declarer's king (East failing to follow suit). Regardless of which of these two developments occurred, it would then become routine to finesse West for his then known queen of clubs.

And, if West's opening lead of the club ten had been a singleton, the hope now would be that West would either shift to a spade or that East would have the ace of spades, resulting in declarer's spade king becoming his ninth trick.

I have presented this deal to five non-expert players and asked them what they would play from dummy on the opening lead of the ten of clubs. Three of them said they would play the jack. The other two are still thinking.

If the finesse of the jack is taken at trick one, East will cover with the queen—and East's nine of clubs will become an entry if declarer persists in leading out the clubs. The spade shift by East will then defeat declarer.

Deal 4:
If one were to look at all four hands below, the fulfillment of the *six-heart* contract would be easy: simply finesse West for the queen of trumps. But again, at the table it's illegal to look at all four hands before you play.

When our actual declarer, the late Sidney Silodor, encountered this deal, he had no trouble whatsoever with it.

```
                ♠ K 9 2
                ♡ K 7 6 2
                ◇ A J 4 3
                ♣ A 4
   ♠ A J 8 5 3       N       ♠ Q 10 7 6 4
   ♡ Q 5 3                   ♡ 4
   ◇ 10 9      W       E     ◇ K 7 6 5 2
   ♣ 7 5 3         S         ♣ Q 6
                ♠ ———
                ♡ A J 10 9 8
                ◇ Q 8
                ♣ K J 10 9 8 2
```

East-West vulnerable. South dealer.

South	West	North	East
1 ♡	Pass	2 ◇	Pass
3 ♣	Pass	5 ♡	Pass
6 ♡	Pass	Pass	Pass

On the opening lead of the diamond ten, Sidney promptly put up dummy's ace (What! No finesse?), and just as promptly dropped the queen from his own hand. A trump was then led to the ace, after which the jack of trumps was finessed successfully. After drawing trumps and felling East's queen of clubs on the second club lead, Sidney waltzed in with all thirteen tricks.

The reader might well ask: "But what if the jack of hearts finesse had lost to *East's* (hypothetical) queen?" All right, that's a fair question. Put yourself in East's seat, having just won the trick with your hypothetical queen of trumps. Be honest. Would you lay down the king of diamonds with Silodor's "singleton" queen having fallen on the opening lead? Couldn't your partner have led the ten-spot from the 10-9-8 combination? Wouldn't you return either a spade or a club?

Sidney, of course, was fully aware of the fact that the jack of hearts might easily have lost to East's queen—but he also foresaw that if this came to pass, East would almost surely *not* return the diamond king. And, whatever else East chose to return, South would have the opportunity of establishing the club suit.

Let's go back to trick one for a brief moment. I believe very few (if any at all) would take the diamond finesse at trick one, for there exists too much danger that it might be a singleton lead; and that upon winning the trick with the king, East would return a diamond for West to trump. Yet, until the truth becomes known and while South is coming to the conclusion to decline the finesse, there will persist the gnawing and lingering thought that West *may* be leading deceptively from the K 10 9 x or K 10 9 x x combination into North's first bid suit, diamonds. And once South begins to reflect on this possibility, he *may* decide to finesse. Will he then recover by guessing the location of the trump queen?

This is another deal that you might try out on some of your friends. Give East the Q 4 of trumps and transfer the four of spades to the West hand. See if your friends, sitting East, will play the diamond king after winning a trick with the queen of trumps.

Deal 5:

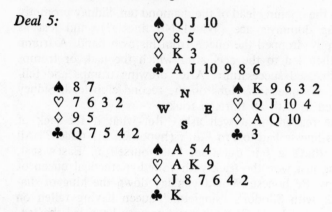

♠ Q J 10
♡ 8 5
◇ K 3
♣ A J 10 9 8 6

♠ 8 7   ♠ K 9 6 3 2
♡ 7 6 3 2   N   ♡ Q J 10 4
◇ 9 5   W   E   ◇ A Q 10
♣ Q 7 5 4 2   S   ♣ 3

♠ A 5 4
♡ A K 9
◇ J 8 7 6 4 2
♣ K

Neither side vulnerable. East dealer.

East	South	West	North
1 ♠	Pass*	Pass	2 ♣
Pass	3 NT	Pass	Pass
Pass			

In response to partner's opening spade bid, West led the eight of spades, dummy's queen was put up, and East followed with a low spade. Evidently delighted to have obtained a "free finesse," declarer permitted the queen to win. The board's jack of spades was then laid down, which won the trick when East again refused to cover with his marked king of spades. Let me spare you the gruesome details that then followed. Eventually South went down two tricks.

It should have been apparent to South that his best chance of making the contract was to establish dummy's club suit. In order to cash the clubs later, an entry to dummy had to be developed in spades (for certainly the king of diamonds could not provide an entry since, based on the bidding, the diamond ace just had to be in the East hand).

*Having no good bid to make, South decided to pass and await developments.

At trick one, South should have overtaken the board's queen of spades with his ace. At trick two, declarer's king of clubs would be overtaken by dummy's ace, and the jack of clubs led, West taking the trick with his queen. Dummy's clubs would all now be high.

Whatever West then returned, he could not prevent declarer from bringing home his contract, for whenever declarer regained the lead, he would simply play a low spade towards dummy's J 10. East would make his king, but he could not stop declarer from reaching dummy via the jack of spades.

In this manner (properly, that is), declarer would have won five club tricks, two hearts, and two spades. And in all systems of mathematics, both past and present, this adds up to nine tricks, which was South's contractual obligation in no-trump.

Deal 6:

```
                    ♠ Q 9 7 5 4 2
                    ♡ ─────
                    ◇ 8 6 4
                    ♣ K J 4 2
♠ 8                         N         ♠ 6
♡ K Q J 10 6 5 2      W         E     ♡ A 8 4 3
◇ Q 9 7 5                   S         ◇ K J 10
♣ 3                                   ♣ Q 10 9 8 7
                    ♠ A K J 10 3
                    ♡ 9 7
                    ◇ A 3 2
                    ♣ A 6 5
```

North-South vulnerable. South dealer.

South	West	North	East
1 ♠	4 ♡	4 ♠	5 ♡
Double	Pass	5 ♠	Pass
Pass	Pass		

West opened the three of clubs; dummy's jack was put up, covered by East's queen, and taken by declarer's ace. It now became impossible for declarer to avoid the loss of two diamond tricks and one club. Down one.

Let's start with this: West's lead of the three of clubs, even though it has the appearance of being a singleton, may be his fourth highest, in which case West may very well have the queen of clubs. But if he has the queen of clubs now, won't he also have it later? Why put up the jack of clubs at trick one? Won't the future be just as good a proving ground as the present?

Look at what develops if the urge to play the jack of clubs at trick one is resisted. Dummy plays low on the opening lead, and declarer takes East's seven with the ace.

A heart is now ruffed by the board, after which declarer returns to his own hand via a trump to ruff his remaining heart in dummy. The two adverse trumps have now been picked up, and both dummy and declarer are void of hearts.

Next the ace of diamonds is cashed, followed by another diamond lead. If West wins the second diamond, he has no choice but to play a third round of diamonds to East's king. (If, instead, West elects to lead a heart, declarer will trump it in dummy while simultaneously discarding the losing club from his own hand.)

If East should decide to win the second diamond lead, he too has no choice but to lead a third diamond. (A club lead away from the queen would make a winner out of dummy's jack; or, a lead of a heart would enable South to discard his losing club while trumping the trick in dummy.)

Whichever of the opponents wins the third diamond lead is a "dead duck": if East wins it and leads either a club or a heart, he enables declarer to avoid the loss of a club trick. If West captures the third diamond trick, he has no choice but to lead either a heart or a diamond; and whichever he selects, declarer will trump in dummy while he discards the losing club from his own hand.

The reader may inquire: "But what if West had won either the second or third diamond lead and had then led another club?" Had this developed, declarer would have had no option but to finesse dummy's jack of clubs. But this uncomfortable position could have developed only *if* West had another club to lead. Certainly there was no good reason to put up the jack of clubs at trick one—and by preserving it (in combination with dummy's king), it would have made it impossible for *East* ever to play a club unless the latter wanted to give declarer a present of a trick.

Had the jack been saved, declarer would have been "forced" to make his contract: West would have no club to lead, and East couldn't afford to lead a club.

Deal 7:
You are sitting South on the following deal and have arrived at a *six–no-trump* contract via the following bidding sequence:

South	West	North	East
1 NT	Pass	6 NT	Pass
Pass	Pass		

♠ A K 8 6
♡ A Q 3
◇ K Q 9 4
♣ 8 5

```
        N
    W       E
        S
```

♠ J 10 7
♡ K 7 5 2
◇ A J 10
♣ A Q J

West opens the nine of spades, which figures to be a "top of nothing" lead. However, if you play low from dummy, and East wins with the queen, your jack of spades will become a winner. So you play low. East wins with the queen and returns a small club.

You have 11 tricks at this point. If you finesse the jack of clubs at trick two, down you go if the finesse loses. And what could be worse than getting to a small slam, taking two finesses at tricks one and two, losing both of them—and discovering subsequently that if you hadn't taken the second finesse, you could have made your contract. As you look at the above North-South hands—prior to playing to trick two—if the six adversely held hearts are divided 3-3, won't South's fourth heart become his twelfth trick? To finesse the club at trick two or not to finesse, that is the question.

Please don't infer that I have recommended—or suggested—that you, the reader, would have taken the *first* finesse in spades at trick one. I sincerely hope that you would not have, for the finesse should not have been taken. To have done so would be wrong.

Look ahead a bit as the opening spade lead is made. It's a cinch that East has the queen of spades. And if he is permitted to capture this trick, won't he automatically lead a club whether he has the king or doesn't? What else can he lead as he views the dummy? And won't you now be compelled to make the decision that will determine your destiny: to finesse the clubs or to play for a 3-3 division of the six adverse hearts?

Is it not proper to capture the opening spade lead in dummy and immediately finesse the queen of clubs? If it wins—which it will 50% of the time—you are home safely. All you now have to do is to give away the jack of spades, establishing your ten-spot as a winner, and you have twelve tricks: three spades, three hearts, four diamonds, and two clubs.

If, after you win the opening spade lead, your club finesse loses at trick two, you still have a good chance to survive. Assuming that the club finesse loses and that West returns a spade, you go up with the board's remaining high spade. (You know—well that East has the queen of spades!) You now have 11 sure winners, the jack of clubs having been created into a trick. You now play for the six

missing hearts to be divided 3-3; or, failing that, for the
opponents to make a mistake and discard a heart as you
cash your four high diamonds.* On this deal, however,
you would have had no problem, for the club finesse would
have been successful.

This deal arose in the National Open Pair Championships of 1955. Here are the four hands:

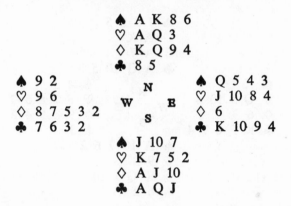

```
                    ♠ A K 8 6
                    ♡ A Q 3
                    ◇ K Q 9 4
                    ♣ 8 5
   ♠ 9 2                N            ♠ Q 5 4 3
   ♡ 9 6                             ♡ J 10 8 4
   ◇ 8 7 5 3 2    W         E        ◇ 6
   ♣ 7 6 3 2          S             ♣ K 10 9 4
                    ♠ J 10 7
                    ♡ K 7 5 2
                    ◇ A J 10
                    ♣ A Q J
```

Deal 8:
This final deal on "to finesse or not to finesse" features
a deal played many, many moons ago by Charles Solomon,** one of the world's finest players. The deal arose in

---

*The expert player would recognize that the possibilities of a "squeeze"
also existed: that if East had four hearts and the queen of spades (the latter being certain), he would be compelled to relinquish a heart or the spade
queen as South cashed his clubs and diamonds. Just interchange East's king
of clubs and West's deuce, and play out the hand as I have just suggested
(the club finesse losing, of course).

**Charlie was playing in a rubber-bridge game some years ago, and his
partner was the declarer at a four-heart contract. After taking two losing
finesses, Charlie's partner went down a trick. I was kibitzing the game and
noted that the contract could have been fulfilled without resorting to any
finesses. Charlie was equally aware of this, and at dinner after the game he
remarked to me: "They ought to change the scoring rules and award an
extra bonus—of, say, 50 points—to anyone who fulfills a contract without
taking a finesse."

Although I doubt that this change will ever take place, the thought is an
enticing one and it surely would tend to make better card players not only
out of our partners who often stake our collective existence on needless
finesses, but also out of all of us who play mechanically at times.

a regional tournament conducted by the Continental Congress Bridge League. I was sitting North and Charlie was in the South seat. East and West were, respectively, Benjamin Franklin and Thomas Jefferson who had arrived that morning to attend a Continental Congress Convention that was scheduled to begin the following week. They were spending the day in relaxation.

```
                ♠ J 9 8 5
                ♡ A K
                ◇ A 7
                ♣ A Q 10 5 3
 ♠ K Q              N          ♠ 4 3
 ♡ Q J 10 4    W       E      ♡ 8 7 6 5 2
 ◇ 6 3             S          ◇ 9 8 5 4 2
 ♣ K 9 8 7 4                  ♣ J
                ♠ A 10 7 6 2
                ♡ 9 3
                ◇ K Q J 10
                ♣ 6 2
```

Both sides vulnerable. North dealer.

North	East	South	West
1 ♣	Pass	1 ♠	Pass
4 ♠	Pass	4 NT*	Pass
5 ♠	Pass	6 ♠	Pass
Pass	Pass		

Mr. Jefferson, knowing that he had a sure trump trick and that his partner, Mr. Franklin, figured to have absolutely nothing except ability, decided that chicanery offered the best hope of defeating the slam. So he opened the nine of clubs into dummy's bid suit.

Charlie was quite unhappy when he viewed the dummy, for no expert likes to stake his existence on a finesse at trick one, especially at a slam contract. But, since the loss of a trump trick was inevitable, there was no alternative

*Jeffersonian Blackwood.

but to finesse. So Charlie put up the queen—and it won *as East dropped the jack.*

I think it is appreciated by all that Mr. Franklin's jack had to be a singleton, especially since everybody knew that Mr. Franklin had coined the expression, "A penny saved is a penny earned." Mr. Franklin was not tossing any jack of clubs to the winds if he had a lower club to toss.

Now Charlie is (and was even in those days) a pretty good mathematician. He knew that the mathematically correct way of playing the trump suit:

$$\spadesuit \text{ J 9 8 5}$$
$$\textbf{N}$$

$$\textbf{S}$$
$$\spadesuit \text{ A 10 7 6 2}$$

was to lead the jack and double-finesse—that is, to assume that East held either the queen or king, or both of these key cards. If the jack lost to West's queen or king (in theory), then when North regained the lead, the nine of spades would be led, and East would be finessed for the missing picture card. This line of play would lose only when West held exactly the doubleton K Q.* It would win (limit the trump loss to just one trick) whenever East held the K Q x or the K Q x x. And, mathematically, East figured to have the K Q 3, or the K Q 4, or the K Q 4 3, more often than he figured to have precisely the doubleton 4-3 (which would leave West with precisely the doubleton K Q).

But Charlie also realized that Mr. Jefferson was quite observant. Mr. Jefferson had seen Mr. Franklin's jack of clubs fall on the opening club lead. Mr. Jefferson didn't need the wisdom of a Solomon (no pun intended) to recognize that Mr. Franklin was now void of clubs.

Hence, if Charlie took the mathematically correct way

---

*If the four adverse trumps were divided 2-2, any line of play would limit the trump loss to just one trick: that is, the double-finesse or the initial play of the ace followed by a second lead of spades would achieve the winning result. And, if West held either the K Q 3, the K Q 4, or the K Q 4 3, two tricks would be lost owing to circumstances beyond one's control.

of playing the trump suit—by double-finessing—Mr. Jefferson figured to win the first trump lead with the queen
or king of spades. The automatic club return would then
be ruffed by Mr. Franklin for the setting trick.

So, in desperation, Charlie banged down the ace of
trumps at trick two, dropping West's queen. He then led
a second round of trumps, West's king winning. The
trumps were now all gone, and the remainder of the tricks
were Charlie's.

As a result of the excellent result on this board, we won
the tournament by three match points. Mr. Jefferson and
Mr. Franklin were second. Had our slam contract been
defeated, Mr. Jefferson and Mr. Franklin would have won
the tournament. And with that victory to spur them on,
who knows to what heights they might have risen in the
world of bridgedom? I have a feeling that, as a result of
their defeat on this deal, they were demoralized and probably retired from active competition to search for greener
and more fertile pastures. I hope they succeeded, for they
deserved a better fate than was meted out to them that
night in Philadelphia.

Through the years gone by, I have often speculated
about this deal. I wonder what would have happened if
Mr. Jefferson had gotten his hand on the queen of hearts
at trick one. Charlie would have won it with dummy's king,
and then, in all probability, would have led the jack of
spades, losing to Mr. Jefferson's queen. Upon winning
West's normal heart return, Charlie would then have led
dummy's nine of spades and would have let it ride, losing
to Mr. Jefferson's king. It's just conceivable that if they
had defeated our slam, Mr. Jefferson might have written a
book on "How to win at bridge." And, I'd wager, it would
have been a pretty good book.

But, as destiny would have it, Mr. Jefferson was a
"Virginia Gentleman," and the thought of putting his
hand on a queen was not only repulsive to him, but also
was in bad taste, especially in public. So far as Charlie
and I are concerned, we agree wholeheartedly with Mr.
Jefferson's philosophy: first a gentleman, then a bridge
player.

chapter 2 The Play from Dummy

♠ If I were given the assignment of procuring just one deal to demonstrate how important the play from dummy at trick one can be, I would select the deal that follows. This deal, which has become a classic in the annals of bridgedom, arose some years ago in the United States National Team-of-Four Championships. To me, the play made by the declarer (Sam Fry, Jr.) from dummy at trick one, is the finest example I have ever seen of convincing the opponents to believe that a certain situation existed— and too late they discovered that what had appeared to be a reality had been a mirage.

Deal 1:

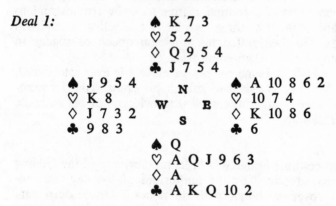

                    ♠ K 7 3
                    ♡ 5 2
                    ◇ Q 9 5 4
                    ♣ J 7 5 4

    ♠ J 9 5 4   N   ♠ A 10 8 6 2
    ♡ K 8   W   E   ♡ 10 7 4
    ◇ J 7 3 2   S   ◇ K 10 8 6
    ♣ 9 8 3   ♣ 6

                    ♠ Q
                    ♡ A Q J 9 6 3
                    ◇ A
                    ♣ A K Q 10 2

Against South's *six-club* contract, West opened the two of diamonds. It was readily apparent to Mr. Fry that if the heart finesse lost, he was doomed to defeat—unless the opponents failed to play back a spade.

So, to take out insurance (at no cost) against West's holding the king of hearts, declarer unhesitatingly put up dummy's queen of diamonds. Of course, this was covered by East's king and taken by declarer's ace.

In playing the diamond queen from dummy, Sam created in the opponents' minds the indelible impression that he himself held at least two diamonds (After all, what "normal" bridge player would play the queen from dummy when in his own hand he held the singleton ace?).

Declarer then led the ten of clubs and overtook it with dummy's jack. A heart was now led, and South's queen was captured by West's king.

Is there a bridge player alive who would censure West for his next play of the jack of diamonds? Did not declarer figure to have started with at least two diamonds? Frankly, would not have declarer made the identical play of the diamond queen *if he had held the A x of diamonds?* Looking at the situation objectively (and *not* in retrospect), one might say that if West had returned a spade instead of the jack of diamonds, he would have made an irrational lead.

With the jack of diamonds lead, which South trumped, it then became a routine matter to draw trumps and to discard dummy's three spades on South's established hearts. He then ruffed his singleton queen of spades in dummy for the slam-going trick.

If a Hall of Fame for bridge players is ever established, and Mr. Fry is asked to submit his credentials, I recommend that he submits this deal as evidence of his entrance qualifications.

Deal 2:

When contract bridge was in its infancy, one of the guiding slogans advocated by the authorities of the day was "always cover an honor with an honor." (In modern parlance, the translation would be: "always cover a picture card with a picture card.") In the majority of situations, the application of this slogan brings beneficial results. But any slogan, or rule, which contains the word "always," has many exceptions, for bridge is a game of judgment; and any rigid, undeviating, adherence to a rule must, on many occasions, turn out to be costly. As an example, witness this deal.

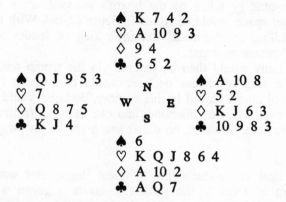

♠ K 7 4 2
♡ A 10 9 3
◇ 9 4
♣ 6 5 2

♠ Q J 9 5 3
♡ 7
◇ Q 8 7 5
♣ K J 4

♠ A 10 8
♡ 5 2
◇ K J 6 3
♣ 10 9 8 3

♠ 6
♡ K Q J 8 6 4
◇ A 10 2
♣ A Q 7

West opened the queen of spades against South's *four-heart* contract, the king was put up from dummy, and East's ace captured the trick. East now shifted to the club ten, declarer finessed the queen, and West won the trick with his king. Later on declarer lost another club, in addition to a diamond, and he went down to defeat.

Those readers who are thinking that declarer's play of dummy's spade king at trick one was a naive play are absolutely correct. In this day and age, no one opens a queen from an A Q combination at trick one. The play of the king could result only in his capture by East's ace.

Declarer was looking at four losers: one spade, one diamond, and two clubs. Of course, if East held the club king, a club loser would be eliminated and the contract fulfilled. But if the club finesse lost, there existed the possibility that the contract could still be salvaged.

This could be accomplished if dummy's king of spades were established as a winner. This hope rested on East's having been dealt either the singleton ace of spades, the A x, or the A x x. If any of these distributions existed, East's ace would fall no later than the third lead of spades.

West's queen of spades should have been permitted to win the opening lead. Let's say that West then chose to lead a diamond. East's king would be taken by declarer's ace. A low trump would next be led to dummy's nine, and a spade ruffed in the closed hand. Another low trump lead would be taken by the board's ten-spot, after which another spade would be ruffed in South's hand. With East's ace falling on this trick, dummy's king of spades would now become supreme.

Dummy would then be entered via the trump ace, and on the king of spades declarer would discard his losing seven of clubs. Played in this manner, declarer would have lost one spade, one diamond, and one club. Unfortunately for declarer, however, he didn't see it the "right" way.

Deal 3:

This deal reintroduces the identical theme that was the subject of Deal 2: the refusal to cover a queen with a king when it is apparent that the king will be captured by the ace. But whereas in the preceding deal the reason for not covering was the hope that the king might subsequently become a winner, in this deal the reason is a different one. Here there is no doubt that the king is hopelessly ambushed, with no escape possible. By not covering, declarer simply gives himself a greater chance for survival, for he keeps East, the dangerous hand, out of the lead.

```
                    ♠ A K 3
                    ♡ K 6 2
                    ◇ A K 7 5
                    ♣ 7 6 4
      ♠ 8 6              N           ♠ 9 4
      ♡ Q J 10                       ♡ A 9 8 7 4 3
      ◇ J 10 9 2    W       E        ◇ 6 3
      ♣ A 9 8 5          S           ♣ Q J 10
                    ♠ Q J 10 7 5 2
                    ♡ 5
                    ◇ Q 8 4
                    ♣ K 3 2
```

North-South vulnerable. North dealer.

North	East	South	West
1 NT	Pass	4 ♠	Pass
Pass	Pass		

West opened the queen of hearts, and declarer properly played the deuce from dummy, West's queen winning. Had declarer put up the king, he probably would have lost the first four tricks, for East, upon winning with the heart ace, undoubtedly would have returned the queen of clubs, thereby developing three club winners for the defenders.

But when declarer played low from dummy, East was not going to take his partner's queen with the ace (our East player was not that clairvoyant!) in order to shift to the queen of clubs. West's continuation of the heart jack at trick two was ruffed by declarer, who then cashed the ace and king of trumps, picking up the adverse pieces. Dummy's last heart was now ruffed by the South hand.

With the hope that the six adversely held diamonds were divided 3-3, declarer now cashed the queen, king, and ace of diamonds. Had the diamonds been divided 3-3, dummy's fourth diamond would have provided a parking place for one of declarer's losing clubs.

When it was revealed that the diamonds were not divided as hoped for and that West still possessed the high jack of diamonds, declarer led dummy's fourth diamond and conceded the trick to West. On this trick, declarer discarded his losing two of clubs. This was the position now, with West being on lead.

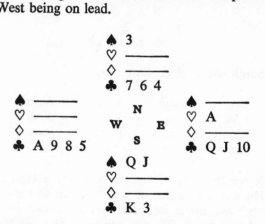

West had no option but to lead a club, making a winner out of South's king of clubs. Even if West had had another heart, it would not have altered the outcome, for a heart lead by West would have been trumped with dummy's three-spot, while declarer was discarding his own three of clubs.

By declining to cover West's queen of hearts at trick one, declarer fulfilled his contract.

Deal 4:
There is a trait all of us possess that is both admirable and essential to our well-being: the non-squandering of our resources. But there are situations where economy can turn out to be an expensive luxury. The following deal serves as an example of "false economy."

```
                    ♠ J 9 7 5
                    ♡ K Q 4
                    ◇ K Q 6
                    ♣ Q 9 2
     ♠ 8 6 4              N          ♠ 2
     ♡ A 7 3 2                       ♡ 10 9 8
     ◇ 8 7 5 3       W       E       ◇ A J 10 9
     ♣ 10 4              S          ♣ A J 7 6 5
                    ♠ A K Q 10 3
                    ♡ J 6 5
                    ◇ 4 2
                    ♣ K 8 3
```

North-South vulnerable. East dealer.

East	South	West	North
1 ♣	1 ♠	Pass	3 ♠
Pass	4 ♠	Pass	Pass
Pass			

East's opening bid of one club is not a typographical error. He was the dealer, it was his turn to bid—and he always bid whenever he held two aces, two jacks, two tens, and two nines. We can condemn him for his transgression from accepted standards, but we should not condemn him for his adherence to a principle.

West dutifully opened the ten of clubs, and declarer, not wishing to squander dummy's queen, instead played the deuce. East properly followed with the seven-spot, and declarer won the trick with his king. When West subsequently obtained the lead via the heart ace, he returned the four of clubs, and dummy's Q 9 of clubs was entrapped by East's A J. All in all, the defenders made two club tricks and the two red aces, thereby defeating declarer.

Declarer's play of the deuce of clubs from dummy at trick one was a thoughtless play. West's lead of the ten-spot had demonstrated beyond a doubt that he did not have the jack of clubs, and that therefore East's club holding was headed by the A J. By putting up dummy's queen, declarer would have compelled East to win the trick with the ace. Declarer's remaining K 8 of clubs—in combination with dummy's nine—then would have been promoted into two winning tricks, for East's remaining J 7 would now be trapped. This should have been apparent to declarer—but evidently it wasn't.

Deal 5:
On this deal and the one that follows (Deal 6), declarer's concern is not how he can best create the maximum number of tricks in the suit led at trick one, but rather how he can prevent the leader from establishing that suit.

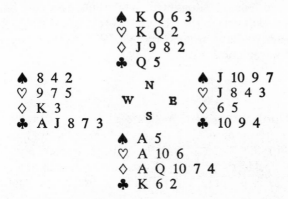

```
                   ♠ K Q 6 3
                   ♡ K Q 2
                   ◇ J 9 8 2
                   ♣ Q 5
   ♠ 8 4 2              N          ♠ J 10 9 7
   ♡ 9 7 5                         ♡ J 8 4 3
   ◇ K 3          W         E      ◇ 6 5
   ♣ A J 8 7 3        S            ♣ 10 9 4
                   ♠ A 5
                   ♡ A 10 6
                   ◇ A Q 10 7 4
                   ♣ K 6 2
```

Against South's *three–no-trump* contract, West opens

his fourth highest club, the seven-spot. If declarer should play low from dummy and take the trick with his own king, he might be very sorry, for he thereby leaves the queen open to decapitation by the defenders.

Obviously declarer is going to attack the diamond suit, for without it he cannot bring home nine tricks. If *East* has the diamond king, declarer has nothing to worry about, for in this situation, by repeated finesses, the entire suit will be brought home without the loss of a trick. But if West possesses that crucial king of diamonds and declarer captures the opening lead with his king of clubs, then when West obtains the lead, he will cash all of his clubs, felling dummy's queen enroute.

To eliminate or minimize the latter possibility, declarer puts up dummy's queen of clubs at trick one, with the hope that West has the club ace. When the queen of clubs wins, declarer leads the jack of diamonds and finesses, losing to West's king. Since declarer still retains the K 6 of clubs, he effectively prevents West from cashing the club suit. The only trick the defenders can win from here in is the ace of clubs.

Admittedly, if *East* were able to obtain the lead, then declarer's K 6 of clubs would not be a stopper. But declarer knew that he was going to finesse the diamonds in such a manner that East could never obtain the lead.

Too often, in situations comparable to the above, a declarer will create the abstract worry that if East obtains the lead, declarer will be ruined. Why worry about what could never come to pass?

Deal 6:
The North-South cards in this deal closely resemble those of the preceding deal. The only difference is that the high cards in the diamond suit have been interchanged. And again, declarer's problem is not how to win as many club tricks as is possible, but rather how best to prevent West from ultimately cashing that suit.

```
                    ♠ K Q 6 3
                    ♡ K Q 2
                    ◇ A Q 10 8
                    ♣ Q 5
  ♠ 8 4                N          ♠ J 10 9 7 2
  ♡ 9 7 5                         ♡ J 8 4 3
  ◇ 6 3            W       E      ◇ K 5
  ♣ A J 9 8 7 3          S        ♣ 10 4
                    ♠ A 5
                    ♡ A 10 6
                    ◇ J 9 7 4 2
                    ♣ K 6 2
```

Again West leads his fourth best club, the eight-spot, against South's *three no-trump* contract. Before playing from dummy, South takes a "time-out" for inventory.

A moment's reflection makes it apparent that a diamond finesse will have to be taken. If West happens to possess the diamond king, the sailing will be smooth, for five diamond tricks then will be brought in via successful finesses. But if East has the diamond king, he will capture the trick when declarer's finesse loses.

Declarer's approach, therefore, should be a pessimistic one: that East may well have the king of diamonds and that, in this case, East will obtain the lead. If this develops, what can declarer do to protect his interests?

To put it simply and in general form, declarer should try to do all in his power *to prevent East from returning a club* when he obtains the lead via the diamond king. To this end, declarer plays the five of clubs from dummy, and when East puts up the ten, he is permitted to capture the trick as declarer follows with the deuce of clubs!

As the reader can see, West will subsequently be unable to cash his club suit, for when East returns his remaining club at trick two, he will have voided himself of clubs. East will thus have been rendered "non-dangerous"; and when he obtains the lead with the king of diamonds, the communication between him and West will have been destroyed. And, as is equally apparent, had declarer captured the opening club lead with either dummy's queen or his own king, he would have been doomed to defeat. For, had he taken the opening lead, when East eventually won a trick with the diamond king, the return of his remaining club would have enabled West to cash five club tricks.

Some proper questions at this point might be: What if West had only five clubs, and East had three clubs? Then when East, upon being permitted to win the opening lead, returned a second club, couldn't West decline to win the trick (dummy's queen winning)? When East regained the lead with the king of diamonds, wouldn't East then be able to return his remaining club, West's ace felling declarer's king and enabling West to cash the entire club suit?

In other words, the questions raised come to this: If the distribution of the eight adversely held clubs had been 5-3 rather than the actual 6-2, would not the defenders have beaten declarer?

The answer is: "Yes." If West had five clubs and East three clubs, the opponents could defeat the three no-trump contract. But if this were the distribution, *then declarer could attribute his defeat to circumstances beyond his control.*

Thus, by refusing to capture the opening club lead (the "hold-up play"), declarer was taking out insurance, at no cost, against a 6-2 division of the adversely held clubs.

The moral of this deal? If there were one, it would be this: one seldom gets "guarantees" in a bridge game—and winning bridge players are those who do the right thing more often than do their opponents.

It might be mentioned, in passing and in conclusion, that if the eight adverse clubs had been divided 4-4, even the worst player in the world would have fulfilled this contract. Had this distribution existed, declarer simply would be unable to lose more than three club tricks and one diamond, no matter how hard he tried.

Deal 7:
On this deal, I believe that most bridge players, upon viewing the dummy, would think to themselves: "It can't make

any difference what I play from dummy." How wrong they would all be!

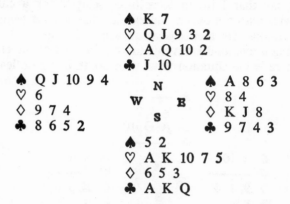

```
              ♠ K 7
              ♡ Q J 9 3 2
              ◇ A Q 10 2
              ♣ J 10
♠ Q J 10 9 4       N        ♠ A 8 6 3
♡ 6            W       E    ♡ 8 4
◇ 9 7 4           S        ◇ K J 8
♣ 8 6 5 2                   ♣ 9 7 4 3
              ♠ 5 2
              ♡ A K 10 7 5
              ◇ 6 5 3
              ♣ A K Q
```

With no adverse bidding, South arrived at a *four-heart* contract, against which West opened the queen of spades.

Had declarer put up dummy's king, he would have been defeated, for East would have won the trick with the ace and returned a spade to West's jack. Gazing at the dummy, West would then have led a diamond as his best hope— and eventually East would have made two diamond tricks.

From declarer's point of view, he knew that the king of spades was hopelessly trapped, for there was no West player who, against a suit contract, would have opened the queen of spades from an A Q combination. Therefore the loss of two spade tricks was inevitable; and declarer accepted it as such.

But look at what happens if declarer properly plays the seven of spades at trick one (as he did in the actual play). What is West to lead next, upon winning the opening lead? If he fails to lead a second spade, whatever else he plays (let's say a diamond) will be won by declarer. Declarer will then draw trumps, and on his third high club he will discard dummy's king of spades. He will then lose only one spade and two diamonds at most.

So, at trick two, West is compelled to lead a second round of spades, the board's king being taken by East's ace. Whatever East now plays back is immaterial—and even if declarer had never heard of an "end-play," he would now be *forced* into making his contract.

Let's say that East, at trick three, plays back a club. South wins with the queen and extracts the adverse trumps in two rounds. He then cashes an ace and king of clubs, discarding a diamond from dummy on the lead of the club king. Here is the situation now, with South being on lead:

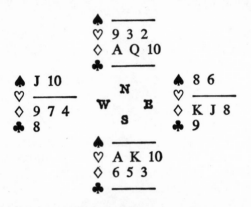

South now leads the three of diamonds and inserts the board's ten-spot (or the queen, if he desires). East wins the ten with the jack.

If East returns either a club or a spade, South discards his five of diamonds while simultaneously trumping the trick in dummy. And obviously, if instead East elects to return a diamond, dummy's queen will become a winner. In bridge parlance, East has become the "victim of an end-play." And there was never anything that either he or his partner could have done about it.

Played in the above way—as was done—declarer lost two spades and just one diamond.

Deal 8:
It goes without saying that a game or a slam made by the employment of deceptive tactics counts exactly as much as a game or slam made by brute force. And, much more often than not, a "stolen" game or slam is valued even higher than its nominal value, especially where the glorifi-

cation of the ego is the yardstick. Here is a case in point.
The deal arose in the 1949 National Championships.

```
              ♠ A 10 9 6 2
              ♡ K J 7
              ◇ J 9 5
              ♣ A 4
♠ 8 5 3                        ♠ Q J 7
♡ 6 2            N             ♡ 9 8 3
◇ Q 2        W       E         ◇ A 6 4 3
♣ K J 8 5 3 2    S             ♣ Q 10 6
              ♠ K 4
              ♡ A Q 10 5 4
              ◇ K 10 8 7
              ♣ 9 7
```

North-South vulnerable. South dealer.

South	West	North	East
1 ♡	Pass	1 ♠	Pass
1 NT	Pass	3 NT	Pass
Pass	Pass		

South's rebid of one no-trump was a pretty bad rebid.
But then, such rebids occur dozens of times every day of
the week in every bridge club in our land. When the hand
was over, however, any criticism of South's rebid would
have been purely academic.

West opened the five of clubs, the dummy came into
view, declarer played the ace from dummy and led the
jack of diamonds to trick two. When East followed with
the three-spot, South put up the king from his own hand.
When it held the trick, he scampered home with his nine
tricks.

We all agree that had East played the ace of diamonds at
trick two when dummy's jack was led, and then returned
a club to his partner, the defenders would have handed
declarer a two-trick set. But did East know that West had
the king of clubs rather than South? Couldn't South have
possessed that card? From East's position, might not South,

in leading the jack of diamonds at trick two, have the intention of finessing East for the queen of diamonds? And, if East climbed right up with the ace, wouldn't he then be establishing declarer's presumed king of diamonds as a winner? And might not that king provide declarer with his ninth and game-going trick?

I do not mean to imply that I am giving South my unconditional stamp of approval for his line of play. Had West held the ace of diamonds, declarer would have suffered a three-trick, vulnerable set. On the other hand, I certainly wouldn't stand up and applaud declarer for his alternative line of play: to win the first trick, take his eight winners and scamper home like a scared rabbit. I am simply presenting the role that deception (plus a little "nerve") can accomplish.

I'm sure that declarer was fully cognizant of the risk he was taking when he led the jack of diamonds and put up his king. If he went down, at least it could be said of him that he went down fighting. And if his chicanery worked, look at the wonderful story he could tell all of his friends about how he "put one over on two of the best bridge players at the club."

Deal 9:
That deception in the play of the cards is mandatory if winning results are to be achieved, is concurred in by everyone. Even those who are categorically opposed to deception in bidding agree that in *play* deception is a must, and that when all seems lost, the effective application of deception and camouflage can often alter one's seemingly apparent destiny. Deceptive tactics in play must be utilized not merely to demonstrate to the opponents that one is not a stereotyped, down-the-middle player at all times, but also, in the long run, for one's preservation.

The following deal, which came up in the Vanderbilt Championships of 1952, illustrates the point that when observation reveals that one is doomed to defeat if the opponents play correctly, one's only salvation lies in the hope that they can be tricked into playing incorrectly. And, although the best-laid plans of mice and men often turn out wrong, as Shakespeare once remarked, there *are* many times when they turn out just as planned.

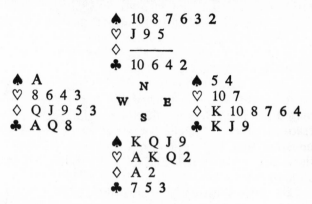

East-West vulnerable. South dealer.

South	West	North	East
1 ♠	Pass	4 ♠	Pass
Pass	Pass		

West led the queen of diamonds, and South, without undue haste or undue deliberation, discarded the five of hearts from dummy as he won the trick in his own hand with the ace. He then led the king of trumps, West's ace winning.

Unquestionably, the discard of the heart five from dummy created, in West's mind, the impression of weakness in hearts. So West now shifted to a heart. Declarer won this with the board's jack, picked up East's remaining trump, and then proceeded to discard two of dummy's clubs on South's ace and king of hearts. He now conceded two club tricks and claimed his "unmakable" contract.

Had declarer discarded a club instead of a heart on the opening diamond lead, West *might well* have shifted to a club at trick three, unappetizing as that lead was. Whether he would have done so or not, will never be resolved, of course. But it is agreed by all that declarer, in discarding the five of hearts, created a stimulus that oriented the West defender to the wrong path.

chapter 3 Championship Bridge: Misplays
by the Dummy

♠ The five deals that comprise this chapter were all played in major National Championship events. Each deal features either a blunder, or an error of commission or omission that was made by a topflight expert. Each of these experts is a potential or current nominee for the Hall of Fame.

Lest the impression be created that I am belittling these experts, or expertdom in general, nothing could be farther from the truth. If any one deal seems to diminish the stature of the expert involved, it is only because I want to illustrate that our "cream of the crop" is mortal, as you and I; and, as such, will blunder, err, or develop blind spots in occasional critical situations. If the sum total of their victories and defeats at the bridge table could be presented, their splendid achievements would far outweigh their infrequent mistakes.

If any lessons—for future application—are to be derived from the exhibitions that will be presented, they should be (1) the realization that not even the upper strata of our bridge society is perfect at all times; and (2) that one becomes a winner not by being brilliant but, rather, by not getting careless on the repetitive, run-of-the-mill hands. This latter point can be confirmed by checking with our experts, who will tell you that tournaments are won by those who make the fewest blunders or errors.

The names of the "wrongdoers" have been omitted deliberately. They have suffered in silence for their individual sins of commission and/or omission, sins of the type that all of us commit with regularity. But unfortunately for our experts, they committed their sins while the eyes of the world were upon them—and they were caught redhanded.

Deal 1:

```
              ♠ Q 9 8 2
              ♡ K 7 2
              ◇ 7 6 4 3
              ♣ Q 5
  ♠ K 4                      ♠ 6 3
  ♡ J 10 8 3        N        ♡ Q 9 5
  ◇ K J 8 5     W     E      ◇ Q 10 9
  ♣ K 7 4           S        ♣ J 10 9 6 3
              ♠ A J 10 7 5
              ♡ A 6 4
              ◇ A 2
              ♣ A 8 2
```

Against South's *four-spade* contract, West opened the jack of hearts, which was won by dummy's king, East following with the encouraging nine-spot. Dummy's queen of spades was then laid down and the trump finesse taken, losing to West's king. A heart continuation by West was captured by declarer's ace. When it was all over, declarer had lost a trick in each suit, for a one-trick set.

South, an acknowledged expert, committed a blunder at trick one. There should have been no hurry about attacking the trump suit. Declarer's correct play was to win the opening lead in his own hand with the ace, in order to lead a club toward dummy's queen. Whenever West possessed the king (50% of the time), the queen would become a winner, as it would have on this deal.

When West takes his club king, whatever he returns is immaterial. Let's say he plays back a heart, which is won by dummy's king. The club queen is now cashed, after which declarer enters his own hand via the ace of trumps. On the ace of clubs, declarer discards dummy's remaining heart. He then ruffs out his last heart. Now he leads a trump—and all the defenders can take from here in is the king of spades plus a diamond trick. Had he played the hand properly, declarer would have lost just three tricks: a club, a diamond, and the trump king.

Had it been revealed in the play that East possessed the

king of clubs, then the success of the contract would have hinged on the trump king being favorably located. But the trump finesse should have been a "last resort" play rather than a "first choice" one.

Deal 2:

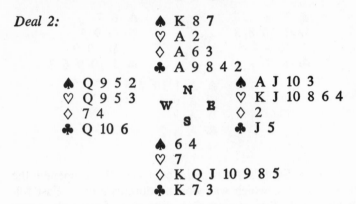

```
                     ♠ K 8 7
                     ♡ A 2
                     ◊ A 6 3
                     ♣ A 9 8 4 2
     ♠ Q 9 5 2                      ♠ A J 10 3
     ♡ Q 9 5 3         N            ♡ K J 10 8 6 4
     ◊ 7 4          W     E         ◊ 2
     ♣ Q 10 6          S            ♣ J 5
                     ♠ 6 4
                     ♡ 7
                     ◊ K Q J 10 9 8 5
                     ♣ K 7 3
```

East-West vulnerable. South dealer.

South	West	North	East
4 ◊	Pass	5 ◊	Pass
Pass	Pass		

West elected to open the three of hearts rather than the two of spades, since his hearts were "stronger" than his spades. This trick was won by dummy's ace, after which the board's remaining heart was ruffed in the closed hand. The king and queen of trumps then picked up the three adversely held trumps.

Declarer now led a club to the ace and then came back another club, East's jack falling to declarer's king. A third round of clubs now followed, West's queen winning. West then played a spade, and South was unable to avoid the loss of two spade tricks.

This is not a simple hand for the average player to handle correctly, but our expert declarer should have fulfilled his contract. When dummy came into view, I'm certain that declarer recognized that he was going to develop the club suit. In doing this, the danger existed that West might regain the lead via the club suit; and if he did, the return of a spade might result in declarer losing two spade tricks. Hence declarer should have played the hand in such a manner as to keep West out of the lead.

As I stated, this is not a simple hand to play. And yet, in retrospect, the proper play at trick one is not a complicated one; simply play the two of hearts on the opening lead instead of the ace!

East will now capture the trick. It does not matter what he returns, so let's assume he plays back a heart. On this, South discards the three of clubs as the board's ace wins the trick. The opponents' trumps are then drawn by declarer's king and queen. Next, declarer cashes the king of clubs, then leads a club to dummy's ace, and ruffs a third round of clubs. Dummy's two remaining clubs have now been promoted into winners, and the ace of trumps is on the board as an entry. On the two established clubs, declarer disposes of his two losing spades.

From declarer's point of view, in conceding the first trick to East, he wasn't losing a thing. What he was really doing was exchanging a trick for a trick: instead of losing a club trick later, he was losing a heart trick now. But in the exchange, he gained a tremendous advantage by allowing *East* to win the trick instead of leaving the avenue open for the West hand to win a club trick later on.

Of course, if when East won the opening lead, he had chosen to cash the spade ace (which he would not have done, what with the ace sitting over the king), that would have been the defenders' last trick.

For those who feel that this is really a tough hand for the average player to handle, they are, of course, quite correct. But again, our declarer was not an average player; he was a professional expert who undoubtedly had encountered this identical type of situation on many previous occasions. Certainly, in these circumstances, he should have come up with the correct solution; and his failure to have done so must be classified as either an inexcusable blunder or a temporary blackout. To him, ignorance could not serve as an excuse—and I don't think he would offer it as one.

And so I think the reader will concur that, on this deal, we should not temper judgment with mercy.

Deal 3:

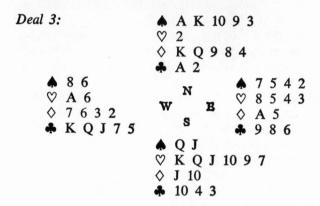

```
                    ♠ A K 10 9 3
                    ♡ 2
                    ◇ K Q 9 8 4
                    ♣ A 2
  ♠ 8 6                N              ♠ 7 5 4 2
  ♡ A 6                               ♡ 8 5 4 3
  ◇ 7 6 3 2       W         E         ◇ A 5
  ♣ K Q J 7 5         S              ♣ 9 8 6
                    ♠ Q J
                    ♡ K Q J 10 9 7
                    ◇ J 10
                    ♣ 10 4 3
```

Both sides vulnerable. North dealer.

North	East	South	West
1 ♠	Pass	2 ♡	Pass
3 ◇	Pass	3 ♡	Pass
4 ◇	Pass	4 ♡	Pass
Pass	Pass		

West made the normal opening of the king of clubs, and declarer made the "normal" play of winning it with dummy's ace. And declarer's "normal" play cost him his contract!

If declarer now led a trump, West would take it with his ace. The defenders would then cash two clubs and the ace of diamonds. Of course, declarer was fully aware of that.

So declarer, as undoubtedly he had planned, led a spade to his jack at trick two, then overtook his spade queen with the board's king at trick three; and led the ace of spades to trick four, hoping to discard a club (which he did). But, as is evident, West ruffed this trick with his six of trumps. He then played the trump ace, removing dummy's only trump, after which he cashed the club queen. Eventually, East won the setting trick with the diamond ace.

As declarer played the hand, he would have made his contract had the six adverse spades been divided 3-3. However, in my opinion, declarer received his just desert, for when six of a suit are missing, they don't figure to be divided 3-3 (a 3-3 division occurs but 36% of the time); and furthermore, declarer had overlooked a much superior line of play, which would have netted him his contract.

All declarer has to do is to permit West to win the opening lead with the king of clubs! West is now helpless. If he returns another club, dummy's ace wins, after which declarer enters his own hand via a spade to ruff his remaining club with dummy's singleton trump. Should West choose to take this line of defense, South's only losers will be a heart, a diamond, and a club.

After West is allowed to win the opening lead, if he plays the ace and another trump, declarer will win the rest of the tricks, for dummy's spades will enable declarer to discard his two diamonds and his losing club.

And if, at trick two, West decides to lead a low trump, declarer will win it and then drive out West's trump ace. And if West doesn't lead a diamond now, declarer again will make the remainder of the tricks. (If West chooses to lead a diamond, declarer will fulfill his contract without the overtrick.)

Why didn't our expert declarer think of these things? Frankly, I don't know. In all probability, I would imagine he had a "blind spot." But if he had thought of them, I wouldn't have had my tale to tell.

Deal 4:
In 1950, the winners of the blue-ribbon Vanderbilt Cup Team-of-Four Championships were Harry Fishbein, Morrie Elis, Charles Lockridge, and Larry Hirsch. But if, on the deal which follows, South had fulfilled his grand slam contract, the above-named winners would have been eliminated in the very first round! The key to the hand was the play from dummy at trick one.

How would you, the reader, like to take a crack at coming up with the right decision? If you make it, you deserve a round of applause. If you don't, do not despair, for when the deal arose in actual play, our South declarer came up with the wrong play. And, in the postmortem discussion of the hand, his teammates told him so.

♠ 9 7 3 2
♥ 10 6 5
♦ A 7 6 3 2
♣ A

      N
W   E
      S

♠ A K J
♥ A K Q 4
♦ ———
♣ K Q J 10 3 2

With no adverse bidding, you, sitting South, arrive at a *seven-club* contract. West opens the five of diamonds. What do you play to this trick?

Assuming you win it with dummy's ace of diamonds, what do you discard from your own hand? If it's the spade jack, you will feel sort of sheepish (putting it mildly) if you later discover that the spade finesse would have worked and that the jack of hearts did not fall. If, instead, you discard the four of hearts and stake your destiny on a successful spade finesse, you will feel just as sheepish if, after it's all over, you find out that the four of hearts would have been a winner—and that your jack of spades finesse cost you your contract. What is the answer? It is: don't play the diamond ace at trick one! Why commit yourself at once when there is no necessity to do so?

The proper play is to trump the opening lead. Now play the ace of spades. Perhaps you'll catch a singleton queen—but you don't catch her.

Next, lead the ace of hearts. Perhaps you'll catch the singleton jack, resulting in dummy's ten-spot being promoted into a winner—but you don't have the good fortune to catch the singleton jack.

Then lead the king of spades. Perhaps one of the opponents was dealt the Q x doubleton of spades. *On the king, East drops the queen!*

You breathe a sigh of relief, get to dummy via the trump ace, and on the ace of diamonds you discard your four of hearts. You come back to your hand by ruffing a diamond, draw the adverse trumps, and claim your grand slam. Here are the four hands:

```
                   ♠ 9 7 3 2
                   ♡ 10 6 5
                   ◇ A 7 6 3 2
                   ♣ A
  ♠ 10 8 6 5             N        ♠ Q 4
  ♡ J 9 8 3                       ♡ 7 2
  ◇ Q 10 5        W         E     ◇ K J 9 8 4
  ♣ 7 6                  S        ♣ 9 8 5 4
                   ♠ A K J
                   ♡ A K Q 4
                   ◇ ————
                   ♣ K Q J 10 3 2
```

It should be pointed out that when you lead the king of spades to the second lead of spades, if you don't catch the queen, *do not play a second round of hearts* to see whether the jack of hearts falls. If, on the second lead of spades (the king) the queen does not drop, you are now committed to discarding the jack of spades on the diamond ace. Why run the risk, however slight, that the king of hearts might be trumped on the second round of that suit?

In the actual play, our South declarer promptly put up dummy's ace of diamonds at trick one—and just as promptly discarded the jack of spades from his own hand! As is apparent, he later lost a heart trick.

Deal 5:

On a goodly number of deals, as soon as the dummy comes into view, observation reveals that there are two alternative lines of play available. And, fairly frequently, the issue of which of them to select can be deferred for a few tricks, to see whether any clues might be revealed that will assist you in arriving at the proper course of action.

On rarer occasions, a deal comes along in which, as soon as the dummy is put down, three apparently optional lines of play present themselves. And again, which of them to select can be postponed for a few tricks.

And, once in a blue moon, a deal is encountered where not only do three different lines of play make themselves evident, but the declarer must make the decision *at trick one* as to which line of play he must choose.

It is this latter type of situation which is presented in this deal. May I again put you into the South seat, as the declarer at a *four-heart* contract.

> ♠ A 9 4
> ♡ Q 6
> ♢ 9 6 4 3 2
> ♣ J 8 5
>
>   **N**
> **W**   **E**
>   **S**
>
> ♠ K 7 2
> ♡ A J 10 7 5 3
> ♢ A 8
> ♣ A Q

West leads the queen of spades. First, do you win it with dummy's ace? If you do, do you then take the trump finesse or the club finesse? And bear in mind that you might now be in dummy for the first and last time.

If you lead the queen of trumps in order to finesse, East will put up the king, which you will win with your ace. But when you next lead the jack of trumps, West will fail to follow suit, and you will know, to your regret, that East started with K 9 8 6 of trumps. A trump trick will eventually have to be lost to East, and you will now go down since you will be unable to escape losing a trick in each of the three other suits.

If, upon winning the opening spade lead with the board's

ace, you decide to take the club finesse rather than the trump finesse, you are making a superior play. For if East has the king of clubs, the finesse will be successful and you will have gained a trick; whereas if East has the trump king, and you finesse successfully, you still haven't gained anything, for East might have four trumps (as he did), and you will be compelled to lose a trump trick. However, if you take the club finesse today, as fate will have it, the finesse will lose to West's king. Although dummy's jack of clubs will now be a winner, unfortunately there will be no way of getting to dummy to cash it, for, with East possessing the king of trumps, dummy's queen will not provide an entry. Thus, by taking the club finesse, as by taking the trump finesse, you go down, losing a trick in each suit. When the deal actually arose, our declarer took the club finesse—and suffered defeat.

Has the third line of play suggested itself as yet? Frankly, it is not easy to find, conceivably because it's too simple and you are looking for something difficult.

Win the opening lead of the spade queen with your own king, preserving dummy's ace as a future entry to the board. Then lay down the ace of clubs and follow up by playing the queen of clubs! West (or East, in theory) will win with the king. The board's jack of clubs has now become established as a winner.

Whatever West returns, you will capture, enter dummy via the spade ace, and on the jack of clubs you will discard one of your losers (either a spade or a diamond).

The reader might say that this line of play involves a risk: that the jack of clubs might be trumped. This is true. But the jack of clubs will be trumped only if the eight adversely held clubs were originally divided in a most abnormal way.

Putting it positively, if the eight outstanding clubs are divided either 4-4 or 5-3, then the lead of the jack of clubs on the third round of the suit will not be trumped. And the mathematicians tell us that when eight of a suit are outstanding in the hands of the two opponents, those eight will be divided either 4-4 or 5-3 approximately 80% of the time.

Thus, if played as suggested, the establishing and cashing of the club jack will enable declarer to fulfill his contract four out of every five times. And, as one of our stage comedians was wont to remark, "In these days, you can hardly ask for anything better."

The deal was:

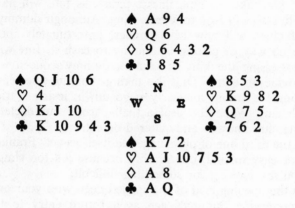

```
                    ♠ A 9 4
                    ♡ Q 6
                    ◇ 9 6 4 3 2
                    ♣ J 8 5
    ♠ Q J 10 6            N            ♠ 8 5 3
    ♡ 4                                ♡ K 9 8 2
    ◇ K J 10        W         E        ◇ Q 7 5
    ♣ K 10 9 4 3         S            ♣ 7 6 2
                    ♠ K 7 2
                    ♡ A J 10 7 5 3
                    ◇ A 8
                    ♣ A Q
```

chapter 4 The Play from Declarer's Hand

♠ It is lamentable that so many bridge players have developed the bad habit of winning the first trick hurriedly and *then* pausing to examine the situation at hand. In these circumstances, it is only natural that the postmortem examination will often reveal that they did the wrong thing: either they should not have won the trick at all; or they should have won it in dummy instead of in the declarer's hand; or they should have won it in the declarer's hand instead of in the dummy; or, perhaps, they played the improper card from either the dummy or the declarer's hand and thereby lost a future trick—or lost the contract.

Why the hurry to seize the first trick? Certainly if declarer intends to formulate some plan of attack, then in terms of elapsed seconds or minutes he isn't losing any time if he does his thinking *before* playing to the first trick instead of thinking *after* he plays to it. But in terms of profit and loss, surely the failure to think *before* playing to trick one must lead to avoidable losses.

When I am instructing an elementary class on the subject of "the play of the cards," I emphasize and reemphasize that after the opening lead is made and the dummy comes into view, the declarer should never capture the first trick—even if no problem or option exists—*until he has first made up his mind what he is going to play to the second trick.* As soon as this good habit is acquired, the student has made an excellent, profit-guaranteed, investment for the future—and at no extra cost. Unfortunately, too many bridge players were never students. Like Topsy, they just "growed up."

Deal 1:
The following deal is a good example of winning the first

trick automatically (which most players would do on this hand), pausing for reflection—and then realizing belatedly that they now find themselves in the position of "locking the barn doors after the horse has been stolen."

Would you, the reader, care to test yourself on this deal? Here it is:

```
            ♠ Q 5 4 2
            ♡ 7 5 3 2
            ◇ A 9 8 4
            ♣ 6
                 N
            W          E
                 S
            ♠ A 7 6 3
            ♡ K Q J 10 9 6
            ◇ 7
            ♣ A 8
```

You are sitting South playing a *four-heart* contract. There has been no adverse bidding.

West's opening lead is the jack of spades. You play low from dummy, and East puts up *the king*. You take the king with the ace—and if you do, you are doomed!

Let's think it over before playing to the first trick. Isn't East's king an obvious singleton? If you take it with the ace, you will undoubtedly lead a trump, which West, as it happens, will win with his ace. Back will come the ten of spades, for after all, *West knows that his partner held a singleton king*. If you cover the ten with the board's queen, East will trump, and eventually you will lose two more spade tricks. And, if you don't cover the ten with the queen, the ten will win, after which West will persist in the spade suit, and dummy's queen will be ruffed by East, either now or later. Your only winner in spades will be the ace.

But suppose you properly permit East's spade king to

win the opening lead! What can he possibly return that
will prevent you from fulfilling the contract? Let's look
at all four hands:

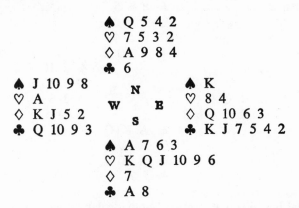

When East is allowed to capture the opening lead with
the king of spades, suppose he returns a diamond (any return he makes cannot defeat declarer). Dummy's ace
takes the trick, and a trump is led, West's ace winning.
Back comes the ten of spades. You play *low* from dummy,
and East trumps, as you follow suit with a low spade.
And that's the end of the line for the defenders. The rest
of the tricks belong to you.

Played in this manner, when East ruffs the ten of spades,
he is ruffing a trick that you would have lost in any (and
all) circumstances, for you have two natural losers in
spades. He is not ruffing your queen of spades—and
therein lies the difference between making your contract
and going down. And, if you went down, no psychiatrist
will be required to trace the cause of your unhappiness.
We laymen—your peers—are all equipped to find it
promptly, for we need go no farther than trick one.

This deal, incidentally, is a good one to try out on some
of your bridge-playing friends. I have used it in attempting
to determine the degree of expertness of potential pupils
who want to take a course with me in "advanced bridge."

If they make the proper play with the South hand at trick one, they qualify.

Deal 2:

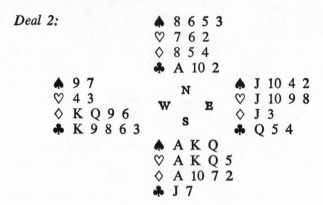

```
              ♠ 8 6 5 3
              ♡ 7 6 2
              ◊ 8 5 4
              ♣ A 10 2
  ♠ 9 7                      ♠ J 10 4 2
  ♡ 4 3           N          ♡ J 10 9 8
  ◊ K Q 9 6     W   E        ◊ J 3
  ♣ K 9 8 6 3     S          ♣ Q 5 4
              ♠ A K Q
              ♡ A K Q 5
              ◊ A 10 7 2
              ♣ J 7
```

Neither side vulnerable. South dealer.

South	West	North	East
2 NT	Pass	3 NT	Pass
Pass	Pass		

West opened the six of clubs, the deuce was played from dummy, East put up the queen, and declarer mechanically followed with his lowest card, the seven-spot. East returned the jack of hearts, South's ace winning.

Declarer had eight tricks going in, and prospects looked bright, for if either the adverse spades broke 3-3, or if the adverse hearts broke 3-3, declarer had his ninth, and game-going, trick.

But when declarer cashed the A K Q of spades, he discovered that the spades did not divide as hoped for; and when he played his top hearts, he learned, to his sorrow, that this suit wasn't divided 3-3 either. (Had he tested the diamonds, he would have found out that this was not the day for suits to divide 3-3). When he next led the jack of clubs, West properly refused to cover with the king—and all declarer could make was one club trick. So he went down.

Admittedly, declarer was unlucky, for one of the two major suits figured to divide nicely and evenly. Nevertheless, despite the "tough luck," the contract was an easy one to make. Declarer had no one to blame but himself.

On the opening lead, declarer should have tossed the jack of clubs, not the seven-spot. Not that he intended to finesse dummy's ten of clubs (playing West for the king) as a first-choice play, but rather, in case necessity demanded that it be finessed, then the avenue would be open for him to do so. And, when the subsequent plays in spades and hearts would reveal that a winner could not be developed in either of these two suits, then declarer would lead his seven of clubs and successfully finesse the board's ten-spot. After declarer's "economical" play at trick one, there was no way to recover.

Deal 3:

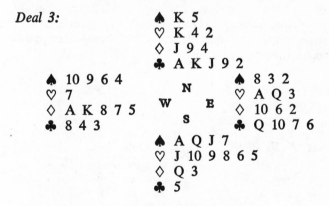

```
              ♠ K 5
              ♡ K 4 2
              ◇ J 9 4
              ♣ A K J 9 2

♠ 10 9 6 4         N         ♠ 8 3 2
♡ 7                          ♡ A Q 3
◇ A K 8 7 5    W     E       ◇ 10 6 2
♣ 8 4 3            S         ♣ Q 10 7 6

              ♠ A Q J 7
              ♡ J 10 9 8 6 5
              ◇ Q 3
              ♣ 5
```

Neither side vulnerable. North dealer.

North	East	South	West
1 ♣	Pass	1 ♡	Pass
2 ♡	Pass	4 ♡	Pass
Pass	Pass		

West led the king of diamonds, East played the deuce, and South false carded with the queen. West then shifted

to the ten of spades, hoping that East could entrap dummy's
king. As is evident, it didn't work out as hoped for. The
board's king captured the trick, after which the ace and
king of clubs were laid down. On the latter card, declarer
discarded his losing three of diamonds. It now became
routine to draw trumps, yielding two tricks to East's ace
and queen.

It is hard to condemn West for falling for South's false
card of the queen. After all, South could have had the
singleton queen, in which case the continuation of the
diamond ace would be ruffed by South—and the board's
jack of diamonds would be promoted into a winner.

Deal 4:
On the previous deal, South's timely false card misled the
West defender. On this deal, had declarer attempted to
deceive a defender by false carding, the false card might
well have boomeranged. Our declarer fully realized this
and perceived that his best chance of deceiving the opposition was by telling the truth.

```
                    ♠ J 7 6
                    ♡ Q
                    ◇ Q J 10 8 5 3
                    ♣ K 4 3
    ♠ A K 10 9                    ♠ Q 3
    ♡ 9 7 5 4          N          ♡ J 10 8 6 3
    ◇ 6 4         W         E      ◇ 7 2
    ♣ A 8 5           S          ♣ J 9 6 2
                    ♠ 8 5 4 2
                    ♡ A K 2
                    ◇ A K 9
                    ♣ Q 10 7
```

North-South vulnerable. South dealer.

South	West	North	East
1 NT	Pass	3 NT	Pass
Pass	Pass		

West led the king of spades, dummy followed with the six, East played the three, and South dropped the deuce. It seemed to West that East had no interest in the spade suit, since the latter's three-spot was the most discouraging card that could have been played by East (declarer had played the deuce). So at trick two, West decided to cash the ace of spades and to continue the suit at trick three (hoping that South had been dealt the Q x x) in order to establish his fourth spade. As is evident, West felled his partner's queen at trick two, thereby creating a winner out of dummy's jack of spades.

It is impossible to predict with certainty what would have happened had declarer false carded with the four or five of spades at trick one. Undoubtedly West would have noticed that the deuce of spades was missing; and he *may* have come to the conclusion that possibly East held the Q 3 2 and was doing his best to give a come-on signal. West, at trick two, *might* then have led a low spade to East's presumed (hoped for) queen. A club return by East would then have defeated the contract.

But, with the deuce and three of spades in evidence at trick one, West felt that it was useless to play a low spade at trick two. In retrospect, West should have decided otherwise—but he didn't know it at trick two.

Deal 5:

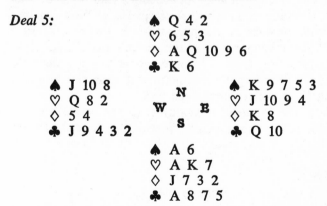

```
              ♠ Q 4 2
              ♡ 6 5 3
              ◇ A Q 10 9 6
              ♣ K 6
♠ J 10 8          N          ♠ K 9 7 5 3
♡ Q 8 2       W     E        ♡ J 10 9 4
◇ 5 4            S           ◇ K 8
♣ J 9 4 3 2                  ♣ Q 10
              ♠ A 6
              ♡ A K 7
              ◇ J 7 3 2
              ♣ A 8 7 5
```

Against South's *three–no-trump* contract, West got off

to the inspired opening lead of the jack of spades. Declarer, hoping that West was leading from some combination headed by the K J 10, put up dummy's queen. East, of course, covered with the king, and declarer declined to take the ace. East returned a low spade, South's ace won, and West made another inspired play: he "unblocked" by tossing the ten of spades on the ace. When South then tried the diamond finesse, it lost to East's king. East now cashed the high nine of spades, West dropping the eight-spot, and then went on to cash two more spades. All in all, East—with West's active cooperation—made four spades and one diamond.

This hand is a simple one to play for those who are not greedy about overtricks. An astute declarer should have foreseen that he was going to take the diamond finesse in such a manner that if the finesse lost, *it could lose only to East*. Hence, if declarer had not put up dummy's queen of spades at trick one and instead had captured West's jack with his ace, then dummy's remaining Q 4 of spades would constitute a second stopper against East. That is, if the diamond finesse lost to East, it would be impossible for the defenders to cash their spade suit, since dummy's Q 4 of spades would effectively prevent that possibility.

Of course, in winning the opening lead with the ace while retaining dummy's Q 4 of spades, *if* West regained the lead, another spade play through the board's Q 4 would (or might) result in the queen's being trapped by East's king. But this could never come to pass, since declarer, in attacking the diamond suit, was not going to permit West ever to obtain the lead.

Thus, the immediate capturing of the spade jack by the ace, preserving dummy's queen, was the only correct play for declarer to make.

Deal 6:
On this deal, which arose in the National Championships of 1938, every South declarer came up with the winning play at trick one. It serves as a good illustration of the technique which has made the expert an expert.

```
                    ♠ A 8 3
                    ♡ K 6
                    ◇ A Q 10 6 4
                    ♣ 9 8 5
  ♠ J 6 5                         ♠ 10 9 4 2
  ♡ J 7 2            N            ♡ Q 10 8 5 3
  ◇ 9 5          W     E          ◇ K 7
  ♣ A 10 7 3 2      S             ♣ Q 6
                    ♠ K Q 7
                    ♡ A 9 4
                    ◇ J 8 3 2
                    ♣ K J 4
```

Against South's *three–no-trump* contract, West led the three of clubs, the eight was played from dummy, and East put up the queen.

Many bridge players would take this trick with the king, then pause to examine the situation—and it would be too late to do anything about controlling it. Upon subsequently taking the diamond finesse, which would lose to East's king, the return of a club would enable West to make four club tricks.

Our declarer foresaw that he was going to finesse for the diamond king and that, if West held this "key" card, there would be nothing to worry about, since the diamond suit could then be brought home without the loss of a trick. Declarer also realized that if East held this vital card, he would win a trick with it. So declarer's objective became the prevention of East returning a club if East happened to possess the king of diamonds.

At trick one, declarer declined to take East's queen of clubs. To trick two, East played back his remaining club, declarer put up his jack—and he was home safely whether West took his ace or didn't.

As declarer viewed the situation—*prior* to playing to trick one—if the adverse clubs were divided 5-2, declarer's holdup play—the refusal to win the opening lead—would pay nice dividends if East held the diamond king. And if the adverse clubs were divided 4-3, no matter how badly declarer played the hand, he just couldn't lose more than three clubs tricks and a diamond.

Thus, the refusal to win the opening lead could never be a losing play, but it could be—as it turned out to be—the only winning play.

Deal 7:
In my opinion, the proper play to trick one on this deal would not be made by the average player. It would be made by both the below-average player and the above-average player, but for different reasons: the below-average player couldn't resist the impulse to win the first trick, while the above-average player would perceive the potential danger that existed if he did not take the first trick.

```
                   ♠ A 4 2
                   ♡ A K 3
                   ◇ A J 10 8 6
                   ♣ J 5
      ♠ 10 6            N            ♠ K Q J 9
      ♡ 8 6 4 2                      ♡ J 7 5
      ◇ 7 5 4      W         E       ◇ K 2
      ♣ K 10 8 2        S            ♣ Q 9 7 3
                   ♠ 8 7 5 3
                   ♡ Q 10 9
                   ◇ Q 9 3
                   ♣ A 6 4
```

Neither side vulnerable. North dealer.

North	East	South	West
1 ◇	Pass	1 NT	Pass
2 NT	Pass	3 NT	Pass
Pass	Pass		

West opens the two of clubs, the five is put up from dummy, and East plays the queen. The question is whether to take the ace or not.

To a partial extent, the proper play depends on the company you keep: if the opposition is "honest," you should certainly take the ace, for West's lead of the deuce of clubs (as his fourth best) indicates that he has precisely four clubs; and that, therefore, East also has four clubs. Upon winning the ace, you finesse in diamonds, and even if it should lose, your only losers will be three clubs and one diamond.

If the opposition—or, more specifically, the West player —has been known to be "dishonest" or "deceptive" on occasion, it then becomes a rougher proposition, for if West is leading the deuce from a five- or six-card suit, to defer taking the club ace until the third round of the suit is led will eliminate clubs from the East hand. In this case, should East subsequently obtain the lead via the diamond king, he will be unable to return a club. However, if against a deceptive West you choose to win the first club lead (hoping that the adverse clubs are divided 4-4), and then lose the diamond finesse to East's king, a club return by East may enable West to cash four or five club tricks.

By and large, I think that one should assume that the opening lead is honest and true, for if this assumption is not made, I believe a greater danger exists, namely, that East, upon winning the opening lead, may decide to shift to a spade. And if he does, what will happen is what did happen.

Our actual declarer did permit East's queen of clubs to win the opening lead, whereupon East promptly laid down the king of spades—and eventually declarer went down, losing one club, three spades, and one diamond.

Deal 8:
If just one deal had to be selected to demonstrate the precarious position of a player's finding himself on the brink of disaster, from which escape seemed impossible, *and extricating himself,* I believe this deal would most vividly portray it. Our heroine (a "her," not a "him") was a diminutive lady who was playing in a game with three big, rough, tough men. The lady was Mrs. Barbara Tepper, of New York City—and her stature increased appreciably after the deal was played out.

```
                              ♠ A K Q 9 7 4 2
                              ♡ 6
                              ◇ A
                              ♣ K J 9 3
        ♠ 6                                    ♠ J 10 8 3
        ♡ K Q J 10 9 5 2        N             ♡ 8 7 3
        ◇ J 6              W         E         ◇ 9 5 4
        ♣ 8 6 2                S              ♣ A 5 4
                              ♠ 5
                              ♡ A 4
                              ◇ K Q 10 8 7 3 2
                              ♣ Q 10 7
```

Both sides vulnerable. West dealer.

West	North	East	South
3 ♡	4 ♠	Pass	5 ◇
Pass	6 ♠	Double	6 NT
Pass	Pass	Double	Pass
Pass	Pass		

West led the king of hearts, and Barbara took a time-out to examine the situation. If she won the opening lead, there would be no way to reenter the South hand to cash the diamonds after dummy's ace of diamonds was played, except via the club suit. Of course, if the latter were attempted, the defenders would hop up with the club ace and run "a few dozen" heart tricks. It was equally apparent to declarer that even if the five adversely held spades were divided 3-2 (which they weren't going to be, based on East's double of the six-spade bid), declarer couldn't honestly make more than nine tricks.

So Barbara allowed West to win the opening lead with his king of hearts! West now made the normal continuation of the queen of hearts, upon which declarer discarded dummy's ace of diamonds, South's ace winning the trick. When South next led the king and queen of diamonds, the queen caught the jack (a most wondrous sight for declarer to behold!). Four more diamond tricks were then cashed, arriving at this position prior to South's leading to trick nine:

```
                    ♠ A K Q 9
                    ♡ ———
                    ◇ ———
                    ♣ K
     ♠ ———                        ♠ J 10 8 3
     ♡ J 10 9         N           ♡ ———
     ◇ ———         W     E        ◇ ———
     ♣ 8 6            S           ♣ A
                    ♠ 5
                    ♡ ———
                    ◇ 2
                    ♣ Q 10 7
```

Barbara now led her remaining high diamond, the deuce, and discarded dummy's king of clubs. East was caught in the vise of a squeeze. If he discarded the three of spades, dummy's nine-spot would be promoted into a winner; if, instead, he threw away the ace of clubs, South's queen would become the highest ranking club. Actually, East did toss away the ace of clubs—the proper discard—hoping his partner held the queen. But declarer then produced the queen of clubs, upon which the board's nine of spades was discarded, after which the ace, king, and queen of spades were cashed, thereby providing declarer with a most satisfactory ending to what had started out to be a most excruciating adventure.

Deal 9:

If one aspires to be a good bridge player, he must at times resort to deception in the play of the cards. I do not mean to imply that deceptive tactics must be used as a replacement for technical skill, for if they are, the quality of one's game must deteriorate. But, since technical skill is not in itself sufficient to yield optimum results, deceptive tactics must be included in one's arsenal of useful weapons, for prompt application when the necessity for their occasional use arises.

The spontaneous, imaginative, deceptive, play that is the theme of this deal, arose many years ago, with the South declarer being Alfred ("Freddie") Sheinwold, world-re-nowned player and authority.

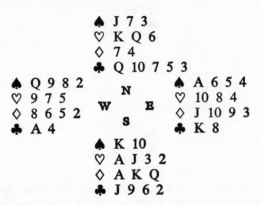

♠ J 7 3
♡ K Q 6
◇ 7 4
♣ Q 10 7 5 3

♠ Q 9 8 2   ♠ A 6 5 4
♡ 9 7 5   ♡ 10 8 4
◇ 8 6 5 2   ◇ J 10 9 3
♣ A 4   ♣ K 8

♠ K 10
♡ A J 3 2
◇ A K Q
♣ J 9 6 2

Against South's *three–no-trump* contract, West led the deuce of spades, which East won with the ace. On this trick, Freddie dropped the king! East now pushed back his chair, and began to reflect on the situation.

It was perfectly obvious to him that South held another spade, since West's opening lead of the deuce had denoted exactly four spades in the West hand (and East knew that his partner was honest). So South was known to possess precisely two spades. Why did he play the king then, East asked himself?

East finally concluded that South's remaining spade just had to be the queen. Why else would he play the king? East therefore abandoned the spade suit, seeing no future in continuing spades, since declarer still possessed the queen (so East thought), and dummy had the jack. He then shifted to the jack of diamonds.

Freddie won this trick with the king and attacked the clubs, East winning with the king. East now continued in diamonds, hoping to establish that suit. As is apparent, South took this trick. It now became routine to establish dummy's club suit by knocking out West's ace. West could then take his queen of clubs, but that would be the defenders' last trick.

Even after East had been hoodwinked into discontinuing spades after the first trick, he still could have defeated declarer had he returned a spade at trick three, when he obtained the lead with the king of clubs. But East was unable to shake off his original conclusion that declarer still possessed the queen of spades.

Sheinwold anticipated East's reaction when he dropped the king of spades at trick one, for Sheinwold knew, from West's lead of the deuce, that West and East had four spades apiece; and that when the king was played at trick one, East would realize that South was false carding and that East's trend of thought would lead to East's concluding that the only apparent justification for the false card was that declarer still had the queen. Going further, East would reason that Sheinwold was trying to get East to continue spades by creating the false impression that South had no more spades. But East, of course, knew that South had another spade. From East's point of view, if Sheinwold was trying to entice East into continuing spades, East was just a little too smart to be taken in by Sheinwold's "obvious" stratagem—and he wasn't going to continue spades! And he didn't—to his regret.

Of course, had spades been continued, declarer would have lost three spade tricks and two clubs.

Incidentally, even if East had diagnosed the situation correctly and had led back a spade at trick two, Sheinwold would still have made one spade trick, since dummy's jack would have become a winner when the ten-spot lost to West's queen. At worst, then, Freddie's discard of the spade king at trick one merely deferred the taking of a spade trick. At best, exactly what did happen: the seduction of the East defender.

Deal 10:
This deal was played in Europe some years ago, and it

serves as a simple but classic illustration of the role that deception can play in reversing one's apparent destiny. The actual South declarer, unfortunately, is unknown.

```
                    ♠ 8 2
                    ♡ J 10 3
                    ◇ 6 4
                    ♣ A 10 9 8 6 4
    ♠ K Q J              N         ♠ 9 7 5 4
    ♡ 9 6 5                        ♡ K Q 8 7 2
    ◇ A J 10 8 3   W       E       ◇ 9 5 2
    ♣ J 2              S           ♣ 7
                    ♠ A 10 6 3
                    ♡ A 4
                    ◇ K Q 7
                    ♣ K Q 5 3
```

East-West vulnerable. West dealer.

West	North	East	South
1 ◇	Pass	1 ♡	Double
Pass	2 ♣	Pass	2 NT
Pass	3 NT	Pass	Pass
Pass			

West led the nine of hearts, the suit his partner had bid. On it dummy's jack was played, East put up the queen—and declarer followed with the four-spot!

Oh yes, it's very easy to return a heart at trick two as you look at all four hands. But East, knowing from West's lead and South's two–no-trump bid that South had the heart ace, felt that South had started with the A x x of hearts. And if this were the set-up (why else should South not take the ace, thought East), then a heart return at trick two would give South two heart tricks.

East therefore played back a diamond, West's opening suit bid. When declarer now put up the queen, he had his contracted-for nine tricks: six clubs, one diamond, one heart, and one spade.

Had declarer taken his heart ace at trick one, then when

West later obtained the lead via his diamond ace, a heart return through the board's remaining 10 3 of hearts would have enabled East to cash four heart tricks.

How many East players are there who would have been that gifted to return a low heart at trick two? If there are such, then in describing them we would be compelled to change the word "gifted" to something else *if declarer had started with the A x x of hearts,* rather than the A x that he actually had.

Deal 11:

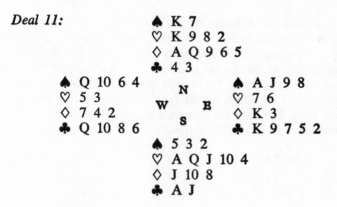

```
                    ♠ K 7
                    ♡ K 9 8 2
                    ◇ A Q 9 6 5
                    ♣ 4 3
   ♠ Q 10 6 4           N           ♠ A J 9 8
   ♡ 5 3                            ♡ 7 6
   ◇ 7 4 2         W       E        ◇ K 3
   ♣ Q 10 8 6          S            ♣ K 9 7 5 2
                    ♠ 5 3 2
                    ♡ A Q J 10 4
                    ◇ J 10 8
                    ♣ A J
```

Both sides vulnerable. South dealer.

South	West	North	East
1 ♡	Pass	3 ♡	Pass
4 ♡	Pass	· Pass	Pass

Had West gotten his fingers on a spade at trick one, declarer would have been doomed, for the defenders could then have made two spades, one diamond, and one club. But West, not being clairvoyant, elected to open the six of clubs. However, our declarer failed to rise to the occasion at trick one—as he really should have without needing to be clairvoyant—and thus doomed himself to defeat.

On the opening club lead East played the king, which South won with the ace. After drawing the adverse trumps, declarer led his jack of diamonds and finessed, losing to East's king. Back came a club, West's queen winning. West, perceiving the futility of leading either a club or a diamond, returned a spade. East now took two spade tricks and declarer was down one.

If declarer had looked ahead, he would have realized that the only danger to his contract was that West might later obtain the lead. If this happened, then declarer might well lose two spade tricks. But if West were prevented from obtaining the lead, then declarer could always discard two of his own spades on dummy's to-be-established diamond suit.

Hence, declarer should have allowed East's king of clubs to win the opening lead. Whatever East returned at trick two, the sailing would now be a smooth one for declarer. Trumps would be drawn and the diamond finesse taken, losing to East's king. And, once again, whatever East returned, the defenders would be powerless to prevent declarer from fulfilling his contract. All they could now cash would be East's ace of spades.

chapter 5 The Play from Declarer's Hand: The Holdup Play

♠ In the preceding chapter there were presented illustrations of various types of plays that declarer makes from his own hand at trick one. These examples embodied judgment situations, the proper handling of which necessitated looking ahead to see what dangers lurked; deceptive or false carding situations; and, with only passing reference to the term "holdup play."

In a broad sense, any holdup play (declining to win a trick) is essentially a judgment situation, as contrasted to a sterotyped, stock play, since its proper application stems from looking over the specific deal at hand to determine whether it will be advantageous to apply a hold up. However, there are many types of recurring, identical situations that demand that the holdup play be employed if optimum results are to be obtained. After examining and analyzing the rationale behind these similar, recurring situations (having encountered them repeatedly in actual play), the better players have memorized these holdup cases and have earmarked them for future reference and application. In so doing, they thus have spared themselves the time and trouble of working them out at the table whenever they arise.

The holdup play, consisting of the refusal to win the opening lead, is based on one or more of these four reasons:

(1) To maintain control of the suit until such time as that control can be relinquished with safety.

(2) To destroy the opponents' line of communication, *i.e.*, to prevent them from reaching each other via the suit they have opened.

(3) To convey to the opponents the misinformation that declarer is weak in the suit led, whereas in

reality he is not—thereby encouraging them to continue playing that suit. And, in so doing, they will present declarer with a trick that he could not obtain on his own power. (The specific reference here is to the Bath coup, which is discussed in detail throughout this chapter.)

(4) To gain time by forcing the defenders to abandon their suit, thus enabling declarer to establish and cash his suit before the defenders can establish and cash their suit. (The specific reference here is also to the Bath coup, a dual-purpose declarer's weapon.)

The holdup play is most frequently employed by declarer in no-trump contracts, although there are many circumstances in which it is used to good advantage in suit contracts. The reason behind the more frequent occurrence in no-trump contracts is this:

Universally, the standard lead against no-trump contracts is in the leader's *longest* suit. The world's best players use this lead, you and I use it, and your opponents use it. We use it because in experience we have learned that our best chance of defeating a no-trump contract usually lies in establishing and cashing our longest suit.

Much more often than not, the leader (against no-trump contracts) will have more cards in his suit than will his partner. (That is, the leader generally has "lots" of his suit, and his partner has "few.") Therefore, if declarer can eliminate the "few" from the leader's partner's hand, then should the latter subsequently obtain the lead, he will have been rendered non-dangerous, for he will be unable to return partner's suit.

And so, when a lead is made against a no-trump contract, and declarer has just one stopper in that suit (say A x x), he will decline to take his ace until the third round of the suit is led. Each time declarer declines to win the trick in that suit, the leader's partner who, let us say, also started with three cards in that suit, is forced to play one of them on the first round, another on the second round, and his last one on the third round. He now has no cards remaining in that suit and has ceased to be an enemy who can hurt declarer. Thus, the holdup play eliminates or, as we shall see, minimizes, the danger of the opponents' to-be-established suit being cashed later on when they regain the lead.

In a suit contract, to hold up one's ace until the third (or even the second) round of the suit can be most dangerous, for the third or second round might be trumped—and declarer's ace goes down the drain. Furthermore, in a suit contract, the necessity does not exist for employing the holdup play in the attempt to prevent the opponents from *cashing* their to-be-established suit. In a suit contract, declarer's trumps, *the controlling cards,* will destroy the opponents' established suit. Nevertheless, there are times when the holdup play is proper in a suit contract.

Let us look at some of these standard, repetitive holdup plays, while at the same time obtaining an insight into the logic and motivation that brought them into being and established them as highly-efficient tools.

The first two deals that follow present the holdup play in its most basic form. I hope the reader will appreciate that I am not insulting his intelligence by presenting these two deals. They are introduced because they depict the holdup play in its simplest and most elementary setting, thereby illustrating and establishing the logical foundation for its repeated application at the bridge table.

Deal 1:

```
                        ♠ Q 6 5
                        ♡ K 8 4
                        ◇ A J 9 8 3
                        ♣ 8 3

                             N
Five of clubs led        W       E
                             S

                        ♠ A K 4
                        ♡ A 7 2
                        ◇ Q 10 4 2
                        ♣ A 7 6
```

You are the South declarer, playing a *three–no-trump* contract. West opens the five of clubs, and East puts up the queen. How do you play the hand?

The proper play is to employ the holdup, permitting East to win the trick. East then continues with the ten of clubs, and again you do not take your ace. When a third round of clubs is led, you have no option but to win it.

By counting your winners, it becomes apparent that you need three diamond tricks to fulfill your contract. So you take the diamond finesse, and your queen loses to East's king. Your contract is now guaranteed, since East has no club to return to partner. The deal was:

```
                    ♠ Q 6 5
                    ♡ K 8 4
                    ◇ A J 9 8 3
                    ♣ 8 3
  ♠ 10 7 3                        ♠ J 9 8 2
  ♡ Q 10 6 5        N             ♡ J 9 3
  ◇ 7            W      E          ◇ K 6 5
  ♣ K J 9 5 4       S             ♣ Q 10 2
                    ♠ A K 4
                    ♡ A 7 2
                    ◇ Q 10 4 2
                    ♣ A 7 6
```

I think it is obvious as to what would have happened had you won either the first club lead or the second. East, upon subsequently obtaining the lead, would have returned a club, and the defenders would have taken four club tricks and a diamond to defeat the contract. But, with the holdup play, each time declarer declined to take his ace, East's club length was reduced by one card, until East reached the point where he had none left—and at that moment he had become non-dangerous. When declarer lost the diamond finesse to East at trick four, his worry about the opponents' established club suit had ceased to exist.

The reader might well ask: "But what if East had had another club to return?" The answer is that if East had another club, then West would have had one club less— and the clubs would, in this case, have been divided 4-4. And, in this situation, declarer would have lost just *three* clubs and one diamond, fulfilling his contract.

The holdup play is designed to protect you in all situations where the adversely led suit is divided either 6-2 or 5-3 or 5-2, with the opening leader having the greater number. Where the suit that is led is divided 4-4 (or 4-3 where 7 cards of the suit are in the hands of the opponents), you require no protection, whether you are the world's best player, the world's worst player, or anything in between these two extremes. When the suit is divided 4-4, you will lose three tricks in the suit whether you capture the first, second, or third round of that suit. In effect, then, the holdup play is insurance at no cost whatsoever and is protection against what is usually the normal circumstance: that the opening leader has more of the suit than does his partner.

The question might also arise: "If the king of diamonds were favorably located (in the West hand), then was not the holdup play a wasted effort?" The answer is "yes." But we all know that finesses sometimes work, and sometimes do not. And so the holdup play is what we might call comprehensive insurance—it takes care of everything.

Deal 2:

Let us now examine the identical deal with one card being changed: dummy has the *diamond king* instead of the ace.

```
            ♠ Q 6 5
            ♡ K 8 4
            ◇ K J 9 8 3
            ♣ 8 3

                N
            W       E
                S

            ♠ A K 4
            ♡ A 7 2
            ◇ Q 10 4 2
            ♣ A 7 6
```

Again the contract is *three–no-trump,* with West opening the five of clubs and East putting up the queen. How about the holdup play now?

The answer is a most positive "yes." As a matter of experience, in virtually every no-trump contract, when a suit is led and you have just one stopper, do not take it until you are forced to.

In this deal, if you fail to employ the holdup play, you will go down unless the eight adversely held clubs are divided 4-4, for upon relinquishing the lead to the opponents' ace of diamonds (which you must do), they will cash at least four clubs. I would estimate that if you take the club ace at trick one, you will go down at your contract 75% of the time—that is, you will make your contract about 25% of the time (when the adverse clubs are divided 4-4).

But suppose you hold up your club ace until the third round, exhausting East of clubs, except if the original club distribution was 4-4, in which case it does not matter what you do since you will in this case always make your contract. What next? You hopefully lead a diamond, and if East has the ace, all is well. If West has the ace, he will cash his clubs; and, if you now go down, you can attribute your defeat to circumstances beyond your control.

There is no guarantee on this hand. But the employment of the holdup play increases your chances of making the contract from 25% to 50% (the 50-50 chance of East's holding the diamond ace). And in bridge as in life, if you can double your chances of fulfilling a venture, you should grasp the opportunity to do so. The complete deal was:

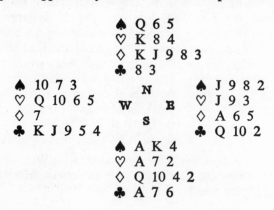

```
                    ♠ Q 6 5
                    ♡ K 8 4
                    ◇ K J 9 8 3
                    ♣ 8 3
   ♠ 10 7 3              N          ♠ J 9 8 2
   ♡ Q 10 6 5                       ♡ J 9 3
   ◇ 7         W           E        ◇ A 6 5
   ♣ K J 9 5 4        S             ♣ Q 10 2
                    ♠ A K 4
                    ♡ A 7 2
                    ◇ Q 10 4 2
                    ♣ A 7 6
```

Deal 3:

This deal introduces the "Bath Coup,"* which is basically nothing more than a holdup play with an A J x combination. That is, when an opening lead of a king is made, declarer, in fourth position, refuses to win the trick:

$$\spadesuit \ 7 \ 5$$

$$\begin{array}{ccc} & \text{N} & \\ \spadesuit \ \text{K Q 10 9} & \text{W} \quad \text{E} & \spadesuit \ 8 \ 6 \ 4 \ 2 \\ & \text{S} & \end{array}$$

$$\spadesuit \ \text{A J 3}$$

West opens the king of spades, and declarer plays the three-spot from his own hand. Should West now play another spade, declarer will win two spade tricks. If West does not continue spades, declarer can make but one spade trick, his ace. It should be apparent that there is an element of deception involved in this Bath coup: that declarer, by holding up, may seduce West into believing that declarer is weak in spades, with the hoped for effect being that West will continue spades.

But there can be an equally important element involved in declarer's refusal to win the opening lead of the king. By declining to capture the trick, declarer compels West, if the latter should diagnose the true situation, to abandon the spade suit, thereby *giving declarer the time necessary to establish his own suit.* For example, if declarer wins the king with the ace and, while attempting to establish his own best suit, he allows East to obtain the lead, a spade return by East will enable West to cash *three* spade tricks. Thus, in not capturing the opening lead, declarer retains control of the spade suit at the expense of one trick, rather than winning the opening lead and running the risk of losing *three* spade tricks.

A good illustration of the above described objectives of

*The name "Bath coup" comes to us from the town of Bath, England, where the play was first observed scores of years ago, when whist was the game of the day.

the Bath coup can be evidenced in the deal that follows. The South declarer was my very good friend and frequent partner, Andy Gabrilovitch, of Silver Spring, Md. Andy, the winner of several National Championships, is one of the nation's top-ranking players. The deal was played in a rubber-bridge game.

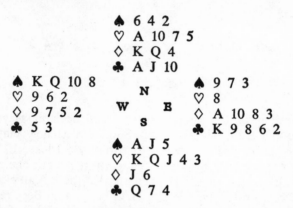

With no adverse bidding, South arrived at a *four-heart* contract. West opened the king of spades, and Andy correctly permitted the king to win. Had West now continued spades, he would have given declarer a present of a trick. But West, seeing that his partner had played the discouraging two of spades, shifted to a club at trick two. Andy, however, was not taking any finesse. Up he went with dummy's ace and drew the adverse trumps with his king, queen, and jack.

He then led the diamond jack, which was taken by East's ace. East played back a spade, Andy's ace winning. A diamond was now led to dummy's queen. On the diamond king, South discarded his spade jack. A club was then conceded to the defenders' king, and that was that. Declarer lost one spade, one diamond, and one club.

There are two fundamental points contained in this deal. First, if declarer had won incorrectly the opening lead of the king of spades, then when East subsequently obtained the lead via the ace of diamonds, a spade return by him would have given West two spade tricks—and declarer would have gone down. And secondly, when West shifted to a club at trick two, Andy hopped right up with the ace, spurning a finesse, which he did not need. Had he taken the finesse, East would have won the trick with his king, after which the return of a spade would have made a loser out of declarer's jack.

In refusing to capture the opening lead, Andy forced West to abandon the spade suit and thereby gave himself the time necessary to establish dummy's diamonds, on one of which the jack of spades was discarded.

All in all, this was really a well-played hand, combining as it did the knowledge of technique (the Bath coup) with the application of judgment (the realization that the club finesse was a luxury that declarer could not afford). Of such stuff are champions made.

Deal 4:
This deal, as the preceding one, illustrates the dual potentialities of the Bath coup in not only decoying the opening leader into continuing his suit, but also, if the decoy does not succeed, in gaining for declarer the time so vitally needed for his preservation.

```
                      ♠ K 8 2
                      ♡ A K J 8 3
                      ◇ Q J
                      ♣ 9 7 2
    ♠ 7 6                  N              ♠ A 5 3
    ♡ 9 5             W         B         ♡ 7 6 4
    ◇ A 8 7 4 2            S              ◇ 10 9 5 3
    ♣ K Q 10 3                            ♣ 8 6 4
                      ♠ Q J 10 9 4
                      ♡ Q 10 2
                      ◇ K 6
                      ♣ A J 5
```

Against South's *four-spade* contract, West made the normal opening of the club king, dummy following with the deuce, East with the four, and declarer with the five. West then cashed his ace of diamonds, after which another diamond was led, South's king winning.

When declarer now played a trump to the king, East took his ace and returned a club. Of course, declarer won this lead, drew the remaining trumps, and discarded the jack of clubs on one of dummy's high hearts.

But the deal would have had a different ending had declarer captured the opening lead of the king of clubs. Had he done this, then when East obtained the lead with the trump ace, the normal club return would have entrapped South remaining J 5 of clubs, resulting in declarer suffering a one-trick set.

Deal 5:
This deal presents a situation where the Bath coup should not be employed. The key to the shelving of the Bath coup comes from listening to, and interpreting, the bidding of the West defender.

```
                    ♠ 8 4 2
                    ♡ A
                    ◇ A 10 8 3
                    ♣ A 10 9 7 5
♠ K Q 10 9 7 5          N          ♠ 6
♡ Q 10 6 4                          ♡ K J 8 7 5 3 2
◇ 7              W         E        ◇ 6 5 4
♣ 8 3                  S            ♣ K 2
                    ♠ A J 3
                    ♡ 9
                    ◇ K Q J 9 2
                    ♣ Q J 6 4
```

Neither side vulnerable. South dealer.

South	West	North	East
1 ◇	2 ♠ *	3 ♣	3 ♡
4 ♣	Pass	4 ♡	Double
Pass	Pass	5 ◇	Pass
Pass	Pass		

*This is one of the modern bids, known as the "weak" jump overcall. Its purpose is to deprive the opponents of bidding space. Technically, the bid shows a six-card suit. In the long run, this "weak" bid is a winning one.

West opened the king of spades, which declarer won with his ace. Three rounds of trumps picked up the adverse pieces, after which declarer took the club finesse, losing to East's king. East returned a heart to dummy's ace. Clubs were then cashed, and on the board's fifth club declarer discarded his three of spades. At trick thirteen the jack of spades was conceded to West.

Had declarer permitted West to win the opening lead, a spade continuation would have been ruffed by East. In this case, the East defender would (eventually) have won a trick with the king of clubs, to defeat the contract.

Just what declarer would have done at trick one had West not made his weak jump overcall can never be determined. But with the overcall, his choice was a clear-cut one: West was marked with a six-card suit, and hence, East had a singleton.

Deal 6:

	♠ A 10 9 8 4 3	
	♡ K 6	
	◇ 5 3 2	
	♣ 7 4	
♠ 5	**N**	♠ J 7 6 2
♡ J 10 8 7 4	**W E**	♡ Q 9
◇ J 8	**S**	◇ Q 10 9 7
♣ K Q 9 8 2		♣ 10 6 3
	♠ K Q	
	♡ A 5 3 2	
	◇ A K 6 4	
	♣ A J 5	

Both sides vulnerable. South dealer.

South	West	North	East
1 ◇	Pass	1 ♠	Pass
3 NT	Pass	Pass	Pass

West's opening lead of the king of clubs was allowed to win the trick, after which West shifted to the jack of hearts, declarer taking it with the ace.

The king of spades was now played, followed by the

queen, which declarer overtook with the board's ace. The ten of spades was then led, East winning it with his jack. Declarer now had ten top tricks.

The result would have been quite different had declarer won the opening club lead, in the optimistic hope that the five adverse spades were divided 3-2 (as they actually figured to be), in which case eleven tricks would have been guaranteed. Had he done this, he would have ended up with just eight tricks, for when East obtained the lead via the spade jack, he would have returned a club, and the defenders would have taken four club tricks.

Deal 7:
On occasion, the opening lead will be in a suit where you, as declarer (fourth hand) have the A J x. When third hand puts up the queen (or king), there is no general rule that will tell you whether you should take the ace or hold up. Only your judgment can determine which is correct.

This deal, and the one that follows, illustrate when (and why) you should win the trick at once, and when (and why) you should decline to do so.

You are sitting South and have arrived at a *three–no-trump* contract:

♠ 5 3
♡ A 9 7
◇ A 8 7 2
♣ 10 9 6 3

N

6 of Spades led   **W**   **E**   Queen of spades

S

♠ A J 4
♡ K Q 10
◇ K 3
♣ A Q J 8 4

West opens the six of spades, and East puts up the queen. Should you take the queen, or hold up?

If you examine the hand, you will perceive that you are going to take the club finesse in such a manner that, if the finesse loses, it can lose *only to West*. That is, if East has the all-important king of clubs, he can never obtain the lead with it.

Since West, then, is the only one who can ever get the lead via the club king, you should capture the spade queen with your ace, after which you get to the North hand to take the club finesse. It loses. You still have the J 4 of spades left as protection against West's K x x x. If West now cashes the king of spades, he will establish your jack. And if he abstains from leading any more spades, you have ten sure tricks: one spade, three hearts, two diamonds, and four clubs. The hands were:

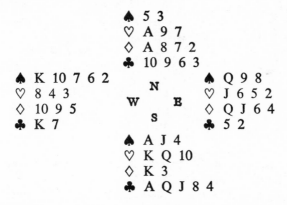

$$
\begin{array}{c}
\spadesuit\ 5\ 3 \\
\heartsuit\ A\ 9\ 7 \\
\diamondsuit\ A\ 8\ 7\ 2 \\
\clubsuit\ 10\ 9\ 6\ 3
\end{array}
$$

♠ K 10 7 6 2   ♠ Q 9 8
♡ 8 4 3   ♡ J 6 5 2
◇ 10 9 5   ◇ Q J 6 4
♣ K 7   ♣ 5 2

$$
\begin{array}{c}
\spadesuit\ A\ J\ 4 \\
\heartsuit\ K\ Q\ 10 \\
\diamondsuit\ K\ 3 \\
\clubsuit\ A\ Q\ J\ 8\ 4
\end{array}
$$

In abstract theory, if you take the spade ace at trick one, and *East* subsequently obtains the lead with the king of clubs, the return of a spade through your remaining J 4 will give West four spade tricks. But this is just abstract theory, with no possibility of its ever developing, for East can never obtain the lead, *since you will not allow it*. So why create a worry that can never come to pass.

If you decline to capture the spade ace at trick one, East will continue spades. No matter what you do from here in, you have lost control, and West will establish his spades. When he subsequently obtains the lead with the king of clubs, he will cash four spade tricks, to defeat your three–no-trump contract.

Deal 8:
The hands in this deal are just about identical to those in Deal 7. The only significant difference is that the North-South club holding has been interchanged, with North's being given South's club suit, and South's being given North's club suit.

Again, South is declarer at a *three–no-trump* contract.

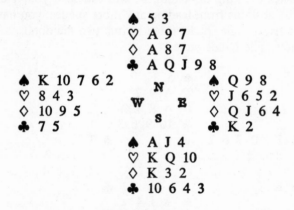

♠ 5 3
♡ A 9 7
◇ A 8 7
♣ A Q J 9 8

♠ K 10 7 6 2
♡ 8 4 3
◇ 10 9 5
♣ 7 5

♠ Q 9 8
♡ J 6 5 2
◇ Q J 6 4
♣ K 2

♠ A J 4
♡ K Q 10
◇ K 3 2
♣ 10 6 4 3

West opens the six of spades, and East puts up the queen. Should South capture this trick?

Looking ahead, South perceives that the development of the club suit is a necessity. Going further, South recognizes that he is going to attack the club suit in such a manner that if the finesse loses, it will lose *only to East*. Hence, if South wins the opening lead, and it should turn out that East has the club king, the latter will play back a spade, trapping declarer's remaining J 4, thus enabling West to cash his spades.

Since South cannot prevent East from winning a trick with the club king should the latter possess that card, his efforts should be directed toward *preventing East from returning a spade*. To achieve this end, South should allow the holdup play, allowing East's queen to win the opening

lead (just as South would have done had he held the
A x x instead of the A J x).

When East next plays back the spade nine, South again
refuses to capture the trick. A third lead of spades then
forces South to take his ace—and East is now void of
spades.

Declarer then attempts the club finesse, which loses to
East's king; and whatever East chooses to return, South's
contract is in the bag.

Had East happened to have held another spade, then
the adverse spades would have been divided 4-4, and South
was always safe although he didn't know it. The holdup
play, in this deal, is designed to protect South against
East's holding either two or three spades—and the protection is free. If East holds four spades, no protection is
required.

Deal 9:
There is a specialized type of situation where the holdup
play is employed in no-trump contracts despite the fact that
you hold *two sure stoppers* in the suit led. The principle
upon which it is based is this:

Whenever you have *two key cards to drive out of the
opponents' hands,* and you have a double-stopper in the suit
that they have led, hold up on the *first* lead of their suit. In
so doing, you will break the communication between their
hands and effectively prevent the leader from cashing his
suit. To illustrate:

```
                    ♠ 7 6 3
                    ♡ J 10 4
                    ◇ J 10 6 3
                    ♣ K 7 5
    ♠ Q J 10 9 4         N          ♠ 8 2
    ♡ A 7 5                          ♡ 9 3 2
    ◇ 9 8 2        W        E        ◇ A 7 4
    ♣ 10 2             S             ♣ J 9 8 4 3
                    ♠ A K 5
                    ♡ K Q 8 6
                    ◇ K Q 5
                    ♣ A Q 6
```

The contract is *three no-trump* against which West opens the queen of spades. As you can see, declarer has to drive out two key cards: the ace of diamonds and the ace of hearts. And, as you will understand in a moment, declarer should permit the queen to win the opening lead.

Let us assume, however, that declarer wins the queen of spades with his king, and that he then leads the king of diamonds, East's ace winning. East will now return a spade, and even if declarer holds up, it will be too late, for West will overtake and lead another spade, driving out declarer's ace. When declarer later leads a heart, West will take his ace to cash his established spades.

The reader may raise the point: "But what if declarer, at trick two, had played a heart instead of a diamond, knocking out *West's* ace? Then West could never regain the lead to cash his to-be-established spades?" Quite right. As I played the hand in the preceding paragraph, had declarer guessed to knock out the heart ace first (instead of East's diamond ace), then he would have made his contract. *The holdup play, when one possesses a double-stopper, with two key cards to drive out, will always eliminate the guess as to which of the two key cards to drive out first.*

Let us now play the hand properly. The queen of spades is permitted to win the first trick, and the second spade lead is captured by declarer's king. Can you see that the contract is now guranteed whether declarer leads a diamond or a heart? If he leads a diamond, East will win it, but he will have no spade to return; if declarer leads a heart instead, West will win it and will play another spade to establish his suit—but he can never regain the lead to cash that suit.

Two more questions may come to mind: (1) What if East had three spades, and (2) what if East possessed both red aces?

On (1), if East had a third spade to return whenever he obtained the lead, then the original spade distribution would have been 4-3 (instead of the actual 5-2), in which case declarer could not have lost more than two spades, a heart, and a diamond, no matter how he played the hand. On (2), if West had held both the ace of hearts and the ace of diamonds (with the spades being divided 5-2), then the contract would have been predestined to defeat, for nobody on earth could have fulfilled it against a spade opening (since three spades and the two red aces would have to be lost).

Whenever the two missing key cards are split in the hands of the opponents, the hold up with a double-stopper in a no-trump contract will assure success.

Deal 10:
This is the final holdup hand, and, as on Deal 9, it illustrates the situation where a hold up is employed with a double-stopper when two of the opponents' key cards are to be driven out (in no-trump contracts only).

```
                  ♠ K J
                  ♡ K 5 2
                  ◊ 10 9 5 4 2
                  ♣ K 4 2
  ♠ 8 6 5                        ♠ 10 9 7 3 2
  ♡ Q 10 8 6 3        N          ♡ J 9
  ◊ K 8 3         W       E      ◊ A 7
  ♣ J 5               S          ♣ Q 9 6 3
                  ♠ A Q 4
                  ♡ A 7 4
                  ◊ Q J 6
                  ♣ A 10 8 7
```

South's contract is *three no-trump,* and West opens the six of hearts.

As declarer views the combined North-South hands, it becomes apparent that he must drive out the ace and king of diamonds to establish that suit.

Let us say declarer plays it incorrectly and wins the opening heart lead. He now leads a diamond, which *East* captures with the ace. East then returns a heart, and even if declarer now holds up, West will overtake the nine with the ten and drive out declarer's last stopper (dummy's king) by continuing the heart suit. When West subsequently obtains the lead with the diamond king, he will then cash his established hearts. All in all, the defenders will make two diamond tricks and three heart tricks.

But if declarer holds up on the opening lead by playing low from both hands, East's jack will win the trick. East will now play back his remaining heart—and declarer has smooth sailing from here in. He leads a diamond: if East wins the ace, he has no heart to return; if, instead, West takes his king, he knocks out declarer's second stopper in hearts. Another diamond is then led, East's ace winning— but East is out of hearts, and dummy's diamond suit is established and cashable.

As mentioned in the previous deal, if East had another heart (three of them at the outset), then the original heart distribution would have been 4-3, guaranteeing the fulfillment of the contract. Had West held both the ace and king of diamonds (and *five* hearts), then the contract would be doomed owing to circumstances beyond declarer's control.

♠ The deals that comprise the contents of this chapter
were all misplayed at trick one by famous experts. Each
of the deals arose in national tournaments.

As the reader views the errors committed by these experts and reads my comments, he may feel that I am being
unduly critical. In a certain sense, I *am* being rather harsh
and possibly going out of my way in not tempering judgment
with mercy. Permit me to explain and justify my position.

The average, non-expert player commits many errors
and blunders during the course of any session of play.
Generally, these can be attributed to either a lack of experience, a lack of interest, or sheer carelessness. These
mistakes are inherent in his immature makeup; he is an
amateur to whom bridge is a pleasant, part-time avocation
or hobby. Quite often he doesn't even know that he has
made a mistake until it is pointed out to him. His mistakes
are expected and understandable, and hence, at least
partly excusable. From my self-appointed judgeship, I
would simply warn the amateur culprit to make an effort
to profit by his mistakes, to be more careful in the future—
and then I would dismiss the case.

But when the identical mistakes are committed by the
professional expert, whose *vocation* is playing bridge, they
are inexcusable—for the expert knew better, or should
have known better. In being perhaps overly critical in
magnifying the expert's error, I again put myself in the
role of judge. This time, however, I find myself convicting
an *expert* of the misdemeanor of "conduct unbecoming an
expert." To each of my individual charges—one per deal—
the expert, if he were permitted to enter a plea, would
plead "guilty as charged." And in none of these deals

would the expert feel bitter toward me for my lack of leniency. He would accept my criticism as his just desert.

Here is the evidence, for the reader to adjudge.

Deal 1:

```
                    ♠ 6 3 2
                    ♡ K 9 4
                    ◊ K 10 7 5 2
                    ♣ 7 5
    ♠ J 10 5              N          ♠ Q 9 7
    ♡ A J 10 8 7    W         E      ♡ Q 6 5 3 2
    ◊ ————               S          ◊ 9
    ♣ A J 9 6 2                      ♣ Q 10 8 4
                    ♠ A K 8 4
                    ♡ ————
                    ◊ A Q J 8 6 4 3
                    ♣ K 3
```

Against South's *five-diamond* contract, West led the jack of spades, the deuce was played from dummy, East followed with the seven-spot, and declarer won the trick with his ace. And, at that precise moment, South had just gotten himself nominated to Bridgedom's Hall of Shame, if such a Hall is ever established.

Having captured the opening lead, declarer now found it impossible to prevent East from ultimately obtaining the lead via a spade. When East then led a club, South lost his contract and the esteem of his partner.

It should have been apparent to our South declarer that the loss of a spade trick was inevitable. And it should have been equally apparent that the danger to his contract was that East might obtain the lead to push a club through South's K 3. Recognizing these things, South should have come up with the right play at trick one!

West's jack of spades should have been permitted to capture the opening lead. For an expert—as South was—this was really such an easy play to make. Even non-expert players have been known to make plays such as this on occasion. Had declarer declined to win the opening lead, his contract would have been in the bag.

Declarer, when he next obtained the lead, would simply draw the adverse trumps and then cash the ace and king of spades. When it became apparent that the six adverse spades were divided 3-3, one of dummy's losing clubs would be discarded on declarer's fourth spade.

Admittedly, the six adverse spades did not figure to be divided 3-3. But what would it have cost declarer to play for this possibility, especially since he had to lose a spade trick somewhere along the line? In so doing, he would be making sure that East did not obtain the lead. If the spades did not split evenly, then as a last resort declarer could fall back on the 50-50 hope that East possessed the ace of clubs. On this deal, the latter hope would not have materialized—but, on this deal, the contract could have been made without the reliance on this hope.

Deal 2:

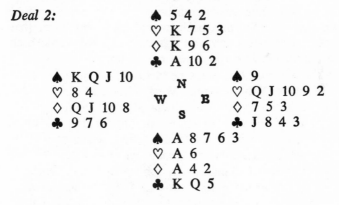

```
                  ♠ 5 4 2
                  ♡ K 7 5 3
                  ◇ K 9 6
                  ♣ A 10 2
  ♠ K Q J 10            N           ♠ 9
  ♡ 8 4                             ♡ Q J 10 9 2
  ◇ Q J 10 8      W         E       ◇ 7 5 3
  ♣ 9 7 6               S           ♣ J 8 4 3
                  ♠ A 8 7 6 3
                  ♡ A 6
                  ◇ A 4 2
                  ♣ K Q 5
```

North-South vulnerable. North dealer.

North	East	South	West
Pass	Pass	1 NT	Pass
3 NT	Pass	Pass	Pass

Against South's *three–no-trump* contract, West opened the king of spades. South won this with the ace and returned the three of spades, West's ten winning. On this trick East discarded the three of diamonds. Perceiving the futility of continuing spades, West properly shifted to the queen of diamonds, dummy's king capturing the trick. The board's last spade was then led, West taking it with his jack, after which he played the jack of diamonds.

Whether declarer took this trick or not was immaterial, for he was now a dead duck. West had established two diamond tricks, which, combined with three spade tricks, was all that any defender needs against an opponent's three no-trump contract. Declarer had commenced operations with eight winning tricks—and he had terminated with the same eight winning tricks.

It is impossible to predict with *absolute* certainty just what would have happened had declarer played the *eight* of spades on the opening lead, instead of winning the trick with the ace. I'm *reasonably* certain that if this had been done, an observant West, perceiving his partner's nine-spot being played to the first trick, would have concluded that partner's nine was a come-on signal. And West would then have continued with the queen of spades.

Declarer would take the second spade lead and fire back a third spade, West winning. West's diamond shift at this point (trick four) would be belated, for declarer would have obtained the timing: upon winning the diamond shift with his ace, he would then lead a fourth round of spades, thereby establishing his fifth spade, while dummy still retained the king of diamonds to control that suit. Declarer would now have his ninth trick—as I'm sure he had it in retrospect. But, unfortunately, they pay off for what happens at the table, and not in retrospect.

Deal 3:
The urge to grab the opening lead whenever the opportunity presents itself is not an impulse confined to non-experts only; experts themselves are equally prone to winning rather than losing the first trick. However, the expert has learned to control this impulse to a much greater extent than the non-expert. But, on occasion, the urge within the expert becomes irresistible. When this happens, expert and

non-expert walk hand in hand—to their collective doom.
Here is a "for instance":

```
              ♠ 8 6 5
              ♡ A 7 2
              ◇ J 8 4
              ♣ A Q J 7
♠ A Q 9 4          N          ♠ J 10 7
♡ 5                           ♡ 6
◇ A K 6 3 2    W     E        ◇ Q 10 9 7 5
♣ 8 6 5            S          ♣ K 9 4 2
              ♠ K 3 2
              ♡ K Q J 10 9 8 4 3
              ◇ ——————
              ♣ 10 3
```

East-West vulnerable. South dealer.

South	West	North	East
4 ♡	Pass	Pass	Pass

West's opening lead of the king of diamonds was ruffed
by declarer, after which the king of trumps picked up the
two adversely held trumps. The ten of clubs was then led
and the finesse taken, losing to East's king. East now made
the natural shift to the jack of spades—and the defenders
lost no time in cashing three spade tricks.

Declarer had no one but himself to blame for the lost
contract, for he failed to make the decisive, expert play at
trick one. The worry on the hand was, of course, that
East might obtain the lead later, to play a spade through
declarer's K 3 2. This worry could have been eliminated
at trick one: on the king of diamonds declarer should have
discarded the three of clubs instead of trumping!

Let's say that West then led another diamond to trick
two (no other lead could alter the outcome). Declarer
would trump this lead, after which he would pick up the
adverse trumps. Now his remaining club, the ten-spot, would
be led and taken with dummy's ace.

Then would follow the queen of clubs. If East covered this with the king, declarer would ruff, enter dummy via the trump ace, and on the established jack of clubs he would discard his losing deuce of spades. If, instead, East declined to cover, the deuce of spades would again be discarded, with the board's queen winning the trick.

The interesting—and instructive—feature of this line of play is that declarer's contract would be guaranteed even if *West* held the king of clubs. Had this been the case, then when the queen of clubs was led (declarer discarding the deuce of spades), West would win the trick with his (hypothetical) king.

If West now led a spade, he would give declarer a present of the latter's king. And whatever else he led, declarer would capture, reenter the board via the ace of trumps, and on the established jack of clubs he would discard his three of spades.

Played properly, declarer had a guarantee that not only would he create a club trick for himself (upon which to discard a losing spade), but also that *East would never obtain the lead.*

Deal 4:

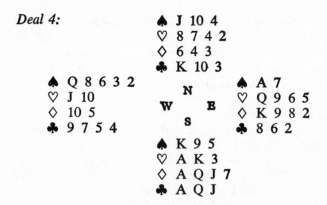

West opened his fourth highest spade against South's contract of *three no-trump.* East won with his ace and played back the seven, South's nine being taken by West's queen. A third round of spades was then captured by South's king.

It was readily apparent to South that he needed three diamond tricks to fulfill his contract. At trick four he led the jack of clubs, which he overtook with dummy's king. The queen of diamonds was then finessed, successfully, after which South, being unable to get to dummy to take another finesse, played the ace of diamonds, and then another diamond, in the hope that the six adverse diamonds were divided 3-3. When it was revealed that the suit was not so divided, South came home with just eight tricks, one short of his contract.

From the beginning, it should have been obvious to declarer that his best hope of fulfilling the contract was to take two diamond finesses, and that in order to accomplish this, he had to get to dummy two times. On the face of it, just one entry to dummy was available—the king of clubs.

But a positive second entry could have been created by discarding the king of spades on East's ace at trick one! Regardless of what East then returned, the board's jack (or ten) of spades would have become a second entry.

Let's say that East played back a heart at trick two. Declarer would win it with the king and lead the five of spades. Whether West took his queen or not, declarer would be able to get to dummy twice, once in spades and once via the king of clubs, to take two finesses in diamonds. And, with the favorable location of the diamond king, he would have his needed three diamond tricks.

It should be noted that, in jettisoning his king of spades at trick one, declarer was *not* sacrificing a trick, since dummy's jack or ten would always be promoted into a winner. From a positive point of view, declarer was simply postponing the winning of a spade trick; and, of much greater importance, he was at the same time creating a vitally needed entry to dummy.

Deal 5:

In introducing the misplay that declarer made on this deal, perhaps I am being unfair to our expert declarer, for I doubt that one out of 1,000 players would have made the right play. But even if the reader will not agree with me

when I say that declarer made a misplay, I'm absolutely
certain that the expert who made it would agree with me.
I should mention that this deal arose in the National
Championships held in Washington, D.C., in 1961, and that
about two hours after it was played, while a group of us
were having coffee, our declarer suddenly screamed out:
"I could have made that five-club contract!!"

Here it is:

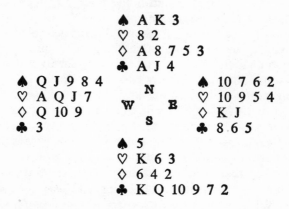

<pre>
                    ♠ A K 3
                    ♡ 8 2
                    ◇ A 8 7 5 3
                    ♣ A J 4
  ♠ Q J 9 8 4   ♠ 10 7 6 2
  ♡ A Q J 7   N   ♡ 10 9 5 4
  ◇ Q 10 9   W   E   ◇ K J
  ♣ 3   S   ♣ 8 6 5
                    ♠ 5
                    ♡ K 6 3
                    ◇ 6 4 2
                    ♣ K Q 10 9 7 2
</pre>

North-South vulnerable. North dealer.

North	East	South	West
1 ◇	Pass	2 ♣	Double*
4 ♣	Pass	5 ♣	Pass
Pass	Pass		

West opened the spade queen, dummy's king winning.
The ace of spades was played next, declarer discarding
the two of diamonds. A trump was then led to South's
nine, after which the four of diamonds was played. West
covered this with the nine, and dummy's ace won the
trick as East dropped the jack. Another diamond was now
led, East's king winning. East next played, quite naturally,

*For takeout, announcing support for both major suits.

a heart—and declarer lost two heart tricks.

What was declarer's "misplay?" you might ask. Well, let's start with an analysis of the situation. Almost surely, on the bidding, West figured to have the heart ace. Hence, it was imperative—from the viewpoint of declarer's self-preservation—that East be kept out of the lead in order to prevent the decapitation of declarer's king of hearts. At the same time, it was obvious that declarer, to make his contract, would have to establish a couple of winners in diamonds. The problem, therefore, was how to establish dummy's diamonds while eliminating, or minimizing, the danger of East's obtaining the lead.

Oh, the simplicity of it all when the battle was ended and contemplation has become the order of the day! Just allow West's spade queen to win the opening lead! No matter what West now leads, South will lose only one more trick.

Suppose West continues the spade suit at trick two. On dummy's A K of spades, declarer discards his two losing diamonds. Then will follow the ace of diamonds, after which declarer will ruff a diamond. With both opponents following suit to these two rounds of diamonds, only the diamond queen is now outstanding. Next the king of trumps is cashed, and a trump is led to dummy's ace. A third round of diamonds is now ruffed—and the board's two remaining diamonds have just become promoted into winners.

Dummy is then reentered via the trump ace—picking up East's last trump enroute—and on the established diamonds declarer discards two of his hearts. At the end West makes his ace of hearts, while declarer makes his contract.

For the average player to come up with the winning line of play would properly be called "a brilliant and imaginative play." For the expert, the failure to come up with the winning line of play must, in my opinion—and by the expert's own admission—be labelled as a "misplay."

Deal 6:
This deal is another good illustration of a declarer who

chose to grab the opening lead without pausing to look ahead. It turned out to be an expensive "grab."

```
              ♠ A J 3
              ♡ Q 6
              ◇ K Q 8 4
              ♣ K 10 9 8
  ♠ 9 8 6 4        N        ♠ K 7 2
  ♡ K 3      W         E    ♡ J 10 9 8 4 2
  ◇ 7 6 3         S         ◇ A 5
  ♣ A 6 5 4                 ♣ 7 2
              ♠ Q 10 5
              ♡ A 7 5
              ◇ J 10 9 2
              ♣ Q J 3
```

Both sides vulnerable. North dealer.

North	East	South	West
1 ◇	1 ♡	1 NT	Pass
2 NT	Pass	3 NT	Pass
Pass	Pass		

West, on lead, opened the king of hearts, and South embraced the king with the ace as though he were greeting a long-lost brother. At trick two, South chose to lead the jack of clubs, but West climbed right up with his ace, in order to return his remaining heart, which was won with the board's queen. At this point, declarer recognized that he had lost his contract, since East, for his vulnerable overcall on a jack-high heart suit, was certain to possess the king of spades and the ace of diamonds. So he cashed his three clubs, East discarding a spade and a diamond on the third and fourth clubs, and then declarer led a diamond. When East had finished running his four heart tricks, he had to lead away from the king of spades, and dummy won two spade tricks. Declarer made exactly seven tricks, for a two-trick set.

In a sense, declarer was unlucky—or, perhaps, simply a bad guesser—for had he decided to attack diamonds rather than clubs at trick two, he would have fulfilled his contract. Had he done this, he would have knocked out *East's* entry card, the diamond ace. And, when East would return a heart, dummy's queen would win, after which the club suit would be attacked. When *West* took his ace of clubs, he would have no heart to play back, and declarer would wind up with nine tricks: one spade, two hearts, three diamonds, and three clubs.

However, even if declarer had made his contract by guessing right (breaking the diamond suit first), I would still accuse him of "conduct unbecoming an expert," for his contract could have been made without relying on guesswork. After all, an expert should be familiar with the holdup play when one possesses a double-stopper in the suit led, with two adversely held key cards to knock out.

Declarer should have permitted West's king of hearts to win the opening lead. A heart continuation would then have been won by dummy's queen, and it then would have made no difference whether declarer went after diamonds or clubs first: if it were diamonds, East would win the trick with the ace and lead another heart to establish his suit, but he could never regain the lead to cash it. And if it were the club suit that declarer elected to attack first, West would win with the ace, but would have no heart to return. Whatever else he chose to return, declarer would have the time to establish his diamond suit (while still retaining the ace of hearts).

Deal 7:
One of the greatest players this world has ever known is Waldemar von Zedtwitz. Many years ago, while discussing with him the general subject of the various types of technical mistakes that bridge players make, "Waldy" made a few remarks that are most significant. He said, in part:

"We cannot isolate all of the various categories of mistakes, for there are certain non-technical mistakes— errors in judgment—which defy pinpointing. For example, have you ever noticed that a poorer player will often be penalized for simply being a poorer player, on a hand where he has not made the slightest semblance of a mistake."

I might add by way of qualification that in using the term, "poorer player," Waldy was not referring to the inexpert player. He was speaking of the "fair" *expert* player, as contrasted to the "very good" *expert* player. His reference was to the encounters between the "fair" and the "very good," in which the "very good" often obtain an advantage over the "fair," an advantage that is not discernible to the naked, untrained, inexpert eye.

The deal that follows is a case in point. I have shown this deal to a good many players and have asked them what "mistake" declarer made that was capitalized on by the East defender. Very few have come up with the proper answer.

```
                  ♠ 7 5
                  ♡ 8 2
                  ◇ Q J 10 9 8 3
                  ♣ A 8 4
  ♠ Q 10 8 6 2         N        ♠ J 9 4
  ♡ K 10 5 3                    ♡ A J 9 4
  ◇ 7 4        W         E      ◇ A 2
  ♣ J 6             S           ♣ 10 9 7 5
                  ♠ A K 3
                  ♡ Q 7 6
                  ◇ K 6 5
                  ♣ K Q 3 2
```

East-West vulnerable. North dealer.

North	East	South	West
3 ◇	Pass	3 NT	Pass
Pass	Pass		

West led the six of spades, and East's jack was taken by declarer's ace. The five of diamonds was then played to the board's queen, East declining to take his ace. On the return of dummy's three of diamonds, East was compelled to win the trick. On this trick, South "unblocked" by discarding the king of diamonds.

After a moment's deliberation, East shifted to a heart, and the defenders rattled off four heart tricks. As is apparent, had East instead played back a spade—West's opening suit—declarer would have romped in with his contract.

What "mistake" did declarer make that motivated East to shift to a heart, rather than to return West's spade suit?

The answer is that East knew that South still retained the king of spades, and that, hence, the return of a spade seemed futile. How did East know that South had "concealed" the king of spades?

The diamond suit was an open book to everybody at the table: South had five diamond tricks once the opponents' ace was knocked out. Why then (reasoned East), if South had held, let us say, the A x x of spades, didn't he hold up the ace of spades until the third round of the suit had been played, so that if East held the ace of diamonds, the latter would be unable to return a spade when he obtained the lead with the ace? Furthermore, East knew that South was a good enough player to hold up the ace if the latter had possessed the A x x of spades. East therefore concluded that South's only justification for taking the spade ace at trick one must have been that South also held the spade *king*. In the face of dummy's established diamond suit, for East to have returned a spade would have been an unthinking, hopeless, defeatist play.

Had South won the opening lead with the king rather than with the ace, East would have had a serious problem as to what to return. The play of the king would have been much less revealing, from East's viewpoint, for West may have been leading away from the ace; and, if he were, South could not afford to hold up his king.*

---

*If South had held the K 8 3 and West had led the six of spades from the A Q 10 6 2, South would have had no option but to win the trick with the king. If he didn't, a spade return would give the defenders five spade tricks.

Presumably, South chose to win the trick with the ace, rather than with the king, to lead East into believing that West held the king. But he created the opposite effect, for our "very good" East defender realized that if South did not have the king, he would have held up his ace, in order to break the defenders' communication.

chapter 7 An Ear to the Bidding

♠ Virtually all textbooks relating to the play of the cards contain a section that presents the mathematical "laws" of suit-division probabilities. For example, the reader is informed that when six of a suit are held by the opponents, those six will be divided 3-3 about 36% of the time; a 4-2 division will occur 48% of the time, etc. In addition, the reader is usually given the proper play of certain standard, frequently recurring combinations of cards. For instance, he is told that the correct way of playing a suit when he has the A J x x x facing the K x x x, is to play the king and ace, hoping to drop the queen, as opposed to leading the king and then finessing for the queen.

All of the data and recommended plays in the above paragraph are correct. But they are correct only out of context, in theory, as proven by mathematical computations *away from* the bridge table. *They are correct only if no clues relevant to the distribution of the opponents' cards have been divulged in the bidding or the play.* For example:

```
             ♠ K x x x
             ♡ x x
             ♢ x x x
             ♣ A J x x
                  N
             W         E
                  S
             ♠ A J 10 9 8
             ♡ x
             ♢ A K Q J
             ♣ K Q 10
```

East-West vulnerable. South dealer.

South	West	North	East
2 ♠	4 ♡	6 ♠	Pass
Pass	Pass		

West opens the king of hearts, everybody following suit. He then leads the ace of hearts, and East *discards* a diamond as you trump.

At this point, there isn't a mathematician alive (nor any good bridge player) who will stand by the mathematical "law" that when four of a suit are held by the opponents (spades in this case), those four will be divided 2-2 about 40% of the time; nor will he wager his life, or a few of his hard-earned pennies, that the king and ace of spades will drop the queen as often as 40% of the time. With West being known to have held *nine* (count 'em!) hearts originally, mathematics, percentages, and tables of probability go into hibernation, to be saved for a future day when they will again become applicable.

The chances of West's having been dealt the Q x of spades in the above deal have just become most remote (the percentage is unimportant). There isn't a decent player who would, in these circumstances, lead the king and ace of spades hoping to catch West with the Q x of spades. Certainly East, in this situation, will possess the spade queen much more often than West. So a spade is led to the king, and on the way back the jack of spades is finessed. Declarer then writes up the score for a small slam bid and made.

Here is the deal, which arose in the National Championships of 1961. Of the thirteen times that this deal was played, twelve South declarers arrived at a six spade contract—*and every one of them finessed East for the queen of spades*. They each realized that the appearance of a nine-card heart suit in West's hand was a reality that had more significance with regard to the situation at hand than out-of-context mathematical probabilities.

This is another deal on which you can test your friends (to see whether or not they take the spade finesse).

```
              ♠ K 7 5 2
              ♡ 8 4
              ◇ 10 7 5
              ♣ A J 3 2
♠ 4                    N        ♠ Q 6 3
♡ A K Q J 10 9 7 5 2      W   E  ♡ 3
◇ 9                    S        ◇ 8 6 4 3 2
♣ 8 5                          ♣ 9 7 6 4
              ♠ A J 10 9 8
              ♡ 6
              ◇ A K Q J
              ♣ K Q 10
```

Obviously, then, the mathematics of normal, expected suit divisions—and when to finesse and when not to finesse for a queen—are not intended by our mathematicians to be adhered to blindly or categorically. The figures advocated for use in normal situations presuppose that no negating hints or clues have been divulged during the bidding or the play. Whenever "contra-mathematical" facts assert themselves, the practical bridge player forsakes his customary reliance on the "approved" mathematical formulae and closely examines the external influences that have entered upon, and affected, the scene.

All of which brings us to the subject at hand, namely *the clues revealed during the bidding that influence declarer's play at trick one.* In this chapter, as in actual combat at the table, mathematics are relegated to a back seat and are correctly replaced by one of the five senses, *the ear.* In each of the deals contained herein, the ear becomes the primary and invaluable aid in directing declarer to the winning line of play.

Deal 1:
In this deal, the play by *a defender* at trick one, combined with declarer's ear to the bidding, directed declarer to what may seem to be, on superficial examination, an illogical, "unmathematical" line of play. However, on

closer analysis, the "illogical" play is the logical, proper, and winning line of play.

```
              ♠ A 10 5
              ♡ 4
              ◇ K Q 7
              ♣ A Q J 10 4 2
  ♠ 7 4                        ♠ 8 6 3
  ♡ A 8 5          N           ♡ K Q J 6 3 2
  ◇ 10 9 8 2   W       E       ◇ A J 5
  ♣ 8 6 5 3        S           ♣ K
              ♠ K Q J 9 2
              ♡ 10 9 7
              ◇ 6 4 3
              ♣ 9 7
```

Both sides vulnerable. East dealer.

East	South	West	North
1 ♡	Pass	Pass	Double
Pass	1 ♠	Pass	3 ♣
Pass	3 ♠	Pass	4 ♠
Pass	Pass	Pass	

West opened the ace of hearts and, upon seeing the dummy, promptly shifted to the ten of diamonds. East took dummy's queen with the ace and played back the jack of diamonds, the board's king winning.

The five of trumps was then led to South's king, after which a heart was ruffed with dummy's ace of trumps. The ten of trumps was now overtaken by declarer's queen, and the jack laid down, picking up East's last trump.

Next declarer led a club, and put up dummy's ace, dropping East's king. The remainder of the tricks belonged to declarer.

How come the "against percentage" play of the club ace, instead of the 50-50 finesse in clubs? To an expert, this was a simple matter: West had passed East's opening one heart bid, and West, at trick one, had shown up with the ace of hearts. Had West also possessed the king of clubs, he would not have passed East's opening bid. So East *had to have* the king of clubs, and declarer's sole hope was that East's king was a singleton. As luck (and "right" living) would have it, the king was a singleton.

Deal 2:

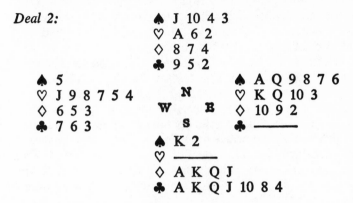

```
                    ♠ J 10 4 3
                    ♡ A 6 2
                    ◇ 8 7 4
                    ♣ 9 5 2
  ♠ 5                            ♠ A Q 9 8 7 6
  ♡ J 9 8 7 5 4      N           ♡ K Q 10 3
  ◇ 6 5 3        W       B       ◇ 10 9 2
  ♣ 7 6 3            S           ♣ —
                    ♠ K 2
                    ♡ —
                    ◇ A K Q J
                    ♣ A K Q J 10 8 4
```

Neither side vulnerable. East dealer.

East	South	West	North
1 ♠	6 ♣	Pass	Pass
Pass			

When West opened the five of spades and dummy came into view, South *knew* that West had a singleton spade, for West, following accepted standard procedure, was leading the highest card of his partner's bid suit. South knew that the five-spot was a singleton because the two, three, and four were in evidence. If the play to the first trick were to go: five by West, three from the dummy, the ace by East, and the deuce by South, East would also know that West had started with a singleton spade, for East would also then be looking at the two, three, four, and five of spades. And, of course, East would then promptly return a spade, for West to trump.

Two lovely, "accidental" cards had come up in dummy: the ace of hearts, and the nine of clubs as an entry to dummy. So declarer followed with the spade three from the board, and when East took his ace, South dropped his king!

East had no way of knowing whether the king was "for real" or not. After all, West might well have started with the 5-2 of spades, and South with the singleton king. After due deliberation, East returned the king of hearts, and declarer, aided and abetted by deception, had just fulfilled an "unmakable" slam.

On the heart lead, South discarded the deuce of spades, dummy's ace winning. The rest of the play was routine.

As to whether East should have been taken in by South's false card is immaterial. The point is that if South had played the deuce on the opening lead, East would automatically have returned a spade, knowing that West had no more spades. With the fall of the king instead, East was compelled to pause for reflection. While East reflected, South prayed that a spade would not be returned.

Deal 3:

```
                    ♠ 6 5
                    ♡ A 10 9
                    ◇ 9 4 3 2
                    ♣ A 10 7 5
  ♠ 3                   N            ♠ 9 4 2
  ♡ 4                                ♡ 8 7 6 5 3 2
  ◇ K Q J          W       E         ◇ 10 8 7 6
  ♣ K Q J 9 8 6 4 2      S           ♣ ———
                    ♠ A K Q J 10 8 7
                    ♡ K Q J
                    ◇ A 5
                    ♣ 3
```

Both sides vulnerable. West dealer.

West	North	East	South
5 ♣	Double	Pass	6 ♠
Pass	Pass	Pass	

Just a brief word on the bidding. North thought he could defeat the five-club contract, so he doubled. And

South felt that if North could beat five clubs, then South ought to be able to make six spades. He was right: six spades was makable—provided declarer did not play hurriedly to the first trick.

West elected to open the king of clubs, dummy's ace was put up—and East trumped! Declarer struggled quietly for the remainder of the play but eventually had to surrender a diamond trick. Tough luck, did I hear you say about the first club being trumped. Not at all, I say. It figured to be trumped.

West, vulnerable, had opened the bidding with *five clubs*. Surely he figured to have "around" an eight-card club suit. East, therefore, figured to have no clubs or, possibly, one club at most.

Declarer should have saved the ace of clubs for later when it would be a certain winner. The proper play at trick one was to permit West to win the opening club lead! West would then lead another club, and again declarer would decline to put up the ace, trumping the trick instead. Trumps would then be drawn, after which dummy would be entered via the heart ace. On the ace of clubs declarer would now discard his losing diamond. Declarer would then claim the remainder of the tricks.

Played in this manner, declarer would simply be exchanging a trick for a trick: instead of giving the opponents a diamond trick later, he would be giving them a club trick now. The logic behind the play was, of course, that it was not safe to attempt to win the ace of clubs at trick one, but that it would be absolutely safe to win it later, after trumps were drawn.

Even if West had not bid anything, the proper technical play would have been to defer the taking of the club ace, since the club ace could be used later for the disposal of South's losing diamond. But with the bidding, it became *mandatory* for declarer not to attempt to take it, for he had been forewarned that it almost certainly would be trumped. But, somehow, either declarer did not hear the warning (I am being gracious), or he paid no attention to it.

Deal 4:

```
              ♠ Q 7 5
              ♡ K Q 8 6 2
              ◇ 5 4
              ♣ J 6 3
♠ A 4 2                      ♠ 8 6
♡ A J 10 9      N           ♡ 7 4 3
◇ Q J 8 7    W     B        ◇ 6 3 2
♣ Q 9          S           ♣ K 7 5 4 2
              ♠ K J 10 9 3
              ♡ 5
              ◇ A K 10 9
              ♣ A 10 8
```

North-South vulnerable. South dealer.

South	West	North	East
1 ♠	1 NT	Double	2 ♣
Pass	Pass	2 ♡	Pass
3 ◇	Pass	3 ♠	Pass
4 ♠	Pass	Pass	Pass

When West opened the queen of clubs, it was quite apparent that (1) he did not have the king; (2) from the
bidding, he had to have the ace of trumps; (3) he almost
certainly possessed a doubleton club, for his no-trump
overcall denoted a balanced hand (hence no singleton),
and he would have led a low club had he held the Q x x.
So South correctly permitted the club queen to win the
opening lead—and there was nothing West could now play
that would prevent South from fulfilling his contract.

At trick two West shifted to the trump ace, after which
he led another trump, declarer taking this trick with his
nine-spot. South then led his singleton heart, and when
West took his ace, that was the last trick for the defenders.
(Later on, declarer finessed East for the king of clubs.)

The result would have been quite different if declarer
had won the opening lead of the club queen. When he
then, or subsequently, led a trump, West would rise with

his ace, to lead his remaining club to East's king. East would then return another club, West ruffing. The ace of hearts would now become the setting trick.

Of course, declarer would probably have made the same play without the adverse bidding—but in this situation, he might have been wrong, for West's queen might have been a singleton. Based on the given bidding, however, declarer's holdup at trick one had to be the right play, for West was certain to have started with a doubleton club.

Deal 5:
On this deal, a false card became the only correct play, for without it declarer knew that he was doomed.

```
                    ♠ Q 9 5
                    ♡ J 10 8
                    ◇ A J 10 3 2
                    ♣ Q 5
   ♠ 4                   N              ♠ 8 7 3 2
   ♡ A Q 9 7 3 2    W         E         ♡ 4
   ◇ 7 5                                ◇ 9 8 6 4
   ♣ A 10 9 8            S              ♣ 7 6 4 3
                    ♠ A K J 10 6
                    ♡ K 6 5
                    ◇ K Q
                    ♣ K J 2
```

North-South vulnerable. West dealer.

West	North	East	South
1 ♡	Pass	Pass	Double
2 ♡	3 ◇	Pass	3 ♠
Pass	4 ♠	Pass	Pass
Pass			

When West opened the ace of hearts, it was a virtual certainty—as South viewed the situation—that West possessed a six- or seven-card heart suit. The only high cards possessed by the East-West defenders were the A Q of hearts and the ace of clubs, which hardly constituted sufficient strength for an opening bid, let alone a rebid opposite a passing partner. Hence, West's only apparent justification for his bidding was that he must have had distributional strength, and a six- or seven-card heart suit formed the basis for his bidding.

On the lead of the ace of hearts, East followed with the four-spot, which eliminated the possibility of West's having held a seven-card suit. Thus, a six-card suit was guaranteed to be possessed by West. So, without undue haste or undue deliberation, the *king* of hearts was dropped by declarer on this trick!

This play "convinced" West that the king was a singleton, and West promptly shifted to the ace of clubs, after which he led another club, dummy's queen winning. It now became a routine proposition for declarer to draw trumps and claim the balance of the tricks (his two losing hearts being discarded on the board's high diamonds).

For those readers who think that declarer was taking an unnecessary gamble when he "needlessly" dropped the heart king on the opening lead, they are wrong. The gamble would have been to drop the five-spot and hope that West would not continue the heart suit. But, then, West might well have continued the heart suit, hoping that (1) East had the heart king, or (2) that East had a singleton heart. With the king's being played by declarer, a different picture was presented: if the king were a "true" play, then a heart continuation would create a winner out of dummy's jack or ten of hearts. Was not the lesser gamble to drop the king? And, with West's accepting the play of the king of hearts at face value, he shifted to clubs, which, of course, was what declarer hoped West would do.

Deal 6:

It has been stated that deceptive play is more effective and less dangerous to employ when it is wielded by declarer, for declarer's partner cannot be deceived. Yet, this does not give declarer the license to be promiscuous; for if he is, much harm can come of it. Too many players, unfortunately, have developed the habit of being tricky in all situations, for practice as it were. For example, whenever they can false card, they do. And in so doing, they point the way for the opposition to register the victory. They do not appreciate that truth can sometimes be more deceptive than fiction.

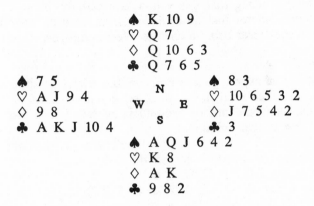

```
                     ♠ K 10 9
                     ♡ Q 7
                     ◇ Q 10 6 3
                     ♣ Q 7 6 5
  ♠ 7 5                              ♠ 8 3
  ♡ A J 9 4          N               ♡ 10 6 5 3 2
  ◇ 9 8          W       E           ◇ J 7 5 4 2
  ♣ A K J 10 4       S               ♣ 3
                     ♠ A Q J 6 4 2
                     ♡ K 8
                     ◇ A K
                     ♣ 9 8 2
```

Neither side vulnerable. South dealer.

South	West	North	East
1 ♠	2 ♣	2 ♠	Pass
4 ♠	Pass	Pass	Pass

When West opened the king of clubs and East followed with the *three-spot, South knew that East's three-spot was a singleton*. Had South "fooled around" by playing the eight or the nine on the trick, West would unquestionably have noticed that the deuce was not in evidence. And he would then have led the ace, for East's three-spot would either have had to have been the beginning of a "high-low" signal with the 3-2, or South possessed the deuce, in which case it was safe to cash the ace of clubs without the fear that it might be trumped by declarer.

But when declarer nonchalantly played the deuce on the opening club lead, West had a legitimate problem, for East could have held the 9 8 3 combination, with declarer's possessing the singleton two-spot. If this were the distribution, then the continuation of the club ace would be trumped by declarer, while simultaneously the board's queen of clubs would be established into a winner.

With nothing positive to guide him, West elected to lead the ace of hearts at trick two. And, despite East's play of the deuce of hearts on this trick, West led another heart, evidently feeling that this was a safe exit for him. As is evident, declarer had no problems from here in, his only subsequent loser being a trick to West's club ace.

Deal 7:
Had a non-expert gone wrong on the trick-one situation that presented itself in this deal, he would be excused. But an expert would not be excused if he failed to come up with the proper solution.

```
                    ♠ 7 5 4
                    ♡ 8 6
                    ◇ K J 10 9 2
                    ♣ A K Q
♠ A Q J 10 9              N          ♠ 8 6
♡ Q J 10                             ♡ 9 7 5 3
◇ 6 4            W         E         ◇ Q 5 3
♣ 9 8 4              S               ♣ 7 5 3 2
                    ♠ K 3 2
                    ♡ A K 4 2
                    ◇ A 8 7
                    ♣ J 10 6
```

Neither side vulnerable. South dealer.

South	West	North	East
1 ♡	1 ♠	2 ◇	Pass
2 NT	Pass	3 NT	Pass
Pass	Pass		

When West opens the queen of spades, virtually every non-expert would win the trick with the king. He would then fulfill his contract only if he were a good guesser and finessed East, rather than West, for the queen of diamonds.

Possibly half of the time he would guess right and half of the time he would guess wrong.

Our expert, on the other hand, would require no guessing ability to bring the contract home safely. Knowing that West, for his overcall, had at least five spades, declarer would permit the spade queen to capture the opening lead!

If West then played the ace of spades and then another round of spades, declarer would win with the king as East failed to follow suit. It would then be routine to lead the ace of diamonds, and then finesse the nine of diamonds, which, if it lost (as it would have), would lose only to East, who was known to be void of spades.

If, at trick two, West chose to lead the jack of spades (instead of the ace), declarer would take it with his king, after which he would again finesse the diamond suit in such a manner that if it lost, it would lose only to East. And, if West had started with a five-card suit (which figured to be), then, again, East was now void of spades and thus harmless to declarer. Even if West had overcalled with but four spades, the contract was nevertheless guaranteed at this point, since, if East had another spade, then the adverse spades would be divided 4-3. In this case, all declarer would lose would be three spades and one diamond.

And if, at trick two, after having been permitted to win the opening lead with his queen of spades, West elected to lead some suit other than spades, declarer would have no problem or worry. Let's say West chose to lead the queen of hearts at trick two, which declarer would win with his ace. Dummy then would be entered via a club, and the diamond jack would be led, and East's queen would be finessed, successfully as it would turn out. But even if this finesse had lost, it would lose *only to West*. And once again West would find himself in the same position in which he found himself at trick two—and in the interim declarer would have established dummy's diamond suit.

By employing the holdup play at trick one, and depending upon what West continued at trick two, declarer would have been enabled to maneuver his diamond finesse in

such a manner as to guarantee that if the finesse lost,
it would lose only to the non-dangerous hand.

Deal 8:

Very often the prime issue at trick one becomes whether
to win the opening lead in dummy in order to take a
finesse in Suit A; or whether to win it in the closed hand
in order to take a finesse in Suit B. Here is one of those
deals.

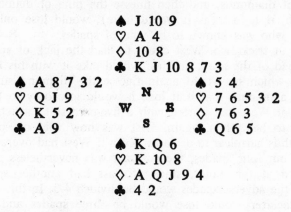

```
                    ♠ J 10 9
                    ♡ A 4
                    ◇ 10 8
                    ♣ K J 10 8 7 3
  ♠ A 8 7 3 2                        ♠ 5 4
  ♡ Q J 9            N               ♡ 7 6 5 3 2
  ◇ K 5 2        W       E           ◇ 7 6 3
  ♣ A 9              S               ♣ Q 6 5
                    ♠ K Q 6
                    ♡ K 10 8
                    ◇ A Q J 9 4
                    ♣ 4 2
```

East-West vulnerable. West dealer.

West	North	East	South
1 ♠	Pass	Pass	Double
Pass	3 ♣	Pass	3 NT
Pass	Pass	Pass	

West opened the three of spades, dummy's nine was
played, East followed with the four-spot, and the issue
became whether to permit the nine to win in order to take
the diamond finesse; or whether to overtake the nine with
the queen in order to attack the club suit. Our declarer
gave it some thought—and came up with the correct answer.

Certainly, on the bidding, West figured to possess both
the king of diamonds and the ace of clubs (in addition to

the spade ace, which was obvious when East played the four of spades at trick one). If declarer took the diamond finesse at trick two, he knew it would lose to West. West would then continue the spade suit by playing the ace and another spade. And, if it turned out that West possessed a five-card suit (which he did), then his two remaining spades would become established. When declarer would subsequently lead clubs, West would climb up with his ace and cash the two good spades, thus handing declarer a one-trick set. The diamond finesse at trick two, therefore, figured to be a losing play.

Our actual declarer overtook the dummy's nine of spades with his own queen and led the four of clubs. When West followed suit with the nine, dummy's king was put up, holding the trick. *Now* the diamond finesse was taken, West's king winning. When West then played the ace of spades, declarer had his nine tricks: two spades, two hearts, four diamonds, and the "stolen" king of clubs.

When declarer led the club at trick two, it would not have mattered (either in theory or in actuality) whether West took his ace or didn't. Let's assume that he did win it immediately. When declarer regained the lead (either via a spade or some other suit), he would lead his remaining club and finesse dummy's jack. If the finesse lost, it would lose only to East, who would have no spade to return (assuming that West had established his spade suit when he took the club ace). And regardless of what East then returned, declarer would again have his contracted-for nine-tricks: two spades, two hearts, one diamond, and four clubs.

Frankly, this is a tough hand to play. But there is one right way to play it, and one wrong way. Thus, there is no choice if the optimum result is to be achieved.

Deal 9:
This deal was played in London, England, in 1958. The South declarer was Ewart Kempson, one of Great Britain's finest players. The deal demonstrates the technique that has brought him many laurels.

```
                    ♠ 9 8 4 3
                    ♡ 7 5 3
                    ◇ A K 6
                    ♣ A J 2
   ♠ J 10 5          N          ♠ 7
   ♡ A Q 10                     ♡ J 9 8 4 2
   ◇ Q J 9 2     W      E       ◇ 10 8 7
   ♣ K 8 5          S           ♣ 10 9 6 4
                    ♠ A K Q 6 2
                    ♡ K 6
                    ◇ 5 4 3
                    ♣ Q 7 3
```

Neither side vulnerable. West dealer.

West	North	East	South
1 ◇	Pass	Pass	1 ♠
Pass	3 ♠	Pass	4 ♠
Pass	Pass	Pass	

West opened the diamond queen, which was permitted to win. A second diamond was then led, dummy's king winning. After trumps were drawn, the board's jack of clubs was finessed. The ace of diamonds was now cashed, then the ace of clubs. The deuce of clubs was next led, South's queen being taken by West's king. This position was thus reached:

```
                    ♠ 9
                    ♡ 7 5 3
                    ◇ ———
                    ♣ ———
   ♠ ———            N          ♠ ———
   ♡ A Q 10                     ♡ J 9 8
   ◇ J           W      E       ◇ ———
   ♣ ———            S           ♣ 10
                    ♠ 6 2
                    ♡ K 6
                    ◇ ———
                    ♣ ———
```

Whatever West now led, he was bound to present declarer with a trick that the latter could not have made on his own power. If West led the diamond jack, declarer would ruff it in dummy while simultaneously discarding the six of hearts from his own hand. And, if West chose to lead a heart instead, South's king would be promoted into a winner.

What motivated Mr. Kempson to play as he did, conceding the first diamond trick and ultimately throwing West into the lead, to make the latter the victim of an end play?

The bidding told the story. West, for his opening bid, was clearly marked as the possessor of the club king, and —more important—the ace of hearts. To hope that East possessed the ace of hearts was nothing more than the enticing delusion of a thoughtless optimism. Thinking ahead, Mr. Kempson perceived that if *East* were to obtain the lead, a heart play by him would result in the defenders' taking two heart tricks. Since the only way East figured to obtain the lead was via the ten of diamonds, declarer immediately eliminated that one possibility by permitting West's diamond queen to win the opening lead.

Had declarer captured the opening diamond lead with the board's king, he would have found it impossible to prevent East from obtaining the lead via the diamond ten; and the normal heart play by East would compel declarer to lose two heart tricks. But, as was pointed out, Mr. Kempson had foreseen this eventuality, and he removed any chance of its developing by declining to win the opening lead.

Such is the functioning of the expert mind.

Deal 10:
This deal is undoubtedly the most difficult one in this chapter on "an ear to the bidding." It is difficult primarily because the proper play consists of deliberately throwing a trick out of the window on the opening lead—and instinctively one rebels at doing such a thing voluntarily. On closer examination, however, it is revealed that in giving away a trick, two tricks are later obtained in exchange.

This one-trick advantage that accrues to the giver represents the difference between victory and defeat.

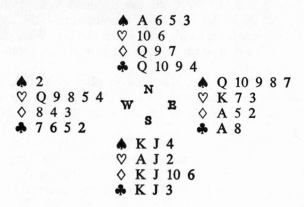

```
                  ♠ A 6 5 3
                  ♡ 10 6
                  ◇ Q 9 7
                  ♣ Q 10 9 4
  ♠ 2                          ♠ Q 10 9 8 7
  ♡ Q 9 8 5 4        N         ♡ K 7 3
  ◇ 8 4 3         W     E      ◇ A 5 2
  ♣ 7 6 5 2          S         ♣ A 8
                  ♠ K J 4
                  ♡ A J 2
                  ◇ K J 10 6
                  ♣ K J 3
```

Both sides vulnerable. East dealer.

East	South	West	North
1 ♠	1 NT	Pass	2 NT
Pass	3 NT	Pass	Pass
Pass			

West opened the five of hearts, the four was played from dummy, East put up the king—and do you take the trick with your ace? If you do, will you now have a second winner in hearts out of dummy's ten and your own jack? Let's see what happens if you take the king with your ace.

Suppose you then lead a club, which East will win with his ace. Back will come a heart, and West will decline to take the trick with his queen, dummy's ten winning. Even with the successful spade finesse, you will have only eight tricks. And when you ultimately lead a diamond, East will take his ace, return his remaining heart, and West will cash three heart tricks.

Let's go back to the bidding. Without any doubt, East has both minor-suit aces. And, without a doubt, West has either a singleton spade or is void of spades, judging from his failure to open a spade, the suit that East bid. From

East's play of the heart king at trick one, West is marked with a heart suit headed by the queen. And it figures to be a five-card suit, for with only a broken-down four card suit, West would not have had the audacity to lead it, as against leading the singleton of partner's bid suit.* Thus, the "worry" on the hand is that West may later obtain the lead to cash his to-be-established heart suit. Declarer's objective should be to prevent this from happening.

Declarer should permit East's heart king to capture the opening lead! Thus the way is paved for the breaking of the communication between the East-West defenders. East, at trick two, will then return a heart, and declarer's jack will be taken by West's queen. A third round of hearts, taken by declarer's ace, will now establish West's suit. (No matter what else West might return at trick three, declarer's victory is assured.)

Upon winning the third heart lead with the ace, declarer knocks out East's ace of clubs. East, of course, has no heart to return. Whatever else he decides to lead, declarer will win, after which he will knock out East's diamond ace. The rest of the tricks will now belong to declarer.

Played as suggested, South's only losers will have been two heart tricks, and the two minor-suit aces. By winning the first heart trick, declarer's losers will have been *three* heart tricks, and the two minor-suit aces.

Deal 11:
This final deal is a most simple one to play from declarer's point of view *if* the habit of counting one's winners before *playing* to the first trick is cultivated. Yet, I'd be willing to wager that at least half of our nation's players would do the wrong thing at trick one—and there would then be no recovery.

---

*For those readers who might say that perhaps West was void of spades, it might be pointed out that if this were the case, then West would have had to have some five-card suit (or longer), in which situation West, on lead against a no-trump contract, would have opened the longer suit. What I am trying to point out is that West could not have had exactly one spade and exactly four hearts, for his heart lead. He had to have at least five hearts, or run the risk of incurring the enmity of partner by not leading a spade.

```
                    ♠ K 8 5
                    ♡ 6
                    ◇ A 6 5
                    ♣ A 10 9 8 5 2
♠ Q 10 9 6 4 3              N              ♠ J
♡ Q 9 7 2                                  ♡ K 10 5 4
◇ 9 4              W           E           ◇ K J 10 8 7
♣ 3                        S              ♣ Q J 6
                    ♠ A 7 2
                    ♡ A J 8 3
                    ◇ Q 3 2
                    ♣ K 7 4
```

North-South vulnerable. North dealer.

North	East	South	West
1 ♣	1 ◇	1 ♡	Pass
2 ♣	Pass	3 NT	Pass
Pass	Pass		

When the deal arose in actual competition, our declarer did not give the hand an expert play. West opened the nine of diamonds, and declarer played low from dummy, East's king winning. Perceiving the hopelessness of returning a diamond—South was known to have the queen, since West's nine-spot was the "automatic" highest of partner's suit—East shifted to the four of hearts, and declarer's contract ascended (or, rather, descended) to the happy hunting grounds of contracts that should have been fulfilled.

On the heart return at trick two, South put up the eight-spot, which was taken by West's nine. West played back the deuce of hearts, East's king forcing declarer's ace. Belatedly, declarer attacked the club suit, East taking the third round with the queen. East, of course, returned a heart, and the defenders took two more heart tricks. All in all, declarer lost three heart tricks, one ~~spade~~ trick, and one club trick.   *DIAMOND*

When West led the nine of diamonds at trick one, it

should have been obvious to our declarer that *East had the king of diamonds*. Dummy's ace should have been put up on this trick, and the club suit attacked at once. At trick four, when East obtained a trick with the club queen, declarer would have had his nine tricks: two spades, one heart, one diamond, and five clubs. And, of course, declarer's remaining Q 3 of diamonds would have effectively prevented East from cashing the latter's diamond suit.

As was stated, even by incorrectly playing a low diamond from dummy at trick one, declarer might still have made his contract. This would have been accomplished had East mechanically returned a diamond at trick two. But, unfortunately for declarer, East was on his toes; and, unfortunately for declarer's partner, declarer failed to perform the simple *duty* of counting his tricks before playing to the opening lead.

chapter 8 Deception

♠ The primary reason that the experts are such consistent winners is that they possess great technical skill in both bidding and play. But the fact remains that the possession and application of all the relevant technical knowledge is not in itself sufficient to make one a really good player. Even if one masters all the principles of sound play and becomes familiar with all of the many and varied involved situations that require special treatment, he cannot become an expert until he has learned *how to deceive*. After all, there continually arise numerous situations where skillful play—and even perfect intuition—are not enough to fulfill some given contracts. And, when observation reveals that you are doomed to defeat if the opponents play correctly, your only salvation lies in the hope that you can trick them into playing incorrectly. In these circumstances, deception becomes mandatory.

Generally speaking, more often than not the practice of deceptive play brings better results when *declarer* applies it, since a defender, by a deceptive play, may easily mislead his partner as to the true state of affairs. The declarer, on the other hand, has no partner to fool, and thus has more freedom of action.

In this chapter, there will be presented various deceptive plays made by declarer at trick one. The purpose of each of these deceptive plays is, of course, to create an incorrect impression in the mind of the opponent whom declarer is attempting to deceive—to make him believe that a mirage is actually a reality—with the hoped for effect that the potential victim will then think and plan as declarer wants him to do.

The deals contained herein all arose in expert games.

From the reader's point of view, his approach should be to analyze and understand the motivation that brought the deceptive plays into being rather than to memorize them in order to earmark them for future reference. In adopting this approach, the reader's imagination will tend to rise to the fore when necessity so demands.

Deal 1:

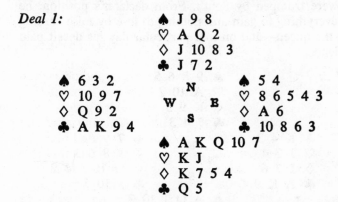

```
              ♠ J 9 8
              ♡ A Q 2
              ◊ J 10 8 3
              ♣ J 7 2
  ♠ 6 3 2         N        ♠ 5 4
  ♡ 10 9 7               ♡ 8 6 5 4 3
  ◊ Q 9 2     W     E     ◊ A 6
  ♣ A K 9 4       S        ♣ 10 8 6 3
              ♠ A K Q 10 7
              ♡ K J
              ◊ K 7 5 4
              ♣ Q 5
```

Against South's *four-spade* contract, West opened the king of clubs, the deuce was played from dummy, East followed with the three, and declarer dropped the queen.

West knew that South's play of the queen might well have been a false card, for this specific type of false card had been occurring daily for scores of years and was accepted as an "old reliable." But he also realized that when South dropped the queen, that card might well have been the only club that South held. And, if the latter were the case, then the continuation of the club ace would be ruffed, and dummy's jack of clubs would become established as a winner. In addition, a factor operating against the continuation of the club ace was that East had followed with the discouraging three of clubs.

Having thought it over, West decided to abandon the club suit and to shift to the ten of hearts at trick two. Declarer took this with his jack, drew the adverse trumps, and then overtook the heart king with dummy's ace. On the ace of hearts, he now discarded his losing five of clubs.

Two diamond tricks were then conceded, and a lost contract had been transformed into a fulfilled one.

Had declarer made the normal "economical" play of the five of clubs at trick one, West undoubtedly would have cashed the ace of clubs at trick two, for in so doing he would not be creating anything for declarer even if the ace were trumped by South. From declarer's position, he had everything to gain and nothing to lose by false carding with the queen—and on that particular day his deceit paid dividends.

Deal 2:

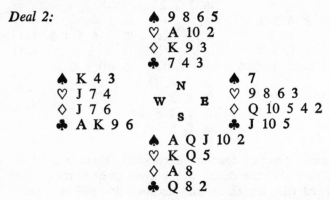

```
                    ♠ 9 8 6 5
                    ♡ A 10 2
                    ◇ K 9 3
                    ♣ 7 4 3
  ♠ K 4 3                          ♠ 7
  ♡ J 7 4          N               ♡ 9 8 6 3
  ◇ J 7 6      W       E           ◇ Q 10 5 4 2
  ♣ A K 9 6        S               ♣ J 10 5
                    ♠ A Q J 10 2
                    ♡ K Q 5
                    ◇ A 8
                    ♣ Q 8 2
```

With no adverse bidding, South reached a *four-spade* contract. On West's opening lead of the club king, South dropped the *eight-spot,* not the deuce. West then laid down his ace of clubs at trick two, declarer's queen had just become a winner, and, as it turned out, his tenth and game-going trick. Had West not led a club to trick two, declarer would have lost three club tricks and a trump trick.

Declarer's false card was most proper. The three and four of clubs were in dummy, and declarer possessed the deuce. So he knew that East's five of clubs was the lowest club East had and that if East had held two clubs, the latter would have initiated a high-low come-on signal at trick one. Hence, South reasoned that if he played the eight-spot on the first trick, West would notice the non-appearance of the deuce, and West might then assume that

East was begining a high-low signal with, for example, the Q 5 2.

Presumably West came to the conclusion South had hoped he would come to, for he did cash the club ace— for which he was quite sorry when the deal had ended.

Deal 3:
The two preceding deals have featured more or less stand-ard, recurring situations where declarer's deceptive false card was quite proper in that it stood to gain a trick while costing nothing even if the attempt failed. Far too fre-quently, however, a declarer will false card from force of habit and at the wrong time. This abuse of the false card then backfires, to declarer's detriment. Here is a situation where a false card proved costly.

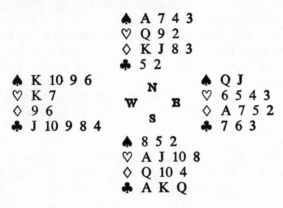

Both sides vulnerable. South dealer.

South	West	North	East
1 NT	Pass	3 NT	Pass
Pass	Pass		

West opened the jack of clubs, which declarer captured with his ace. He then led the queen of diamonds, East's ace winning. Instead of returning a club, East shifted to the queen of spades, which held the trick. The continuation of the jack of spades was overtaken by West's king—and declarer was all through. When he eventually lost the heart finesse to West, the defenders were able to claim the victory, with three spade tricks, a heart, and a diamond.

When declarer incorrectly won the opening lead with the *ace* of clubs, he passed on vital information to the East defender. East knew that West's opening lead of the jack of clubs was being made from a suit containing a J-10 sequence. Hence, South was known to possess the queen of clubs. Why then, thought East, did South capture the opening lead with the ace rather than with the queen? The answer was, of course, obvious: South also had the king of clubs, in which case it cost South nothing to win the opening lead with the ace. East, therefore, recognized the hopelessness of continuing clubs at trick three, and hopefully switched to the spade suit, with the desired result being obtained.

Had declarer captured the opening lead with the queen of clubs, then East, when he won trick two with his diamond ace, would almost certainly have played back a club. From East's position, West might well have had the A J 10 x x of clubs originally, with South holding the K Q x; or West might have held the K J 10 x x, and South the A Q x. In either of these situations a club return would be proper, and would establish West's suit.

But when declarer chose to win the opening lead with the ace of clubs, he gave the show away, and the East defender took full advantage of the situation.

Deal 4:
This deal came up in a National Championship event some years back, and while it may be argued that the expert East defender should not have fallen for South's deceptive false card, the fact is that without the chicanery, the East defender would not have had a chance to fall. From declarer's position, the situation boiled down to, simply, a matter of realizing that if the East defender played properly, declarer was doomed to defeat. It thus became a matter of creating a hope for himself, as opposed to playing with no hope.

```
            ♠ Q 5
            ♡ A Q 6
            ◇ 8 6 5 4 2
            ♣ J 9 3
♠ 9 3               N            ♠ 7
♡ 9 7 5 2       W       B        ♡ J 10 8 3
◇ 3                 S            ◇ A J 10 9
♣ K 10 7 6 5 4                  ♣ A Q 8 2
            ♠ A K J 10 8 6 4 2
            ♡ K 4
            ◇ K Q 7
            ♣ ———
```

Neither side vulnerable. South dealer.

South	West	North	East
2 ♠	Pass	3 ♡	Pass
3 ♠	Pass	4 ♠	Pass
4 NT	Pass	5 ◇	Pass
6 ♠	Pass	Pass	Pass

West opened the three of diamonds, dummy followed with the deuce, East took his ace—and South parted with the king! East then put down the ace of clubs, and South ruffed it. Trumps were now drawn, and declarer's losing seven of diamonds was discarded on the board's ace of hearts. Had East returned a diamond at trick two, of course West would have ruffed it, for the setting trick.

There are a few interesting and instructive points in this deal. First, if South had made the normal play at trick one—of following suit with the seven of diamonds—East promptly would have returned a diamond for West to trump. In this "normal" situation, East would have been certain that West's lead of the three-spot had been a singleton, for only the king and queen of diamonds would not have been in evidence; and no West player would have led the three-spot from the K Q 3, or from the K 3, or from the Q 3. But with the king's falling, it was quite conceivable that West had elected to lead the three from the Q 7 3 combination. Thus, South's false card was a fine deceptive play.

Nevertheless, our expert East should not have been misled, for the bidding had provided a most important clue to the proper defense. South had employed the Blackwood four–no-trump bid and, upon learning that North possessed *only one ace,* had promptly contracted for a small slam in spades. Surely South, had he held a losing club in addition to the losing king of diamonds (which had been played to the first trick), would not have gone on to a slam with these two positive losers. Hence East, holding the two minor suit aces, should have known that South *had to be void of clubs* to have undertaken the six-spade contract voluntarily.

A diamond return, then, should have been made at trick two, not because this return was guaranteed to defeat declarer, but rather because the ace of clubs was certain to be a losing play, since declarer was a cinch to trump it.

Deal 5:
This deal features a very pretty false card that was just about guaranteed to create an incorrect impression in the mind of the East defender—and it did just that.

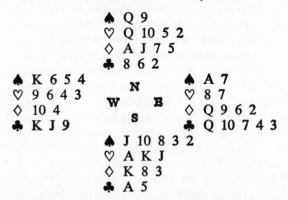

South arrived at a *three–no-trump* contract, against which West opened the four of spades, East winning with the ace. On this trick declarer dropped the *eight-spot!*

Through East's eyes, the eight was "naturally" the lowest spade South possessed. Hence West had a six-card suit, since the deuce and three were "obviously" in the West hand; and, West, by definition, was leading his fourth-highest spade, the four-spot. So East returned a spade, South followed with the deuce, and West took his king. Declarer now had three spade winners—and ten winners. Had East shifted to a club at trick two, declarer could not have established and *cashed* his spade suit, for the defenders would have established and cashed their club suit first.

From declarer's point of view, his false card at trick one was "on the house." Declarer knew that West had *exactly* a four-card spade suit: West's four-spot was the fourth highest, and he could have none lower, since declarer himself held the two and three of spades. In concealing the two and three, declarer, by discarding the eight-spot, hoped to mislead East into believing that West held both the two and three, so that in case East might have any ideas about shifting to a club, he wouldn't. And he didn't.

Deal 6:

```
                    ♠ 9 5
                    ♡ A Q 6
                    ◇ Q J 10 9 5
                    ♣ 8 7 4
    ♠ K 10 7 3 2           ♠ J 6 4
    ♡ 7 5 2         N       ♡ 10 9 4
    ◇ K 3        W     E    ◇ 7 6
    ♣ 10 9 6         S      ♣ A K J 3 2
                    ♠ A Q 8
                    ♡ K J 8 3
                    ◇ A 8 4 2
                    ♣ Q 5
```

Both sides vulnerable. South dealer.

South	West	North	East
1 NT	Pass	3 NT	Pass
Pass	Pass		

West led the three of spades, and East's jack was taken

by declarer's *ace!* Just imagine the thought that is now running through West's mind: "My partner has the queen of spades, for surely if declarer had held the queen, he would not have wasted the ace."

Declarer then entered dummy via the heart ace, led the queen of diamonds, and finessed, West's king winning. West now returned a low spade to East's "marked" queen —after which East would play another spade for West to cash his entire suit.

As is apparent, South won West's spade return with his concealed queen and wrapped up ten tricks. As is equally apparent, had West shifted to a club upon taking his diamond king, East would have rattled off five club tricks, after which a spade return (trapping declarer's queen) would have enabled West to cash four spade tricks. From the defenders' point of view, it would have been much nicer if *they* had made ten tricks, in the manner outlined, instead of permitting declarer to make ten tricks. But declarer, in winning the opening lead with the ace, rather than with the queen, "convinced" West that East possessed the queen of spades and thereby changed the end result to the diametric opposite of what it would have been had the West defender diagnosed the true situation.

As seen through the eyes (and thoughts) of our declarer, here is his justification for the "abnormal" line of play he took: First, if East had the king of diamonds, then the contract was always guaranteed, since by repeated finesses declarer would bring home five diamond tricks. This, combined with four heart tricks, spelled "mission accomplished." True it is that if East held the diamond king, then by winning the opening lead with the ace instead of with the queen, declarer was tossing away an extra trick worth 30 points.

Declarer, however, was perfectly willing to pay these 30 points as a premium to guard against West's holding that most vital card, the king of diamonds. In this case, West would surely assume that South's failure to win the opening lead with the queen indicated that South did not have the queen and, therefore, East held that key card; that, hence, a thinking West would assuredly return a low spade when (and if) he took a trick with the diamond king.

Is there anyone who will quarrel with South for his fancy play at trick one?

Deal 7:
This deal and the one that follows contain virtually the identical type of deceptive, false-carding play. All of the better players have incorporated this play into their arsenal of useful weapons, for in its use it can never be a losing play but can (and usually is) a winning play.

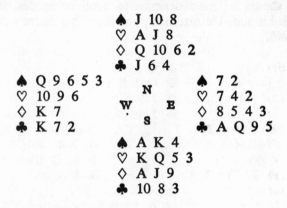

```
                    ♠ J 10 8
                    ♡ A J 8
                    ◇ Q 10 6 2
                    ♣ J 6 4
  ♠ Q 9 6 5 3            N          ♠ 7 2
  ♡ 10 9 6                          ♡ 7 4 2
  ◇ K 7          W         E        ◇ 8 5 4 3
  ♣ K 7 2               S           ♣ A Q 9 5
                    ♠ A K 4
                    ♡ K Q 5 3
                    ◇ A J 9
                    ♣ 10 8 3
```

East-West vulnerable. South dealer.

South	West	North	East
1 NT	Pass	3 NT	Pass
Pass	Pass		

West led the five of spades, the jack was put up from dummy, East followed with the deuce, and declarer won the trick with his *king.* Dummy was then entered via the heart ace, and the diamond finesse taken, losing to West's king. West now paused to examine the lay of the land.

Surely, figured West, declarer had started with precisely the doubleton A K of spades, for had he possessed a third spade, he would have won the opening lead with the board's jack, instead of overtaking the jack with the king.

And so, there being no attractive shift for West to make, he returned a spade to drive out South's presumed now-singleton ace. But, to his surprise, the trick was taken by the board's ten-spot; and West belatedly realized that he had been duped.

South's "unnecessary" overtaking of the jack with his own king was a well-designed strategem. He was going to take the diamond finesse in such a manner that if it lost to West, West would "recognize" that declarer's original spade holding had to be the doubleton A K (West assuming that South was a rational being). And, in this case, West should be most desirous to continue spades, to establish his suit. Unfortunately for West, his desire was not gratified.

Deal 8:

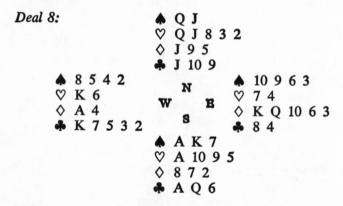

```
                    ♠ Q J
                    ♡ Q J 8 3 2
                    ◇ J 9 5
                    ♣ J 10 9
  ♠ 8 5 4 2              N          ♠ 10 9 6 3
  ♡ K 6                             ♡ 7 4
  ◇ A 4         W          E        ◇ K Q 10 6 3
  ♣ K 7 5 3 2          S            ♣ 8 4
                    ♠ A K 7
                    ♡ A 10 9 5
                    ◇ 8 7 2
                    ♣ A Q 6
```

Neither side vulnerable. South dealer.

South	West	North	East
1 NT	Pass	2 NT	Pass
3 NT	Pass	Pass	Pass

West opened the three of clubs, the jack was played from dummy, East followed with the four, and declarer took his own jack with the queen. This play was calculated to create in West's mind the "fact" that declarer had started with the doubleton A Q of clubs.

A spade was then led to the board's jack, after which

the queen of hearts was laid down, and the finesse taken, losing to West's king.

"Convinced" that declarer had just the singleton ace of clubs left—why else would declarer have overtaken his jack and then entered dummy by means of the jack of spades?—West continued clubs, the trick being won by dummy's ten. Ten tricks were now there for the taking.

Had dummy's jack of clubs won the opening lead, West would have had no choice but to discontinue leading clubs, since declarer, in this case, would be known to have the A Q remaining. In all probability, West would then have switched to diamonds—and the defenders would have captured five diamond tricks. But the wool that declarer pulled over West's eyes at trick one prevented West from seeing anything but a continuation of the club suit.

Deal 9:

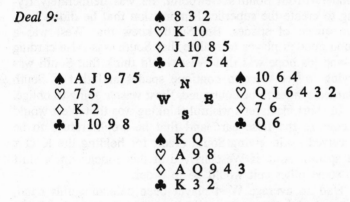

```
              ♠ 8 3 2
              ♡ K 10
              ◇ J 10 8 5
              ♣ A 7 5 4
♠ A J 9 7 5        N        ♠ 10 6 4
♡ 7 5                       ♡ Q J 6 4 3 2
◇ K 2       W        E      ◇ 7 6
♣ J 10 9 8        S         ♣ Q 6
              ♠ K Q
              ♡ A 9 8
              ◇ A Q 9 4 3
              ♣ K 3 2
```

Against South's *three-no-trump* contract. West led the seven of spades, East put up the ten, and declarer won the trick with his *king*. He then crossed over to dummy via the king of hearts and laid down the jack of diamonds, which lost to West's king.

It is perfectly obvious that if West now lays down the ace of spades, he will fell South's queen and then go on to make three more spade tricks. But he didn't lay down the ace, for what he thought was a very good reason.

As West viewed the situation, it was perfectly apparent to him that South still possessed the queen of spades, for if East had held that card, he would have played it at trick one. West therefore knew that South had false carded on the opening lead. Why? West asked himself.

West finally concluded that South had false carded because South had the K Q x of spades, and that by false carding, he was trying to create the impression in West's mind that South didn't have the queen. Thus (said West to himself) South was trying to get West to lay down the ace of spades, thereby making a winner out of declarer's queen. Since South was "obviously" attempting to put something over on West, the latter was not going to be sucked into it. So West shifted to the jack of clubs. After breathing a sigh of relief, declarer then took his nine tricks.

Very simply, declarer "outpsychologized" the West defender. From South's viewpoint, he was deliberately trying to create the superficial impression that he didn't have the queen of spades. But South knew that West was a good enough player to realize that South was false carding —and his hope was that West would think that South was trying to get West to continue spades and that if South wanted spades to be continued, West wasn't going to oblige.

In short, declarer's wishful thinking was that West would recognize the false card and that he would refuse to be deceived by it, giving South credit for holding the K Q x of spades. And, if West arrived at this conclusion, a shift to some other suit would be in order.

Had an average West player been defending this hand, he undoubtedly would not have gone through the thinking that our actual West defender indulged in and in all probability would have laid down the spade ace, felling South's unguarded queen. But then, if an average West player had been defending, our expert South declarer would probably have won the opening lead with the queen, thus openly announcing that he still possessed the king. Would West then have diagnosed the true situation?

Deal 10:
On this deal, at trick one, declarer made a simple decep-

tive play that every West defender in the world would have fallen for. Our West defender was no exception.

```
                    ♠ 8 5 2
                    ♡ 7 6 4 3
                    ◇ Q 10 2
                    ♣ Q 6 4
    ♠ J 10              N        ♠ Q 9 6 4 3
    ♡ K Q 8 2     W         E    ♡ A 9 5
    ◇ 7 4 3              S       ◇ 9 8 6 5
    ♣ J 10 9 7                   ♣ 8
                    ♠ A K 7
                    ♡ J 10
                    ◇ A K J
                    ♣ A K 5 3 2
```

North-South vulnerable. South dealer.

South	West	North	East
2 NT*	Pass	3 NT	Pass
Pass	Pass		

West opened the jack of clubs, the four-spot was played from dummy, East put up the *eight,* and declarer followed with the five.

Is there a West defender who, in this situation, would not have construed his partner's eight-spot as a come-on signal, especially since the deuce and three of clubs were not in evidence? Was it not the normal play for West then to lead the ten of clubs at trick two? When he did, declarer made ten tricks.

Had declarer won the opening lead and continued the club suit, East would have failed to follow to the second round, and the cat would have been out of the bag. When West subsequently won the fourth round of clubs, he assuredly would have led a spade or a heart. And, if it were a heart, the defenders would cash four heart tricks. But,

---

*Not a "book" bid, with the unprotected jack of hearts. But, then, is there a better opening bid!

when declarer false carded at trick one, West made the normal and logical play at trick two: the ten of clubs.

Deal 11:
This final deal presents a situation where a thinking expert declarer outsmarted a thinking expert defender. The deal arose in the Vanderbilt Championships of 1954.

```
                    ♠ Q 9
                    ♡ 5 4 2
                    ◇ A Q 8 7
                    ♣ 10 8 3 2
    ♠ 10 3                          ♠ A J 7 6 5 2
    ♡ A Q 10 9         N            ♡ K J 3
    ◇ 10 6 5 4 2    W     E         ◇ J 9 3
    ♣ 9 5              S            ♣ K
                    ♠ K 8 4
                    ♡ 8 7 6
                    ◇ K
                    ♣ A Q J 7 6 4
```

Both sides vulnerable. East dealer.

East	South	West	North
1 ♠	2 ♣	Pass	3 ♣
Pass	3 NT	Pass	Pass
Pass			

West opened the ten of spades, and our South declarer perceived that he could obtain two spade tricks by putting up the board's queen (with the ten of spades lead, East was known to possess the A J). But declarer felt that East would then surmise that South had two spade tricks and that when East took the queen with the ace, he would surely shift to the heart suit.

Hoping to prevent the heart shift, South played dummy's nine of spades on the opening lead. East, recognizing that he could now prevent declarer from winning two spade tricks, played the encouraging seven-spot on dummy's nine, South's king winning.

Declarer next led the king of diamonds, which he overtook with the board's ace. He then played the ten of clubs—and joyfully greeted the appearance of East's king. Declarer now had his nine tricks.

From East's point of view, if declarer were willing to throw away a spade trick, shouldn't East have been delighted to help him? Actually, I think not. I believe that we should condemn East, who, knowing that South was a very good player, should have realized that South wouldn't be tossing away a spade trick unless there were a good reason for so doing—namely the fear of a heart shift if the spade queen were played, to be captured by East's ace.

chapter 9 The Rule of Eleven

♠ The conventional, standard lead of the fourth highest card of a long suit goes back many centuries, to the days of whist, the great grandparent of contract bridge. This lead is still being diligently observed and applied by virtually all players, since in experience it has amply demonstrated its practicality.

The use of the fourth highest lead makes possible the application of the Rule of Eleven, which was discovered in 1889 by R. F. Foster. This rule is a kind of magical arithmetical gadget designed to interpret the opening lead. It is a tool available to both declarer and the defenders, and it is an extremely valuable one to know. Many problems that develop during the play can be solved through the use of the Rule of Eleven. Whenever the fourth highest card of a suit is led, the rule is infallible.

It should be emphasized that the Rule of Eleven is not a sometimes workable, sometimes unworkable convention. It is an exact, scientific mathematical equation. Here is the way it works:

Whenever the card led is the leader's fourth highest of a suit, subtract the denomination (number) of that card from the number 11. The result will be the total number of cards, higher than the card led, held by the other three players.

For example, if West should open the *seven* of clubs (as his fourth highest) against South's three–no-trump contract, by subtracting the denomination of that card (7) from the number *11*, it becomes a fact that North,

East, and South possess exactly *four* cards higher than the seven-spot. From the viewpoint of the partner of the opening leader, it is a routine matter to determine how many of these four higher cards are possessed by the declarer, for the leader's partner sees his own hand and the dummy, and whichever of the four higher cards in circulation are not in evidence *must be* in declarer's hand. And conversely, declarer can utilize the Rule of Eleven in precisely the same way as the leader's partner does: by subtracting the denomination of the card led (7) from the number 11, declarer knows that dummy, the leader's partner, and declarer himself, have exactly four cards higher than the seven-spot. Since declarer sees his own hand and the dummy, whichever of the four higher cards are not in evidence must be in the leader's partner's hand. Permit me to illustrate the above in diagram form.

From the Leader's Partner's Seat

♣ K 5 2

N

7 of clubs is led   W   E   ♣ A J 9 3

S

On the lead of the seven of clubs against South's three-no-trump contract, the deuce is played from dummy. By subtracting 7 from 11, East knows that the North, East, and South hands have 4 cards higher than the seven-spot. Since the king is in dummy, and East is looking at the ace, jack, and nine, all four higher cards have been accounted for. Therefore South can have no card higher than the seven-spot. And so, on the play of the deuce from dummy, East follows with the three-spot, knowing that West's seven of clubs will win the trick.

Actually, of course, East could have come to the same conclusion by counting on his fingertips: West must have started with the Q 10 8 7 for the seven-spot to have been the fourth highest (of course, West might also have had the 6 and/or 4 of clubs). But isn't it simpler—and more polite—to subtract 7 from 11 than to count on your fingertips in public?

From the Declarer's Seat

♠ Q 9 2

N

7 of spades is led   W   E

S

♠ A 10 3

On the lead of the seven of spades against South's three–no-trump contract, South knows that dummy, East, and South have four cards higher than the seven-spot. Since South (declarer) is looking at the queen and nine in dummy, and the ace and ten in his own hand, he knows that East can have no card higher than the seven-spot. So South finds himself in the catbird's seat: if he wants the lead in the North hand, he simply puts up dummy's nine-spot, which must win the trick; or, if he wants the lead in his own hand, he can let the seven ride around to his ten.

Again, declarer could have figured it out on his finger-tips: for the seven-spot to be the fourth highest spade, West had to have the K J 8 7. But there will be days when your fingernails are a bit dirty, and you're reluctant to show them in public. Certainly, in this situation, the application of the Rule of Eleven will save you embarrassment.

For those who are interested in understanding *why* the "magic" number 11 is used, here is how it is worked out:*

---

*For those not interested, I might point out that they should be, for some-day your son or daughter will come along and ask: "Daddy, how does the Rule of Eleven work?" How would it sound if you said, "I don't know."?

Assign the proper numerals to the unnumbered cards, according to their rank:

Jack .... is No. 11
Queen ...... is No. 12
King .... is No. 13
Ace .... is No. 14

Hence, each suit, if all the cards were thus numbered, would be designated as follows:

2 - 3 - 4 - 5 - 6 - 7 - 8 - 9 - 10 - 11 - 12 - 13 - 14

Assume that the leader opens the *6,* his fourth highest card of a suit. There are obviously *8* cards outstanding higher than the *6.* Since the 6 is, by definition, his fourth highest card in the suit, *the leader himself must automatically hold 3 of the 8 higher cards.* That leaves exactly *5* outstanding higher cards in the hands of the other three players at the table.

There are in circulation in each suit:

12 cards higher than the 2.
11 cards higher than the 3.
10 cards higher than the 4.
9 cards higher than the 5.
8 cards higher than the 6.
7 cards higher than the 7.
6 cards higher than the 8.
5 cards higher than the 9.
4 cards higher than the 10.
3 cards higher than the 11 (Jack).
2 cards higher than the 12 (Queen).
1 card higher than the 13 (King).
0 cards higher than the 14 (Ace).

When opener leads his fourth highest in a suit, quite obviously he therefore has *exactly 3 cards higher* than the one he has led.

Hence:

If opener leads the *2,* there are *9* higher cards in the other three hands.

If opener leads the *3*, there are *8* higher cards in the other three hands.

If opener leads the *4*, there are *7* higher cards in the other three hands.

If opener leads the *5*, there are *6* higher cards in the other three hands.

If opener leads the *6*, there are *5* higher cards in the other three hands.

If opener leads the *7*, there are *4* higher cards in the other three hands.

If opener leads the *8*, there are *3* higher cards in the other three hands.

If opener leads the *9*, there are *2* higher cards in the other three hands.

If opener leads the *10*, there is *1* higher card in the other three hands.

If opener leads the *11* (Jack), there are *0* higher cards in the other three hands.*

And if opener leads the 12, 13, or 14 (Queen, King, and Ace respectively), the lead cannot be the fourth highest, and the Rule of Eleven is inoperative.

Thus, if you subtract the denomination of the card led from the "magic number" 11, the figure you obtain *must always* equal the number of cards (higher than the one led) that are in circulation in the three other hands.

Let us now look at some illustrations of the Rule of Eleven as they arose in actual competition. The deals that follow were all played in expert games. The reader will note that on some of the deals, familiarity with the Rule of Eleven operates to the advantage of the declarer; and, on other deals, to the advantage of the defenders. All of the deals presented depict "type situations" that arise regularly in every session of bridge.

*The reader will note that the *italicized* figures on each line always total 11.

Deal 1: Rule of Eleven—Defenders' Play

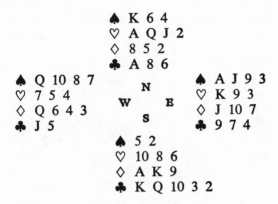

♠ K 6 4
♡ A Q J 2
◇ 8 5 2
♣ A 8 6

♠ Q 10 8 7   ♠ A J 9 3
♡ 7 5 4   ♡ K 9 3
◇ Q 6 4 3   ◇ J 10 7
♣ J 5   ♣ 9 7 4

♠ 5 2
♡ 10 8 6
◇ A K 9
♣ K Q 10 3 2

North-South vulnerable. South dealer.

South	West	North	East
1 ♣	Pass	1 ♡	Pass
1 NT	Pass	3 NT	Pass
Pass	Pass		

West opened the seven of spades, the four-spot was played from dummy, and East, applying the Rule of Eleven, followed with the three. Upon winning the trick with the seven, West led the queen of spades, and the defenders had themselves four spade tricks. Eventually East made his king of hearts, for the setting trick.

From East's point of view, he knew that South had no spade that could beat the seven-spot. This conclusion was arrived at by subtracting seven from eleven, which left four cards higher than the seven in the North, East, and South hands. Since East was looking at the king in dummy, and at the ace, jack, and nine in his own hand, South could have no spade higher than the seven.

Had East not been familiar with the Rule of Eleven, he undoubtedly would have played either the nine or the jack on the opening lead—and South would have avoided the loss of four spade tricks, to fulfill his contract.

Deal 2: Rule of Eleven—Defenders' Play

```
                    ♠ A J 8
                    ♡ 4
                    ◇ A Q J 9 3
                    ♣ Q 9 8 5
♠ K 10 6 5 2           N          ♠ Q 9 7
♡ A Q 10                          ♡ J 9 6 5 3 2
◇ 10 6 4          W     E         ◇ K 8 2
♣ 4 2                 S           ♣ 7
                    ♠ 4 3
                    ♡ K 8 7
                    ◇ 7 5
                    ♣ A K J 10 6 3
```

Neither side vulnerable. North dealer.

North	East	South	West
1 ◇	Pass	2 ♣	Pass
4 ♣	Pass	5 ♣	Pass
Pass	Pass		

West's opening lead was the five of spades, and the eight was played from dummy. East, figuring out that there were outstanding six spades higher than the five-spot (11—5=6) and perceiving those six in dummy and his own hand, correctly put up his nine to win the trick. He then returned the queen of spades, dummy's ace winning. On this trick, West followed with the deuce of spades.

Declarer then drew trumps, after which he finessed the jack of diamonds, East's king winning. Had East now played another spade to West's known king, declarer would have fulfilled his contract: he would have trumped the spade lead and then discarded all of his hearts on the board's established diamonds.

But East's familiarity with the lead of the fourth highest guided him to the proper play. West's lead of the five of spades had been his fourth highest; and on the second spade lead, West had followed with the deuce, which indicated that he had started with five spades. Hence, declarer had started with just two spades, and he had no more spades left.

So, logically, East shifted to a heart. The result was most satisfactory.

Deal 3: Rule of Eleven—Declarer's Play

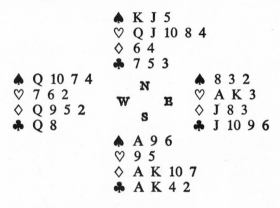

```
                    ♠ K J 5
                    ♡ Q J 10 8 4
                    ◊ 6 4
                    ♣ 7 5 3
  ♠ Q 10 7 4              N          ♠ 8 3 2
  ♡ 7 6 2           W          E     ♡ A K 3
  ◊ Q 9 5 2              S          ◊ J 8 3
  ♣ Q 8                              ♣ J 10 9 6
                    ♠ A 9 6
                    ♡ 9 5
                    ◊ A K 10 7
                    ♣ A K 4 2
```

Neither side vulnerable. North dealer.

North	East	South	West
Pass	Pass	1 ◊	Pass
1 ♡	Pass	2 NT	Pass
3 NT	Pass	Pass	Pass

West led the four of spades, dummy's five-spot covered it, East put up the eight—and South paused for reflection.

Since the standard, universal lead against no-trump contracts is the fourth highest, it became a simple matter to interpret the spade situation around the table: North, East, and South possessed seven spades higher than the four-spot. Since North and South had six of these, East's eight had to be the only one he had that was higher than the four. So *West had to have* the spade queen.

Having figured it out, South captured East's eight with the ace and not with the nine, since South knew that the queen of spades was in the West hand and that it could be finessed if an additional entry to dummy were needed.

South then led the nine of hearts, and East declined to take it. The five of hearts was led next, and East took dummy's queen with his king. East then shifted to a club, declarer winning. Now the six of spades was led, dummy's jack being finessed successfully. Then came the jack of hearts, driving out East's ace. The heart suit was now established, and the king of spades was in dummy as an entry to cash the suit. All in all, declarer made three hearts, two diamonds, three spades, and two clubs.

Try winning the opening spade lead with the nine instead of with the ace. Down you go if you do. When you next lead the nine of hearts, East will decline to take it (as was done). The following lead of the five of hearts will be captured by East's king.

When declarer then takes East's club return, his only entry to dummy will be the king of spades, since dummy will have the K J of spades opposite declarer's A 9 of spades. It will now be impossible to establish and cash dummy's heart suit, since to accomplish that declarer requires two entries to dummy, and he has but one. By winning the opening spade lead with the nine instead of with the ace, declarer winds up making only one heart trick instead of the three he can make by capturing the opening lead with the ace of spades.

Deal 4: Rule of Eleven—Defenders' Play
This deal presents an everyday, recurring type of play. Through repeatedly encountering this situation, most bridge players have learned to handle it instinctively and correctly. But there are undoubtedly some players who either handle it incorrectly or spend a needlessly lengthy period of time working it out at the table when it arises. The twin objectives of this deal, then, are to "educate" and to save some time for the bridge players of the world.

```
              ♠ K 7 3
              ♡ K 4 2
              ◇ A 7 4 2
              ♣ K 7 5
♠ A 10 8 6 5       N        ♠ Q J 4
♡ 9 5                       ♡ 8 7
◇ 6 3        W       E      ◇ K J 10 9 5
♣ J 8 6 4          S        ♣ A 10 9
              ♠ 9 2
              ♡ A Q J 10 6 3
              ◇ Q 8
              ♣ Q 3 2
```

Both sides vulnerable. South dealer.

South	West	North	East
1 ♡	Pass	2 NT	Pass
3 ♡	Pass	4 ♡	Pass
Pass	Pass		

West opens the club four, the five is played from dummy, and East should automatically put up the nine-spot. Except for one extremely rare possibility out of thousands of possibilities, the play of the nine cannot be the losing play. And much more often than not, it will be the only winning play. Let us see why.

East knows that North, South, and East have seven cards higher than the four-spot (11—4=7). Between dummy and East, six of these seven higher cards are in evidence. Hence, declarer has just one higher card.

If East puts up his ace, he establishes dummy's king as a winner 100% of the time and gives declarer two club tricks whenever declarer happens to have the queen. And, if West happens to be leading his fourth highest from Q J x x, the play of the ace gives declarer a present of dummy's king as a winner. If, instead, East properly puts up the nine, should declarer possess either the queen or the jack, declarer will be restricted to just one club

winner, for when West regains the lead, a club play
through dummy's king will enable East to win two club
tricks with his remaining ace and ten.

On the above deal, had East put up his club ace at
trick one, declarer would have fulfilled his contract. But
when East played the nine instead, declarer lost two clubs,
one spade, and one diamond.

The one extremely rare situation where the play of the
nine at trick one *may* lose a trick is where declarer has a
singleton queen. But, in my experience, even where this
unlikely possibility exists, usually nothing is lost by playing the nine-spot, for if the ace had been played instead
(felling declarer's queen), dummy's king would have been
promoted into a winner, and declarer would have been
able to discard one of his other losers on the established
king.

Deal 5: Rule of Eleven—Declarer's Play

```
                    ♠ K 10 3
                    ♡ 8 5
                    ◇ 5 2
                    ♣ Q J 10 9 8 6
     ♠ J 8 7 6 2         N          ♠ 9 5
     ♡ Q 9 7 4      W         E      ♡ K J 6
     ◇ J                S            ◇ Q 10 9 8 3
     ♣ 7 3 2                         ♣ A 5 4
                    ♠ A Q 4
                    ♡ A 10 3 2
                    ◇ A K 7 6 4
                    ♣ K
```

East-West vulnerable. North dealer.

North	East	South	West
3 ♣	Pass	3 NT	Pass
Pass	Pass		

On West's lead of the six of spades the three was played

from dummy, and East's nine was taken by declarer's ace. It was apparent to South that East's nine was the only spade the latter held that was higher than the six-spot: there were five higher spades in the North, East, and South hands (11—6=5), and dummy and declarer had four of them.

To trick two, the king of clubs was laid down, and East correctly declined to capture it. South's next play was the four of spades, and when West followed with the seven-spot; dummy's ten was inserted with the guarantee that it would win. It now became a routine proposition to establish the club suit by knocking out East's ace, and then overtaking the spade queen with the board's king, to cash the suit.

Deal 6: Rule of Eleven—Defenders' Play

```
            ♠ J 8 3
            ♡ Q 10 5 2
            ◇ 8 6 5
            ♣ A K 2
♠ K 10 7 6        N        ♠ Q 9 5
♡ 7 3                      ♡ 9 6
◇ K 10 4 2    W     E      ◇ Q J 9 7
♣ 9 7 6           S        ♣ Q 8 4 3
            ♠ A 4 2
            ♡ A K J 8 4
            ◇ A 3
            ♣ J 10 5
```

Both sides vulnerable. South dealer.

South	West	North	East
1 ♡	Pass	2 ♡	Pass
3 ♡	Pass	4 ♡	Pass
Pass	Pass		

West opened the six of spades, the three was played from dummy, and East mechanically put up the queen,

declarer's ace winning. After drawing trumps, declarer
then led a low spade toward dummy—and the jack of
spades had just been promoted into declarer's game-going
trick.

Had East been familiar with the Rule of Eleven, South
would have gone down to defeat. It was rather apparent
that the six of spades was a fourth best lead, which meant
that North, East, and South possessed five cards higher
than the six. Since dummy had two of these cards, and
East himself had two of them, South could have but one
of them. That card certainly figured to be the ace, for
what sane West player would be underleading the spade
ace at trick one on the given bidding? Had East correctly
played the spade nine on the opening lead, South would
have gone down (owing to the adverse location of the club
queen).

Deal 7: Rule of Eleven—Declarer's Play

```
                    ♠ K 8 4
                    ♡ A J 2
                    ♢ J 10 9 5
                    ♣ A 8 6
   ♠ Q 7 2                        ♠ 10 6 5 3
   ♡ 9 5 4             N          ♡ 10 8 7 3
   ♢ A 6         W         E      ♢ K 4 2
   ♣ K 9 7 5 3         S          ♣ J 4
                    ♠ A J 9
                    ♡ K Q 6
                    ♢ Q 8 7 3
                    ♣ Q 10 2
```

Neither side vulnerable. North dealer.

North	East	South	West
1 ♢	Pass	2 NT	Pass
3 NT	Pass	Pass	Pass

On West's opening lead of the club five, dummy's six
was played, East covered with the jack, and South won the

trick with the queen. He then led the diamond eight, West played low, and East's king took the trick. East returned his remaining club, South played low, and West's nine forced dummy's ace. (It would not have mattered if dummy had deferred the taking of the ace.) A diamond was then led off the board, and when West took his ace, he also cashed three club tricks to inflict a one-trick set on declarer.

While this hand is not a simple one to play, South could have made it had he brought the Rule of Eleven into play. When East put up the jack of clubs at trick one, that had to be the only club he had that was higher than the five-spot that West had led. Declarer was looking at three higher clubs in dummy and two higher clubs in his own hand; and there were exactly six higher in circulation in the North, East, and South hands (11—5=6). The king of clubs therefore *had to be* in West's hand—and South should have permitted East's jack to win the opening club lead!

Whatever East now returned, South was home. If it were a club, West's king would be entrapped; and when East subsequently obtained the lead, he would be unable to return another club. If, at trick two, East played back some suit other than clubs, South would also have smooth sailing; and he would, of course, later finesse West for the marked king of clubs.

The proper play of this hand also embodies the knowledge of a theme that was introduced earlier, namely the holdup play with a double-stopper when there are two key cards to knock out. On this deal South had to knock out the ace and king of diamonds; and, if East had been allowed to win the opening lead, South would have created for himself a double-stopper in clubs.

chapter 10 The Philosophy and Approach
of the Defenders

♠ Every bridge player, from the topflight expert down through the rankest neophyte, will agree that of the three departments of bridge—bidding, declarer's play, and defenders' play—the most difficult to master is defensive play. And, going further, there is unanimous concurrence in the oft-repeated assertion that more mistakes are made in defense than in either of the other two departments of bridge. There are two major reasons accounting for this deficiency in the techniques of defense.

First, when declarer is playing out a hand, he sees the 26 cards that belong to him and his partner, the dummy. He knows exactly how many cards of each suit his side possesses, what the quality of the cards is, and what his specific future problems are. In brief, he knows his *precise* strength and weakness and is thereby enabled to deploy his resources in an intelligent manner while waging his campaign. The defenders, on the other hand, do not see their 26 cards, but only the 13 that each of them holds. Thus, the defenders' task is automatically much more difficult, since each must try to figure out, or deduce, or imagine (or guess!) what his partner is holding.

And secondly, it is an established "fact" that "scientific development" in the field of defense has lagged far behind the scientific development of bidding methods and techniques of declarer's play. There are relatively few guiding principles to point the way to proper defense. As a consequence, a defender is frequently on his own because the pattern of correct defense varies greatly from deal to deal. Many diverse defensive situations arise where there exists no precedent to take a defender by the hand and lead him to the desired objective. In these situations, judgment and/or imagination must operate independently of any established, governing law.

From the defenders' point of view, in order to attack and counterattack successfully, they must rely on the few scientific principles that are available to them. These consist of a system of "conventional leads" and a system of "signals." With the application of these principles of standard leads and standard signals, the defenders are able to convey to each other the proper line of defense. It is mandatory, for their self-preservation that each partner be continuously on the alert to receive and correctly interpret whatever "scientific" information his partner is trying to transmit. If this approach is adopted, the natural difficulties that are inherent in proper defensive play can be reduced substantially, for knowledge, mutual understanding, and partnership cooperation will then tend to minimize guesswork and rugged individualism. In brief, each defender must point the way to the other; and while this will not eliminate guesswork, it will narrow the areas where guesswork will otherwise exist, thereby resulting in fewer mistakes. And, as any expert will confirm, victories are not won by being "brilliant," but rather by making fewer mistakes than one's competitors.

Although there is a relative dearth of defensive techniques and guiding principles, nevertheless there have been "invented" a sufficient number of practical defensive conventions (leads and signals) to enable the defenders to reduce to a minimum the hazards of looking skyward for divine guidance. Let us take a brief and more or less cursory look at two of the major defensive conventions *as relate to trick one:* (1) conventional opening leads and (2) conventional signals at trick one by the opening leader's partner.

The Opening Lead

In the opinion of our expert players, about 40% of all game contracts are either *fulfilled* or *defeated* on the opening lead! This figure, of course, can never be proven, but it is nevertheless an obvious fact that a proper or improper opening lead will frequently spell the difference between victory and defeat. Thus, the paramount importance of the opening lead in the defenders' campaign to defeat declarer is obvious. Yet, as was mentioned, despite this most critical importance of the opening lead, there is more uncertainty and less scientific data in the department of defense than in either the department of bidding or in the department of declarer's play.

There are some principles and some methods of approach to the opening lead that have been evolved from experience, that are of valuable practical assistance to the student of the game.

The best opening lead that you can make is to *lead your partner's suit*. This is what is called a "directed" lead, and the reason that it is the prime choice is apparent: when your partner has bid a suit, either as an opening bidder or as an overcaller, he has done so because he has a suit in which he can win tricks immediately, or by virtue of your lead, he can create future tricks in his suit. As to which card of partner's suit you will lead—and the logic behind the various choices—would require many chapters to explain to the reader's satisfaction; and space limitation precludes any detailed discussion of this subject within this book. Suffice it to say, and *generally speaking,* when you have two or three little cards (*e.g.,* 9 6 2; 5 3, etc.) in your partner's bid suit, you will open the *highest card* in his suit. When your holding in his suit consists of a doubleton headed by the ace, king, queen, jack, or ten (A 3; J 8, etc.), you will lead the highest card in his suit. Where you have three or more cards in his suit, headed by the ace, king, queen, jack, or ten (K 7 5; Q 6 2; J 8 6 4, etc.), you will lead the third highest if you have three cards, and the fourth highest if you have four or more. When you have either the A x x or the A x x x in his bid suit, against the opponents' *suit* contract you will lead the ace; against the opponents' *no-trump* contract, you will lead the lowest (third highest if you have three, and fourth highest if you have four or more).

So, when your partner has bid a suit, it becomes a relatively simple matter to make the right lead, for your partner has directed (and commanded!) you to lead *his* suit.

More often than not, however, when the opponents have purchased a contract, your partner will not have bid. In these circumstances, you have nothing to guide you, except the experiences of those who have gone before. Your lead, in these cases, will be what is termed "a lead in the blind." What to lead in these situations will depend, first, on whether the final contract is in a suit or in no-trump. And again, it is impossible within the confines of this book to discuss the advantages and disadvantages of possibly a dozen types of leads that might properly be made in different circumstances. If the reader is interested in a complete presentation of this subject, any book devoted to the play of the cards will cover it thoroughly. However, a brief presentation of the most effective (in the long run) blind leads is in order.

Against *no-trump* contracts, one's most practical "blind" lead is in his *longest suit*, the hope being to ultimately make winners out of the low cards in that suit. The card that is normally led is the fourth highest. The only exception to this lead comes about when in your *longest suit* you have a sequence of three or more high cards, in which case the top card of the sequence is led. For example, with the K Q J 7 3, the king is led and not the seven-spot; with the Q J 10 6, the queen is led, not the six; and with the J 10 9 5 4 2, the jack is led.

Against *suit* contracts, one's best blind lead is from a sequence of three high cards:

The *king* from an A K x, A K x x, A K x x x, etc.
The *king* from a K Q J, K Q J x, K Q J x x, etc.
The *queen* from a Q J 10, Q J 10 x, Q J 10 x x, etc.
The *jack* from a J 10 9, J 10 9 x, J 10 9 x x, etc.

Against *suit* contracts, the blind lead from a sequence

of *two* adjacent high cards is also a recommended lead
(with no guarantee being given on any specific deal):

The *king* from an A K x, A K x x, A K x x x, etc.
The *king* from a K Q x, K Q x x, K Q x x x, etc.
The *queen* from a Q J x, Q J x x, Q J x x x, etc.
The *jack* from a J 10 x, J 10 x x, J 10 x x x, etc.

Against suit contracts, many situations arise where partner has not bid, and you don't have a sequence to lead from.
In these cases, you are usually confronted with an option
of second-rate leads. But, you must lead something, for
you can't just sit all night and hold up the game. In these
situations, your lead will depend on what the opponents'
bidding might have revealed in the way of clues; or you
might even have a hunch and decide to obey your impulse.
In these circumstances, you might then lead either a singleton, the top card of a worthless doubleton, or a card in a
suit in which you possess a worthless tripleton; or you
might lead a trump; or you might lead an unbid suit, with
the wishful thought that your partner has winners in this
suit. If I appear to sound unenthusiastic about these
second-rate leads, it is because they warrant no enthusiasm.
And if you make one of these leads and it happens to
bring about a good result, don't expect that the next time
you make the identical type of lead, it will also turn out
well. It probably will not, for the probability of an inferior
lead turning out well twice in a row is quite unlikely.

So the lead at trick one is the first aggressive blow struck
by the defenders in their struggle to defeat declarer's contract. Usually, when the lead is a class-A lead (*i.e.*, partner's
suit, the top of a three-card sequence, etc.), the defenders
will have gained an advantage. But, probably more often
than not, the defenders' opening lead—their attacking first
blow—is just a shot in the dark that misses its objective
since, as was described above, the choice of an opening
lead does not usually fall into the category of scientific
selection.

However, *after* the opening lead has been made and

the dummy becomes exposed, the defenders come into possession of much meaningful and useful information. Factual data regarding declarer's (dummy's) strong points and his (dummy's) vulnerable spots not only become evident but are brought into focus. It is at this point that the defenders can really start to operate in intelligent fashion, to map out their strategy and tactics, and to get their offensive rolling in high gear. Thus, the scene now shifts to *the leader's partner,* who, at trick one, after the opening lead has been made and the dummy comes into view, assumes the responsibility for directing the defenders' attack. Especially does this hold true when it is apparent that the defending side is going to capture the opening lead, although third hand's position of becoming the commanding general can be equally important even if the lead will be relinquished at trick one. But, regardless of the fate of trick one, the leader's partner is almost always in the position of being able *to signal* the leader as to how to continue the future attack.

As should be quite apparent at this stage, the play at trick one can irrevocably determine the destiny of the combatants. From the viewpoint of the leader's partner, a misleading, or untimely, or thoughtless signal can be the deathblow to the defenders. Similarly, the failure to have listened to the bidding can ruin the defense even before it gets started. In a word, third hand must never play mechanically or automatically if optimum results are desired.

Let us now examine the standard, conventional signals the partner of the opening bidder employs at trick one. Also discussed will be the signals that the leader's partner uses at *trick two,* when these latter signals are necessary in order to interpret the trick-one signal.

The Come-On Signal and the No-Interest Signal

The come-on signal is probably the most important single weapon that the defenders possess in their arsenal of aggressive warfare. When your partner opens a suit, and you want him to continue playing that suit, *you play an unnecessarily high card on his lead.* For example:

♠ J 10 4
♡ K 7 2
◇ K 10 6
♣ K 9 5 2

West leads
the king
of spades

N
W   E
S

♠ Q 9 2
♡ J 8 3
◇ Q 7 5 3
♣ J 6 3

Suppose that South has purchased the contract at *four hearts,* and your partner, West, opens the king of spades, upon which the four-spot is played from dummy. You know that an opening lead of a king is made from either an A K combination or from a K Q combination. Since you yourself hold the queen, you therefore know that your partner has led from an A K combination. Your proper play on his king, to encourage the continuation of the spade suit, is to *play the nine-spot.* West will then lead the ace, upon which you will play the deuce. West will now realize that your "abnormal" play in spades—putting up the nine first and then playing the two on the next trick— indicates your desire to have that suit played again. He will then lead a third spade to your high queen. Your come-on signal will have accomplished its purpose: to get partner to continue the suit that he started originally. This come-on signal is also known as a "high-low signal:* playing a higher-than-necessary card first, and then playing a lower one on the next lead of that suit.

Another illustration:

♠ A 5 2
♡ 7 4 3
◇ Q J 8 2
♣ J 6 4

West leads
the queen
of hearts

N
W   E
S

♠ 9 3
♡ K 8 2
◇ 10 7 4 3
♣ Q 7 3 2

*This high-low signal is also known as "The Echo."

South has become the declarer at *three no-trump,* and West, your partner, opens the queen of hearts. When it comes your turn to play, you will put up the *eight-spot,* an unnecessarily high card, to urge your partner to continue that suit when he again obtains the lead. Of course, should you yourself subsequently obtain the lead, you will lead the king of hearts, followed by the deuce, since you know that your partner has led from a Q J combination in hearts.

Had you played the deuce of hearts on his opening lead, the two-spot would properly have been interpreted by partner as a most discouraging card, for there is nothing lower than a deuce. *Just as an unnecessarily high card is an encouraging come-on signal, so, in diametrically opposite fashion, the playing of the two, or any low card, is a negative signal, telling your partner that you have "no interest" in the suit led and would he please discontinue leading it unless he can afford to continue on his own.* One more example of a come-on signal:

```
                    ♠ 9 3
                    ♡ Q 7 5
                    ◇ A 6 5 4
                    ♣ K 6 4 3
                                    ♠ 10 8 6 4
    West leads       N             ♡ A 8 4 3
    the king      W     E          ◇ J 7 2
    of diamonds       S            ♣ J 5
```

South's contract is *four spades,* and West leads the king of diamonds, which dummy captures with the ace. Since your partner, West, is known to have started with the K Q of diamonds, you play the *seven-spot,* so that when he next obtains the lead, he will continue playing the diamond suit. Had you held instead, let us say, the 7 3 2 of diamonds, you would have played the most discouraging two-spot, as a negative signal.

This come-on signal has been extended to another recurring situation. You are sitting East.

```
              ♠ Q 6 4
              ♡ 10 8 6 3
              ◇ Q 9 5 2
              ♣ A 10
West leads         N        ♠ 9 2
the king       W       E    ♡ 7 4 2
of spades          S        ◇ A J 6 3
                            ♣ 8 7 4 3
```

Against South's *four-heart* contract, your partner, West, opens the king of spades, upon which you play the *nine-spot,* a come-on signal. His king wins, and he then continues with the ace, upon which you play the deuce. He then leads a third round of spades, and you capture the trick by trumping. Playing the nine-spot first and then following with the deuce on the next spade lead is a high-low come-on signal. This signal is a command to partner to continue the suit that he originally led.

A few paragraphs back there was presented a reference to a "discouraging" signal, when your partner opened the queen of hearts, upon which you had the choice of playing an "encouraging" eight-spot, or a "discouraging" deuce of hearts. Always remember that when your partner opens a suit, he will carefully observe what card you play, so that he can be guided in continuing or discontinuing that suit. Therefore, as you observe his lead, scan the dummy, look at your own cards, and make the decision as to whether you want to signal him to continue his suit or to discontinue it.

Let us now look at these conventional signals from the leader's position.

```
                        ♠ Q 8 5
                        ♡ K Q 8 2
                        ◇ Q 2
                        ♣ 7 6 4 3
♠ A K 9 4 2      N        East plays
♡ 10 3       W       E    the ten
◇ 8 7            S        of spades
♣ J 10 9 5
```

Against South's *four-heart* contract, West opens the king of spades, dummy plays the five-spot, and East puts up the *ten-spot*, South dropping the six. Since the ten is an unusually high card (an encouraging one), West then continues with the ace, upon which East drops the three. Observing that East has played high-low, as a come-on signal urging the continuation of the spade suit, West plays a third round of spades—and East trumps. As will be evident in a moment, had East not signalled West to continue spades and had East not trumped the third round of that suit, declarer would have fulfilled his contract.

The actual deal was:

```
              ♠ Q 8 5
              ♡ K Q 8 2
              ◇ Q 2
              ♣ 7 6 4 3
 ♠ A K 9 4 2        N        ♠ 10 3
 ♡ 10 3                      ♡ 6 4
 ◇ 8 7        W       E      ◇ A 10 9 6 5 3
 ♣ J 10 9 5        S         ♣ Q 8 2
              ♠ J 7 6
              ♡ A J 9 7 5
              ◇ K J 4
              ♣ A K
```

After winning the spade lead by trumping, East now lays down his ace of diamonds and thereby defeats South's *four-heart* contract.

Another hand:

```
              ♠ Q 8 6 5
              ♡ K 9 8 2
              ◇ 9 2
              ♣ Q 6 4
 ♠ A K 9 4        N        East plays
 ♡ 10        W       E     the two
 ◇ 8 7 4          S        of spades
 ♣ J 10 9 5 2
```

South has again arrived at a *four-heart* contract, and again West opens the king of spades, upon which East plays *the deuce*, the most discouraging card he can play. Accepting this warning not to continue spades, West then leads the jack of clubs—and defeats declarer's contract, as it turns out. Had West continued playing the spade suit, declarer would have fulfilled the contract.

This deal, by the way, arose in the National Open Pair Championships of 1960. At each table where South arrived at a four-heart contract, he was defeated when the West defender opened the king of spades and then shifted to the jack of clubs at trick two.

Here is the complete deal:

```
                     ♠ Q 8 6 5
                     ♡ K 9 8 2
                     ◇ 9 2
                     ♣ Q 6 4
    ♠ A K 9 4            N          ♠ J 10 7 2
    ♡ 10                            ♡ 5
    ◇ 8 7 4         W       E       ◇ A K 6 5 3
    ♣ J 10 9 5 2        S           ♣ K 8 7
                     ♠ 3
                     ♡ A Q J 7 6 4 3
                     ◇ Q J 10
                     ♣ A 3
```

At trick two, West leads the jack of clubs, dummy puts up the queen, East covers with the king, and South captures the trick with his ace. It now becomes impossible for declarer to avoid the loss of one club trick (to West's ten-spot), two diamond tricks (to East's ace and king), and the spade trick that he has already lost. It would have been a different story if West had continued with the ace of spades at trick two.

South would have trumped the ace of spades, after which he would have drawn the adverse trumps. Now, on the established queen of spades, declarer would have discarded his losing club. From here in, the play would have been routine, and South would have lost only two more tricks, to East's ace and king of diamonds. As is rather evident, then, the observance of signals can well spell the difference between victory and defeat.

Quite often, the defenders will give signals by their *discards*. Virtually every bridge player is familiar with this, but a few simple illustrations are in order to complete this presentation of signals. When a suit is played of which you have none, if you discard *an unnecessarily high card* in another suit, you are telling your partner that you desire that latter suit to be led.

For example:

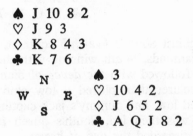

♠ J 10 8 2
♡ J 9 3
◇ K 8 4 3
♣ K 7 6

               ♠ 3
N   ♡ 10 4 2
W   E ◇ J 6 5 2
S   ♣ A Q J 8 2

South is the declarer at a *four-spade* contract, and your partner, West, opens a spade (trump), which declarer captures with his nine-spot. Declarer then lays down the ace of trumps, upon which your partner follows suit. You have a discard to make—and it should be the *eight of clubs,* an unusually high card, telling your partner that when he obtains the lead, he should play a club. Otherwise, if you do not make this discard, your partner will have to guess which suit to lead. Since you desire clubs to be played, you must encourage your partner to lead that suit—hence, the "going out of your way" to discard the eight of clubs.

As you play more and more, you will discover that frequent situations arise when you want to get your partner to lead a certain suit, but you do not possess an unnecessarily high card that you can discard to let him know about it. In these cases, you have at your disposal a "negative" signal that you can employ, and partner will understand it. Here is an illustration of this negative signal.

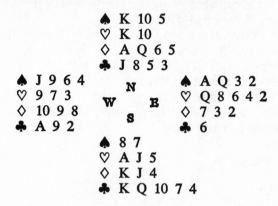

♠ K 10 5
♡ K 10
◇ A Q 6 5
♣ J 8 5 3

♠ J 9 6 4
♡ 9 7 3
◇ 10 9 8
♣ A 9 2

♠ A Q 3 2
♡ Q 8 6 4 2
◇ 7 3 2
♣ 6

♠ 8 7
♡ A J 5
◇ K J 4
♣ K Q 10 7 4

Against South's *five-club* contract, West opened the ten of diamonds, South winning with the jack. On this trick, East followed with the *deuce* of diamonds.

Declarer then played a low club (trump), West also played low, and dummy's jack captured the trick. Another club was then led, South's queen falling to West's ace. East discarded the *two of hearts*.

West now had to lead. From East's plays to the first three tricks, a few things were apparent to West: East did not want diamonds led and he did not want hearts led (on the original diamond lead, East had followed suit with the deuce; on the second club lead, East had discarded the deuce of hearts, stating that he did not want hearts led).

By elimination, therefore, West led a spade, since that seemed to be the sole hope of defeating the contract—and East cashed two spade tricks. Had West, instead, led any other suit, declarer would have fulfilled his contract, for after drawing West's last trump, he would have played his king of diamonds and then his last diamond to dummy's ace. On dummy's queen of diamonds, he would then have discarded one of his two losing spades. But West's spade lead prevented South from getting rid of one of his losing spades.

From a signalling point of view, East would have liked

to give West a more *positive* signal to lead spades. That is, East would have enjoyed possessing the A Q *9* 2 of spades (rather than the A Q *3* 2), for in this case he would have signalled by playing the nine-spot as his discard, an unnecessarily high card. But unfortunately, East had been dealt the A Q 3 2, and he correctly felt that if he played the three-spot, an unusually low card, West would construe it as a discouraging signal. So East was "forced" to make a few negative signals, trusting that his partner would be able to make the proper deductions and would then lead the spade suit. And so it worked out well, with two negatives equalling one positive.

So much for the academic theory behind the defenders' opening lead and the communicative signals that they transmit to each other. Let us now come to their real-life application at the bridge table, where the approach to the defensive problem of "planning at trick one" can be viewed and understood. In studying "history"—critically examining what other defenders have done at trick one—the reader will gain an insight into the *thinking processes* that motivated our actual declarers into doing what they did.

In reading through the remaining chapters of this book—all devoted to *defense at trick one*—it should be noted how vital a role the thinking process plays in the defenders' campaign to outmaneuver declarer; and that if victory is to be achieved, thinking must be made a continuous process, and not merely a one-shot, short-lived, hope-springs-eternal proposition.

chapter 11 The Opening Lead: An Ear to the Opponents' Bidding

♠ In the preceding chapter there was introduced the subject of conventional opening leads. It was stated that, generally speaking, the best opening lead one can make is to lead partner's suit; and that when partner has not bid, one is confronted with options of various opening leads: blind leads such as the top of a sequence lead, the lead of a singleton, the lead of the fourth highest, etc. These blind leads form the primary theme of this chapter.

In the majority of deals that arise, the sole clue as to what to lead is obtained *by interpreting the bidding of the opponents,* at times even if partner has bid. When the logical interpretation is made, the winning lead will be found more often than not. In certain cases, this "ear to the bidding" will indicate that the normal, conventional, automatic lead is actually the incorrect lead. On occasion, the logical lead will turn out to be the losing lead. But, even if the latter should develop, the conscience of the leader will be clear: he did what he *reasoned* was the right thing to do.

Let us now look at the different types of blind opening leads that were made by our expert players under the stress and strain of highly competitive play. In examining these leads, the reader will understand the logical motivation that inspired them.

Deal 1:
On this deal, I imagine that most of our West defenders would make the normal opening lead—and they would thereby present declarer with his contract.

♠ 10 7 6 3
♡ 8 4 2
◊ K J 5 4
♣ 5 2

♠ K 8 2
♡ K 5
◊ A Q 10 9 8 6
♣ 6 3

N
W **E**
S

♠ 9 5 4
♡ Q J 10 9 7 6 3
◊ 2
♣ 10 7

♠ A Q J
♡ A
◊ 7 3
♣ A K Q J 9 8 4

Both sides vulnerable. South dealer.

South	West	North	East
2 ♣	2 ◊	Double	2 ♡
5 ♣	Pass	Pass	Pass

West opened the ace of diamonds and, despite his partner's discouraging deuce, continued with the six of diamonds, East ruffing. Eventually West won a trick with his
king of spades, and declarer went down.

The key to West's winning defense was found in the
bidding. When West's two diamond overcall was doubled
by North, East had "run" to two hearts. No self-respect-
ing partner would have run from the double if he had held
two or more cards in partner's suit. Thus, East was marked
with either a void or a singleton diamond. And, when East
followed with the deuce of diamonds at trick one, West
properly assumed that East had no more diamonds.

Had West made any opening lead other than the diamond ace, or had he played anything but another diamond
at trick two, declarer would have fulfilled his contract.

Deal 2:
When partner bids a suit, the normal lead when one holds
four or more of that suit is the fourth from the highest.
If West had made the normal lead on the deal that follows, declarer would have walked in with his contract.

```
                          ♠ K 10 2
                          ♡ A K J 7 3
                          ◊ J 10 8 4
                          ♣ 4
         ♠ 7 5 4                            ♠ A Q J 9
         ♡ 9 6 5 2          N              ♡ 8 4
         ◊ 6            W         E         ◊ 7 2
         ♣ K 9 6 3 2                        ♣ A Q J 8 5
                          S
                          ♠ 8 6 3
                          ♡ Q 10
                          ◊ A K Q 9 5 3
                          ♣ 10 7
```

East-West vulnerable. North dealer.

North	East	South	West
1 ♡	2 ♣	2 ◊	Pass
3 ◊	Pass	5 ◊	Pass
Pass	Pass		

As West looked at his hand prior to making the opening lead, he knew that he would be on lead for the first and last time if he made the conventional opening of the fourth best of partner's club suit. Realizing—from past experiences—that it might be most advantageous for the defenders if he (rather than his partner) might be able to lead to trick two after the dummy came into view, West elected to open the king of clubs. When this won the trick, West shifted to the seven of spades, thereby enabling East to win two spade tricks.

Had West chosen to open a low club, East would have won the trick—and the defenders could then have made no more than East's ace of spades, for declarer's remaining spades would have been discarded on dummy's hearts.

A moral? Don't allow a general principle to serve as a dogmatic principle. Learn to be flexible.

Deal 3:
The following deal illustrates the lead by a process of elimination: the opponents had bid three suits, so our West defender led the fourth suit.

```
                    ♠ Q J 7 2
                    ♡ A K Q 9 8
                    ◇ K Q
                    ♣ 5 3
   ♠ 8 6 3              N          ♠ 5
   ♡ J 10 5 2      W       E       ♡ 7 4 3
   ◇ 9 7 5 3           S           ◇ 10 6
   ♣ K 10                          ♣ A 9 8 7 6 4 2
                    ♠ A K 10 9 4
                    ♡ 6
                    ◇ A J 8 4 2
                    ♣ Q J
```

Both sides vulnerable. North dealer.

North	East	South	West
1 ♡	Pass	1 ♠	Pass
2 ♠	Pass	3 ◇	Pass
4 ♠	Pass	4 NT	Pass
5 ◇	Pass	6 ♠	Pass
Pass	Pass		

West opened the club king, and when it won the trick, he made haste to lead the ten, East's ace winning.

Having listened to the bidding (he had nothing else to do), West concluded that if North-South had any weak spot, it was in clubs. Despite the unorthodoxy of the lead of a king from a doubleton K 10, West unhesitatingly made it, thereby bringing about declarer's downfall.

I imagine that all bridge players, had they been in the West seat, would have given consideration to the lead of the club king. But I don't know how many, having the courage of their convictions, would have led it.

Deal 4:
On this deal, our West defender had a perfectly safe lead to make in his partner's suit. But he spurned the safe lead, for his "ear" told him that a better lead seemed to be indicated.

```
                    ♠ 7 3
                    ♡ J 5
                    ◇ K 10 9 4
                    ♣ K J 9 7 2
   ♠ 6 5 2                          ♠ A Q J 8 4
   ♡ 10 3            N              ♡ 9 8 6 2
   ◇ A Q 2      W        E          ◇ 7
   ♣ Q 10 8 6 5        S            ♣ A 4 3
                    ♠ K 10 9
                    ♡ A K Q 7 4
                    ◇ J 8 6 5 3
                    ♣ ———
```

Neither side vulnerable. South dealer.

South	West	North	East
1 ♡	Pass	1 NT	2 ♠
3 ◇	3 ♠	4 ◇	Pass
5 ◇	Pass	Pass	Pass

Had West made the normal lead of the six of spades, East would have won the trick with his ace. When declarer subsequently obtained the lead, if he guessed that West possessed the queen of trumps, and successfully finessed the queen, he would have fulfilled his contract. But he never got to that stage.

West, with an ear to the bidding, properly concluded that dummy was short of hearts, South's first bid suit. With a view towards cutting down dummy's ruffing ability, he opened the ace of trumps, East following with the seven-spot. To trick two he led the deuce of trumps, and declarer had a serious problem: were the adverse trumps divided 2-2 originally (if they were, then East now had the singleton queen remaining); or was West leading from an original holding of A Q 2? He decided that it was more likely that they were divided 2-2 than for West to have made the "fancy" lead of the ace from the A Q 2 combination, and then followed up by making the deceptive lead of the deuce.

So declarer went up with dummy's king of trumps at trick two, figuring to catch East's queen. When East's queen did not fall, declarer led the jack of hearts, then a heart to his ace, and then the king of hearts, hoping that the adverse hearts were divided 3-3. If they were, he could discard one of dummy's two spades on the king of hearts, and then he could discard dummy's remaining spade on the queen of hearts, while West was ruffing the trick with his high queen of trumps.

But, unfortunately for declarer, West trumped the third round of hearts and led a spade to his partner's ace, thus defeating declarer.

It should be pointed out that West's opening lead of the trump ace couldn't really ever have cost anything. If, when dummy came into view, the king of trumps was not in evidence, West would abandon trumps, since his remaining guarded queen (Q 2) would be a sure winner. In this case, he would have shifted to spades. But, when dummy showed up with the king, West realized that his queen was (and always had been) "finessible" and that the continuation of the trump deuce was now directed not toward cutting down dummy's ruffing power but toward talking declarer out of taking the finesse for the queen.

Now be honest: would you have finessed for the queen of trumps at trick two, when West led the deuce?

Deal 5:

All of us recognize that guesswork often plays a predominant role in the selection of an opening lead. Here is a deal where a lucky lead defeated a vulnerable slam contract. Yet, the lucky lead was not just pure luck, for it had its origin in an ear that was attuned to the bidding.

```
                    ♠ K 4 2
                    ♡ K 10
                    ◇ 7 5
                    ♣ A K Q J 7 6
    ♠ 9 8 3              N        ♠ 5
    ♡ 7 6 4 3                     ♡ A Q 8 5 2
    ◇ 8 6 4 2      W       E      ◇ Q 10 3
    ♣ 5 2              S          ♣ 10 9 8 4
                    ♠ A Q J 10 7 6
                    ♡ J 9
                    ◇ A K J 9
                    ♣ 3
```

North-South vulnerable. North dealer.

North	East	South	West
1 ♣	Pass	1 ♠	Pass
3 ♣	Pass	3 ♠	Pass
4 ♠	Pass	6 ♠	Pass
Pass	Pass		

Our West defender was the world's greatest woman player, Helen Sobel. Based on the bidding, she realized that to lead a spade or a club was tantamount to conceding defeat. By ear, therefore, the correct lead had to be a diamond or a heart. Which to lead? She chose to lead a heart, and declarer was down one. When a kibitzer commented on Helen's excellent lead, Helen quite naturally refused to take any credit for it.

If this deal proves anything, it is that diamonds are not necessarily a girl's best friend.

Deal 6:

To know the bidding habits of one's opponents can be a tremendous asset. In this deal, South was known frequently to bid suits he did not possess, his aim being to deceive the opposition. The West defender, B. Jay Becker, fortunately was familiar with this trait of South's. The deal arose in the Vanderbilt Championships of 1950.

```
            ♠ A Q 4
            ♡ K J 9 4 3 2
            ◇ K 3
            ♣ K 4
♠ 8 7              N              ♠ J 10 6 5
♡ A 8 7      W         E         ♡ 10 6
◇ A 7 6 5 2        S              ◇ Q 8 4
♣ 7 6 3                           ♣ J 10 9 8
            ♠ K 9 3 2
            ♡ Q 5
            ◇ J 10 9
            ♣ A Q 5 2
```

Neither side vulnerable. North dealer.

North	East	South	West
1 ♡	Pass	2 ◊ (!)	Pass
2 ♡	Pass	2 NT	Pass
3 NT	Pass	Pass	Pass

Mr. Becker led the five of diamonds, the trick being won by dummy's king, as East played the eight of diamonds. A heart was then led off the board, South's queen falling to West's ace. Convinced that South's diamond bid was phony, Becker now led the deuce of diamonds, East's queen winning. East then returned his remaining diamond, and Becker rattled off three more diamonds, to defeat declarer.

Deal 7:
In many bidding sequences where the opponents have displayed that they possess an overwhelming preponderance of high cards, one is usually reluctant to make an aggressive opening lead—for example, away from a K x x or a Q x x, etc., combination—for fear of giving declarer a present of a trick that he could not obtain on his own power. More often than not in these situations, the expert will make what he considers to be a neutral, safe lead. At times, the safe lead turns out to be the most disastrous one, whereas the aggressive, presumably dangerous lead would have been the winning one. Here is an example. The deal arose in the National Team-of-Four Championships of 1958.

```
                   ♠ 10 3
                   ♡ A K J 10 3 2
                   ◊ 3 2
                   ♣ 10 9 4
     ♠ K J 7 5          N          ♠ A 6 4 2
     ♡ Q 9 7 4      W       E      ♡ 8
     ◊ 10 5 4          S          ◊ Q 9 8 6
     ♣ J 3                         ♣ 8 7 5 2
                   ♠ Q 9 8
                   ♡ 6 5
                   ◊ A K J 7
                   ♣ A K Q 6
```

South	West	North	East
1 ◇	Pass	1 ♡	Pass
2 NT	Pass	4 NT	Pass
6 NT	Pass	Pass	Pass

West didn't think it advisable to lead a spade away from his king against the slam contract, for fear of leading into an A Q combination that he figured was possessed by North-South. So he led a diamond, and declarer, by taking two heart finesses, fulfilled his slam contract.

When the deal was subsequently replayed, the bidding proceeded as follows:

South	West	North	East
1 ◇	Pass	1 ♡	Pass
2 NT	Pass	4 NT	Pass
Pass	Pass		

The West defender in this situation felt that an aggressive lead was called for, so he led his fourth highest spade. After the first four tricks had been played, declarer was down one.

Deal 8:
In the two deals that follow (8 and 9), the theme is the blind opening lead of *a low card* in a suit that is headed by an *ace* (A x x; A x x x, etc.). This is probably the most dangerous lead that one can make, especially against a suit contract, for either dummy or declarer might have a singleton king—which will, of course, win the trick. Then, when the ace is led subsequently, it will be trumped.

Nevertheless, there are situations where the bidding indicates that the underlead of an ace is called for. When these situations arise, the underleader usually gets away with it, for declarer cannot quite believe that anybody would dare to take such a risk at the very outset of play.

The underleading deals that follow arose in topflight expert games.

```
              ♠ K J 4
              ♡ A K Q
              ◇ K J 8
              ♣ A Q J 2
♠ A 9 2            N          ♠ Q 10 8 5
♡ J 8 6 5 3 2  W     E        ♡ 10 9 7
◇ 3                S          ◇ 6 4
♣ 9 6 5                       ♣ 8 7 4 3
              ♠ 7 6 3
              ♡ 4
              ◇ A Q 10 9 7 5 2
              ♣ K 10
```

North	East	South	West
2 NT	Pass	3 ◇	Pass
4 ◇	Pass	6 ◇	Pass
Pass	Pass		

From West's point of view, he had no attractive lead to make. He was reasonably certain that North, as part of his two–no-trump opening, possessed the king of spades. With the hope that East possessed the queen of spades, West opened the deuce of spades.

Declarer chose to put up dummy's jack, East's queen winning. East hurriedly returned a spade, and the slam was defeated before declarer ever won a trick.

From declarer's point of view, I am quite sure that if he ever even gave a passing thought to the possibility that West was underleading the spade ace, he quickly dismissed it. After all, people just never (well, hardly ever) underlead aces against slam contracts. But a lead away from the queen is fairly normal. Hence his play of the jack of spades at trick one.

Deal 9:

```
                        ♠ K J 9 5
                        ♡ J 6 2
                        ◇ K 6
                        ♣ K Q J 6
    ♠ A 4 3                              ♠ Q 10 7 2
    ♡ 7 5 4          N                   ♡ A 3
    ◇ 10 8        W     E                ◇ 7 5 3 2
    ♣ 8 5 4 3 2        S                 ♣ A 10 9
                        ♠ 8 6
                        ♡ K Q 10 9 8
                        ◇ A Q J 9 4
                        ♣ 7
```

Neither side vulnerable. South dealer.

South	West	North	East
1 ♡	Pass	2 NT	Pass
3 ◇	Pass	3 ♡	Pass
4 ♡	Pass	Pass	Pass

West, on lead against the four-heart contract, found himself in the position that all of us find ourselves at times: no good lead seemed available. He elected to open the three of spades, as a least-of-evils lead in a sense, and also as a lead that offered hope, since North figured—on the bidding—to possess the king of spades, and the lead of a low spade presented the possibility of deceiving North as to the location of the spade ace.

South realized that West might be underleading the ace of spades. But at the same time, South figured that it was more likely that West was underleading the queen. So he played dummy's jack of spades, and East won the trick with his queen. Eventually the defenders took their three aces and handed declarer a one-trick set.

Had West led any other card in his hand at trick one (except a low spade), declarer would have made his contract, for he would then have lost one spade trick at most (dummy's clubs providing a trick or two).

Deal 10:
The two preceding deals have been concerned with the question of the *blind* opening lead away from an ace. But

even when leading partner's suit, there is much doubt about the practicality of leading the ace of his suit automatically, constituted authority to the contrary. Traditionally, all textbooks have advocated the leading of the ace of partner's suit, rather than underleading the ace. Nevertheless, there arise numerous situations when logic demands that an underlead of partner's suit be made, just as there are times when logic demands the underlead of an ace in a suit that has not been bid.

Admittedly there is a normal reluctance and hesitancy about making an unorthodox lead, especially when one recalls the tongue lashings he has received in the past for being imaginative but not practical. Nevertheless, if one is of the opinion—determined by his interpretation of the bidding—that unorthodoxy is called for, he should not hesitate to become unorthodox.

Here is a good example, taken from the National Championships of 1954. The West defender was Alphonse (Sonny) Moyse, the editor of *The Bridge World*.

```
              ♠ Q J 7 3
              ♡ A 10 9 6
              ◇ 7 5 4
              ♣ 10 2
  ♠ A 6 2            N        ♠ K 10 9 8 5
  ♡ 7 5 4 3 2     W     E     ♡ K 8
  ◇ 6 2              S        ◇ Q J 10
  ♣ 8 5 4                     ♣ 9 7 3
              ♠ 4
              ♡ Q J
              ◇ A K 9 8 3
              ♣ A K Q J 6
```

North-South vulnerable. South dealer.

South	West	North	East
1 ◇	Pass	1 ♡	1 ♠
3 ♣	Pass	3 NT	Pass
4 ♣	Pass	4 ◇	Pass
5 ◇	Pass	Pass	Pass

Had Moyse opened the ace of spades, declarer would have had a cinch. Even if West then shifted to a heart, the defenders could not recover. Dummy's ace of hearts would win, after which the queen of spades would be laid down. If East declined to play the king, declarer would simply discard his losing heart. And if West chose to cover the queen with the king, declarer would simply trump it, reenter dummy via the ten of clubs, and discard his losing heart on the established jack of spades.

In the actual play, Moyse opened the deuce of spades, dummy's jack being taken by East's king. There was now no way for declarer to establish a spade trick for a discard of his losing heart. When South ultimately took the heart finesse, it lost. East's sure trump trick then enabled the defenders to defeat the five-diamond contract.

There is no way of proving what would have happened, but if dummy had turned up with the K J x of spades (East possessing the Q 10 9 x x), I'm certain that on West's opening lead of the deuce of spades, dummy's jack would have been put up on the sound assumption that East, for his overcall, figured to have the ace of spades. Whereas if West opened the ace, dummy's (hypothetical) king would have been promoted into a winner.

In most situations, where dummy (sitting in front of your partner) has bid no-trump after your partner has bid a suit, announcing a stopper in partner's suit, the lead of the ace of partner's suit has little to recommend it. In my opinion, the underlead of the ace will bring favorable results more often than will the lead of the ace.

The Commanded-By-Partner Lead

Whenever your partner has doubled a final contract in either *no-trump* or a *slam* and you are on lead, his double commands you to make a specifically prescribed, conventional lead. In these situations, your judgment concerning what you would like to lead is superseded by what partner has *commanded* you to lead. Here are these conventional leads:

(1) When neither you nor partner has bid, a double of a final *no-trump* contract by partner *demands that you lead the first suit bid by dummy.*

(2) When your partner has doubled a final contract in *no-trump* and *he* has bid a suit, his double is an inviolable command to you *to lead his suit.*

(3) When your partner has doubled a final contract in *no-trump* and *you* have bid a suit, his double is an inviolable command to you *to lead your suit.*

(4) If both you and your partner have bid, and the opponents arrive at a *no-trump* contract, which your partner doubles, your opening lead becomes a matter of judgment. There is no accepted convention to cover this one specific situation.

(5) When your partner has doubled a *slam contract,* whether you or he (or both of you) have or have not bid, it is an accepted convention that his double commands the lead of *the first suit bid by dummy.*

The four deals which follow (11, 12, 13, and 14) illustrate these conventional leads.

Deal 11:

```
                    ♠ K J 10
                    ♡ J 9 5 3
                    ◇ 8 5 4 2
                    ♣ Q J
    ♠ 7 5 4 3              N           ♠ 9 8 6
    ♡ 4 2                              ♡ A K Q 10 8
    ◇ 10 6        W           E        ◇ 9 7
    ♣ K 10 7 3 2          S           ♣ 8 6 5
                    ♠ A Q 2
                    ♡ 7 6
                    ◇ A K Q J 3
                    ♣ A 9 4
```

Both sides vulnerable. South dealer.

South	West	North	East
1 ◊	Pass	1 ♡	Pass
3 NT	Pass	Pass	Double
Pass	Pass	Pass	

In obedience to East's double, West dutifully opened the four of hearts, dummy's bid suit. As is apparent, East took the first five tricks. And, as is equally apparent, had East not doubled, then West, left to his own resources, would probably have opened his fourth highest club. Of course, had West opened anything but a heart, declarer would have scored an easy game.

A point to bear in mind is that if you are sitting East, in a position analogous to the above, don't double on scattered high-card strength simply because you feel that you can defeat the opponents. A double by you is a categoric command to partner to lead dummy's *first-bid suit.* So, if you "can't stand" that lead, then don't double.

Incidentally, if there are those who have no love for North's heart bid, they are not alone. But just as often as not, such bids pay dividends, as would have been the case had not East made his conventional double.

Deal 12:

```
                 ♠ A K 7 4 3
                 ♡ 7 5
                 ◊ K 10 7 2
                 ♣ K Q
  ♠ J 9 8 6 5 2       N          ♠ ——————
  ♡ J 9 6 3                      ♡ A K Q 10 8 2
  ◊ ——————      W       E        ◊ 8 6 4
  ♣ 7 5 3           S            ♣ 10 8 6 4
                 ♠ Q 10
                 ♡ 4
                 ◊ A Q J 9 5 3
                 ♣ A J 9 2
```

North-South vulnerable. North dealer.

North	East	South	West
1 ♠	2 ♡	3 ◇	3 ♡
4 ◇	4 ♡	4 NT	Pass
5 ◇	Pass	6 ◇	Pass
Pass	Double	Pass	Pass
Pass			

When East doubled South's six-diamond bid, West properly led a spade, dummy's first-bid suit. East, of course, trumped, after which he cashed the king of hearts, for the setting trick. (Had East underled the A K Q of hearts at trick two, West would have won the trick with the jack, after which he would have led another spade for East to trump. But just imagine what West would have said had declarer possessed the jack of hearts!)

If East had not doubled, West would have made his normal lead of a low heart, the suit in which East had overcalled. And when East won this trick, the defenders would have made their first and last trick.

Again, a warning: don't double the opponents in a slam contract unless you want your partner to lead dummy's first-bid suit. If you double, that's what he is going to lead.

Deal 13:

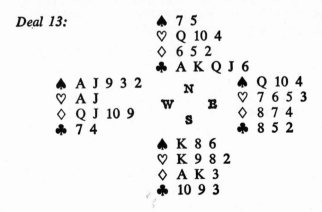

Both sides vulnerable. West dealer.

West	North	East	South
1 ♠	2 ♣	Pass	3 NT
Pass	Pass	Double	Pass
Pass	Pass		

East's double was about as optimistic a double as I have ever seen. However, its conventional meaning was unmistakable. It said: "Partner, lead the suit you bid!"

So West opened the three of spades, and East's queen forced declarer's king. Declarer could now make but eight tricks: one spade, two diamonds, and five clubs. Had East not doubled, West would probably have led the queen of diamonds, feeling that the spade lead might present declarer with a trick.

As presented earlier, the principle involved here is that when you have bid a suit and your partner subsequently doubles the opponents in a three no-trump contract, his double is an inviolable command to you to lead your suit.

I am not recommending that doubles such as East's be made—if one makes them, he figures to go "broke." On this particular deal, the combination of luck and nerve just happened to pay handsome dividends.

Deal 14:
In this deal, the *failure* to double a slam contract enabled declarer to fulfill a contract that, had it been doubled for a *specific* lead, would have been defeated.

```
                        ♠ K 2
                        ♡ J 5
                        ◇ A Q J 8 4
                        ♣ Q 10 3 2
 ♠ J 10 8 7 5 4 3              N        ♠ A Q 9
 ♡ 9                                    ♡ Q 10 7 6 4 2
 ◇ 6 5 3 2           W             E    ◇ K 7
 ♣ 7                          S        ♣ 6 4
                        ♠ 6
                        ♡ A K 8 3
                        ◇ 10 9
                        ♣ A K J 9 8 5
```

East-West vulnerable. North dealer.

North	East	South	West
1 ◇	1 ♡	2 ♣	Pass
3 ♣	Pass	3 ♡	Pass
4 ♣	Pass	4 NT	Pass
5 ◇	Pass	6 ♣	Pass
Pass	Pass (!)		

West made the normal opening lead of the nine of hearts, dummy's jack was put up, East covered with the queen, and South won the trick with his king.

The ace of trumps was then led, followed by another trump to dummy's queen, picking up the adverse trumps. Now came the five of hearts, East played the six, and South put in the eight, knowing it would win (East's opening lead of the heart nine had marked the ten as being in the East hand).

Next came the ace of hearts, upon which the board's two of spades was discarded. Declarer's fourth heart was then trumped in dummy, and this position was arrived at:

```
              ♠ K
              ♡ ——
              ◇ A Q J 8 4
              ♣ 10
  ♠ J 10 8           N           ♠ A Q
  ♡ ——          W         E      ♡ 10 7 4
  ◇ 6 5 3 2          S           ◇ K 7
  ♣ ——                           ♣ ——
              ♠ 6
              ♡ ——
              ◇ 10 9
              ♣ K J 9 8
```

The king of spades was now led, East's ace winning—and East had just become the victim of an end play! If he led either a spade or a heart, declarer would discard his nine of diamonds while simultaneously trumping the trick in dummy. And, if East chose to lead a diamond (at gun point!), declarer would obtain a "free" finesse.

East should have doubled the six-club contract. This would have commanded West to lead a diamond, dummy's first-bid suit—and East's king would figure to become a winner, as it would have been. And declarer then would have been unable to avoid the loss of a diamond trick and a spade trick.

Admittedly, South, rather than North, might have held the diamond ace, but this was a gamble that East should have taken. Certainly a heart lead by West figured to be the worst possible lead, which it turned out to be.

Deal 15:

At the outset of this chapter it was stated that on occasion the perfectly logical lead, which is based on an ear to the opponents' bidding, will turn out to be the losing lead. Here is a dramatic illustration of this point—and the West defender who made the unfortunate lead was one of the world's greatest players. The North player, who talked him into making the lead, was Oswald Jacoby, the world's top-ranking player as of 1964.

```
              ♠ A 9 6 5 3
              ♡ 6 3
              ◇ A K J 8 7 4
              ♣ ——

   ♠ 4 2           N           ♠ 7
   ♡ J                         ♡ A K Q 10 7 5 4 2
   ◇ 10 9 6 2   W       E      ◇ 3
   ♣ A 8 6 4 3 2   S          ♣ J 10 9

              ♠ K Q J 10 8
              ♡ 9 8
              ◇ Q 5
              ♣ K Q 7 5
```

Neither side vulnerable. North dealer.

North	East	South	West
1 ◇	4 ♡	4 ♠	Pass
7 ♠ (!)	Pass	Pass	Pass

West made the normal, natural (and enthusiastic) lead of the ace of clubs, which was ruffed in dummy. The grand slam was now there for the taking. Had West opened a heart, partner's bid suit, the defenders of course would have taken two heart tricks.

To the reader who is a neophyte, Jacoby's bid of seven spades would appear to be a product of a psychopathetic mind. But listen to the way Jacoby explained it: "It was either a game at four spades or a grand slam at seven spades. If I bid six, I figured West would lead a heart and wait with his ace of clubs, if he had it. In that case we'd have to be down. But against a grand slam, the temptation to cash an ace for fear that otherwise you might never get it, is more than any of us can resist."

Deal 16:
This final deal is, in my opinion, a most amusing one, despite the opinion to the contrary of our declarer. East had heard his partner bid diamonds, so he made the proper opening lead of the queen of diamonds—which was fine, except that it wasn't his turn to lead! What happened to declarer as a result I wouldn't wish on anyone, including my worst enemy. The deal arose in the National Open Pair Championships of 1939.

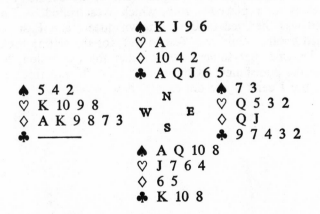

```
                    ♠ K J 9 6
                    ♡ A
                    ◇ 10 4 2
                    ♣ A Q J 6 5
   ♠ 5 4 2                          ♠ 7 3
   ♡ K 10 9 8          N            ♡ Q 5 3 2
   ◇ A K 9 8 7 3   W       E        ◇ Q J
   ♣ —                 S            ♣ 9 7 4 3 2
                    ♠ A Q 10 8
                    ♡ J 7 6 4
                    ◇ 6 5
                    ♣ K 10 8
```

Both sides vulnerable. North dealer.

North	East	South	West
1 ♣	Pass	1 ♠	2 ♦
3 ♠	Pass	4 ♠	Pass
Pass	Pass		

As was stated, *East* opened the queen of diamonds, out of turn, whereupon the tournament director was called upon for a ruling. The rule (at that time) was that declarer could command the lead of *any* suit from West, the proper opening leader, *or* he could treat the queen of diamonds as an exposed card (which meant that the queen *had* to be played at East's first legal opportunity).

Declarer elected to call a club lead from West, feeling that the lead up to his K 10 8 could be most profitable to him. (Declarer, of course, did not see the dummy prior to calling the lead.) West promptly announced that he had no clubs. Declarer had no further rights, and West could now lead anything he wished. He wisely chose to lead a low diamond, knowing (having observed) that his partner held the queen of diamonds. East won this trick with his *jack* (when declarer had exercised his alternative option of commanding West to lead a club, the queen of diamonds ceased being an exposed card and had been put back into the East hand). East, having heard that his partner had no clubs, now played a club, which West ruffed. A diamond was then led to East's known queen, and East returned another club, for West to ruff, for the setting trick.

I imagine that somewhere or other the expression "to make the punishment fit the crime" must fit into this picture, but I can't figure out exactly how or where.

chapter 12 The Opening Lead: Shunning the Natural, Normal Lead

♠ In this chapter there are presented 12 deals in each of which the various defenders could have made the perfectly normal, natural lead, and they would have known that their leads could not be criticized. Yet, had our defenders clung to the sanctuary that was being offered gratuitously by orthodoxy, they would have made the losing lead. In the eyes of the world at large, they would have been adjudged as "not guilty of conduct unbecoming a bridge player." But in the eyes of the world of expert players, in which everyday actions "above and beyond the call of duty" are the prerequisite for admission into the classification of "expert player," the normal lead would have been deemed to be an "ill-advised" lead, for it would have had its roots and motivation in accepted, traditional convention and not in the application of independent, logical judgment to the specific situation at hand.

Deal 1:

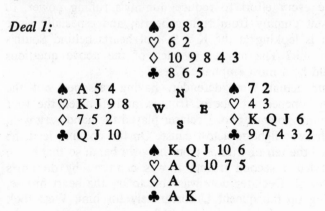

```
               ♠ 9 8 3
               ♡ 6 2
               ◇ 10 9 8 4 3
               ♣ 8 6 5
   ♠ A 5 4         N         ♠ 7 2
   ♡ K J 9 8   W       E     ♡ 4 3
   ◇ 7 5 2         S         ◇ K Q J 6
   ♣ Q J 10                  ♣ 9 7 4 3 2
               ♠ K Q J 10 6
               ♡ A Q 10 7 5
               ◇ A
               ♣ A K
```

Neither side vulnerable. South dealer.

South	West	North	East
2 ♠	Pass	2 NT	Pass
3 ♡	Pass	3 NT	Pass
4 ♡	Pass	4 ♠	Pass
Pass	Pass		

What could be more normal than to open the queen of clubs? If this lead is made, declarer will win it and promptly bang down the ace of hearts, after which he will lead another heart, West winning. Belatedly, West will shift to the ace and another trump, South winning the latter lead. A third round of hearts will now be ruffed with dummy's last trump (while West's jack of hearts falls). The closed hand will then be reentered via the diamond ace, West's last trump will be picked up and a heart conceded to West's remaining king. Played in this manner, declarer's only losers would be two hearts and the ace of trumps.

From South's bidding, is it not apparent that he has a minimum of five spades and a minimum of five hearts? From North's bidding, is it not a "fact" that he prefers (however mildly) spades to hearts as the trump suit? Does not the "ear" indicate that North figures to have either a doubleton heart or a singleton heart or, conceivably, no hearts at all? From West's seat, should he not immediately make every effort to reduce dummy's ruffing power, to prevent dummy from ruffing hearts; and especially since West is looking at the K J 9 8 of hearts behind South's rebid suit? The answer to each of the above questions should be a most emphatic "Yes!"

Our actual West defender, having reasoned out the above, opened the ace of trumps, and then led the four of trumps to trick two. Declarer played the hand very well, but he was fighting a lost cause. On the opening lead, he played the ten of trumps from his own hand, so that when West led a second trump, it was captured by dummy's eight-spot. Declarer now was able to try the heart finesse, putting up the queen. Unfortunately for him, West took the queen with the king and played a third round of trumps, removing dummy's last trump. West could not now be prevented from winning two additional heart tricks that, combined with the heart trick won earlier, plus the ace of trumps, gave the East-West defenders four tricks.

Deal 2:

You are sitting West, on lead against South's *three–no-trump* contract. Let's interpret the bidding before leading:

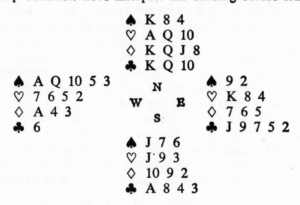

```
                    ♠ K 8 4
                    ♡ A Q 10
                    ◇ K Q J 8
                    ♣ K Q 10
  ♠ A Q 10 5 3           N         ♠ 9 2
  ♡ 7 6 5 2                         ♡ K 8 4
  ◇ A 4 3         W         E       ◇ 7 6 5
  ♣ 6                   S           ♣ J 9 7 5 2
                    ♠ J 7 6
                    ♡ J 9 3
                    ◇ 10 9 2
                    ♣ A 8 4 3
```

Both sides vulnerable. North dealer.

North	East	South	West
1 ◇	Pass	1 NT	Pass
3 NT	Pass	Pass	Pass

South, for his courtesy one–no-trump response, is known to have a poor hand, in the area of 6–9 points. North's three no-trump rebid figures to denote about 20 points. Who figures to have the king of spades, North or South?

South's one no-trump response has promised nothing in the way of stoppers in the unbid suits. North's leap to three no-trump in the face of South's negative response must surely indicate that the former feels he can take care of the unbid suits, including the spade suit. Certainly North figures to possess the spade king much more often than South.

If you make the normal opening lead of the five of spades—the fourth highest—South will win it with the jack and then proceed to knock out your ace of diamonds. If you then continue spades, dummy's king will provide declarer with his ninth trick. And if you lead any other suit instead, declarer will be able to develop his ninth trick in either spades or hearts.

But if, after having analyzed the bidding and having concluded that North probably has the king of spades, you properly open the queen of spades, you are in good shape. North will win the trick with the king as your partner follows suit with the discouraging deuce. Declarer will now attack the diamond suit, and you will take your ace. Avoiding a spade continuation—having been forewarned by partner's deuce—you will return either a diamond, a heart, or a club—and declarer will make but eight tricks. When your partner obtains the lead via the king of hearts, his natural return of the nine of spades will entrap South's remaining J 7, and you will cash your spade suit.

When this deal arose in real life, our West defender, Dr. LeRoy Robins, of Washington, D.C., correctly opened the queen of spades, and declarer went down to defeat.

Deal 3:
In expert circles, the lead that West made on this deal has become a standard type of lead.

```
                       ♠ Q
                       ♡ J 5
                       ◇ 9 4 3 2
                       ♣ A Q J 9 4 3
  ♠ K J 10 8 4 3              N          ♠ 9 7 6 2
  ♡ Q 7 6                              ♡ A K 9 3
  ◇ K 5            W              E      ◇ 8 7 6
  ♣ 8 6                   S            ♣ 7 5
                       ♠ A 5
                       ♡ 10 8 4 2
                       ◇ A Q J 10
                       ♣ K 10 2
```

East-West vulnerable. North dealer.

North	East	South	West
Pass	Pass	1 ◇	1 ♠
2 ♣	2 ♠	3 NT	Pass
Pass	Pass		

Looking at the South hand, we all agree that his jump
to three–no-trump was overly aggressive. And I think that
all of us will also agree that, if we were holding the West
hand, we would be absolutely certain, beyond any doubt,
that South possessed the *ace of spades*.

Further, I think we would all lead a spade against the
three–no-trump contract, for in this suit would appear to
be our best chance of gaining the victory. And now, I imagine, there would come a parting of the ways, for most
of us would lead either the eight of spades (our fourth
best) or the jack of spades, the top of our inner sequence.
If either of these leads is made, declarer breezes in with
his contract: two spades, one diamond, and six clubs.

Since you have made up your mind *to lead a spade*, is
not the lead of the *king* of spades proper? If declarer happens to have both the ace and queen of spades, what difference which spade you lead, since in this case he will
make two spade tricks? If dummy has, let us say, the Q x
or the Q x x of spades (facing declarer's A x or A x x),
again will not declarer make two spade tricks regardless
of whether you open the eight or the jack of spades? But if
dummy happens to have the singleton queen of spades, will
not your lead of the king limit declarer to just one spade
winner while simultaneously establishing your spade suit?
Surely the lead of the spade king puts you in the position
of standing to gain everything while standing to lose nothing.

In the actual play, West opened the king of spades, and
the appearance of the singleton queen in dummy was a joy
to behold. When the play was completed, declarer was a
most unhappy fellow, since all he could make was eight
tricks. And there wasn't a thing he could have done about it.

Deal 4:
The West defender on this deal was the world-renowned Lee Hazen, of New York City. No voices whispered to him that this was a tricky hand and that he had to make an unusual lead to defeat declarer's contract. Nevertheless, he came up with the lead of the only one of his 13 cards that could have achieved the desired result.

```
                    ♠ 10 9 2
                    ♡ K 6
                    ◇ J 6
                    ♣ A Q J 9 7 4
   ♠ J 5 4 3            N            ♠ ——
   ♡ Q J 10 9 8      W     E         ♡ 7 4 3 2
   ◇ 10 7              S             ◇ Q 9 8 5 4 2
   ♣ K 6                             ♣ 10 5 3
                    ♠ A K Q 8 7 6
                    ♡ A 5
                    ◇ A K 3
                    ♣ 8 2
```

Neither side vulnerable. South dealer.

South	West	North	East
1 ♠	Pass	2 ♣	Pass
3 ♠	Pass	4 ♠	Pass
4 NT	Pass	5 ◇	Pass
5 NT	Pass	6 ◇	Pass
6 ♠	Pass	Pass	Pass

Had Lee made the normal opening lead of the heart queen, declarer would have chalked up a small slam, bid and made. He would have won the opening lead with his king, drawn trumps (receiving the bad news that West had a trump winner), and then would have been forced to take the club finesse—successfully. South's only loser would have been the jack of trumps.

But Hazen knew something that declarer could not possibly know or foresee (or expect, on the bidding), namely,

that Hazen had a trump trick. Surely, reasoned Hazen,
dummy figures to have a club suit headed by the ace, and
declarer is not going to risk a finesse on the very first
trick unless no better line of play is available. If (Hazen
still reasoning) I lead the queen of hearts, then when
declarer subsequently discovers that the loss of a trump
trick is inevitable, he may be forced to resort to a club
finesse as his sole remaining hope.

And so, Hazen opened—the six of clubs! What would
you have done had you been sitting in the South seat?
Would you not have won the opening lead with dummy's
ace for fear that West was leading a singleton; and that
if you didn't win the trick with dummy's ace, East would
capture the trick with the club king and return a club for
West to trump? After all, wasn't the trump suit "solid,"
with no losers? And, after drawing trumps, couldn't you
simply concede the queen of clubs to the king, and on
dummy's jack of clubs discard your losing diamond?

At trick one, declarer—even as you and I—put up
dummy's ace of clubs and led a trump, East failing to follow suit. And gloom descended on declarer.

Deal 5:
This deal arose in the National Masters Pairs Championships of 1952. I was sitting East, and my partner, the West
defender, was Edgar Kaplan.

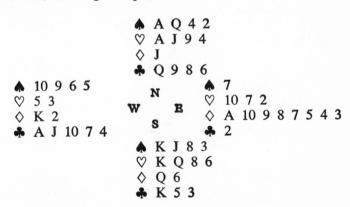

East-West vulnerable. North dealer.

North	*East*	*South*	*West*
1 ♣	2 ♦	2 ♥	3 ♦
3 ♥	Pass	4 ♥	Pass
Pass	Pass		

Edgar opened the ace of clubs and, despite my discouraging deuce (nobody ever deals me singleton nines or tens!), continued with the four of clubs, which I ruffed. I then returned a low diamond to his king (he *had* supported my suit), after which he led another club, which I ruffed for the setting trick.

From West's point of view, he realized that my "weak jump overcall" was based on distributional strength (by definition), with virtually little (if *any*) high-card strength outside of my bid suit. So he hoped that my club was a singleton. When it turned out to be as hoped for, the rest was routine.

How easy (and justifiable) it would have been for Edgar to have made the normal lead of the diamond king—after which there would have been no way of defeating declarer.

Deal 6:
To finesse or not to finesse, that is the question.

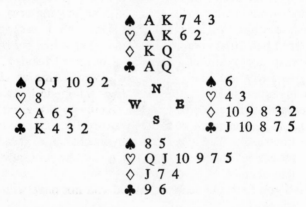

Both sides vulnerable. North dealer.

North	East	South	West
2 ♠	Pass	2 NT	Pass
3 NT	Pass	4 ♡	Pass
6 ♡	Pass	Pass	Pass

It was perfectly obvious to our West defender that
North's hand was equivalent to at least an opening bid of
three no-trump: South's two no-trump response might have
been made on a hand that didn't contain even a jack—of
which North was aware—and North had then gone to bid
three no-trump all by himself. When South then bid four
hearts, it was apparent that his whole hand consisted of a
six or seven card heart suit, with almost certainly no outside
values, since his original two no-trump response was a negative bid; and, had he possessed the obvious heart suit and
some outside strength, he would have bid the heart suit
immediately.

West also knew (or, rather, *felt)* that North's two-spade
opening indicated a respectable spade suit—and West *knew*
(not "felt") that when dummy came into view, if declarer
entertained any hopes of establishing that spade suit, those
hopes were not going to materialize. And further, West,
looking at the ace of diamonds in his own hand, knew that
dummy would come down with the three missing aces, for
how else could North have bid the slam with a reasonably
balanced hand that contained no void (North had bid three
no-trump all by himself, denoting a balanced hand)?

It seemed most likely, then, that West's king of clubs
was in a finessible position and that, when declarer discovered that the spade suit was not going to divide nicely,
he would be (or might be) forced to stake his destiny on a
club finesse. So West gave declarer no chance to discover
the "miserable" division of the spade suit: he promptly led
the three of clubs!

Had you been the declarer, would you not have won the

opening lead with the ace and then attacked the spade suit? After all, if the six adverse spades were divided no worse than 4-2, it would be a routine matter to cash the ace and king and then ruff out two spades, thereby establishing the fifth spade into a winner.

When South won the opening lead with the board's ace of clubs and played the ace and king of spades, East trumped the latter lead. He now went down two tricks. He could have saved a trick if he had played it otherwise, but once he had failed to take the club finesse at trick one, he was doomed to defeat.

Of course, if West had opened anything but a low club, declarer would have made his contract—and without taking a club finesse! On his jack of diamonds—to be established —he would have discarded dummy's queen of clubs.

Deal 7:

As to what the technically proper, "normal" lead is on the following deal, I do not know. But I do know that West's opening lead was not the normal one; and her abnormal lead, plus an abnormal follow through, resulted in declarer's defeat. The deal occurred in a rubber-bridge game in 1935, with the West defender being Josephine Culbertson and the South declarer being P. Hal Sims. Mr. Sims, incidentally, was very rarely outguessed at the bridge table, but on this deal he came out second-best. However, it should be mentioned that he was not ashamed of his misguess in this case, for Josephine Culbertson was one of the world's finest players.

The play embodied in this deal, incidentally, was illustrated in the preceding chapter, on Deals 9 and 10, wherein were presented two illustrations of the blind opening lead away from an ace. It was pointed out that this is a highly dangerous lead against a suit contract, but one which quite often proves successful, for declarer cannot quite bring himself to believe that the leader is that "nervy" as to under-lead an ace. This deal is a good case in point, and demonstrates that one of the requisites of winning defense is active imagination—and "nerve".

```
              ♠ K J 3
              ♡ 7
              ◇ A Q 7 4
              ♣ K Q 9 4 2
  ♠ A 5 4           N        ♠ Q 10 7 6
  ♡ 8 4 3 2      W     E     ♡ 10 5
  ◇ K 9 6                    ◇ J 10 5 3 2
  ♣ A 10 7         S         ♣ 6 3
              ♠ 9 8 2
              ♡ A K Q J 9 6
              ◇ 8
              ♣ J 8 5
```

Both sides vulnerable. North dealer.

North	East	South	West
1 ♣	Pass	1 ♡	Pass
2 ◇	Pass	3 ♡	Pass
3 NT	Pass	4 ♡	Pass
Pass	Pass		

Mrs. Culbertson opened the four of spades, the jack was played from dummy, and East won the trick with his queen. A club return was then made, West winning with her ace. She now led the five of spades and Mr. Sims, assuming (hoping) that West's spade holding was headed by the ten, followed with dummy's three-spot. As is apparent, East took the trick with the ten, and returned a spade, Mrs. Culbertson cashing the setting trick with her ace.

Had Mr. Sims put up dummy's king of spades at either trick one or trick three, he would have fulfilled his contract —and you would never have heard of this hand. But I imagine that Mr. Sims couldn't believe that Mrs. Culbertson had the nerve to underlead the spade ace twice in a row. Would you have believed it had you been in the South seat?

Deal 8:
The West defender on this deal was Alfred Sheinwold, and the East defender was Edgar Kaplan.

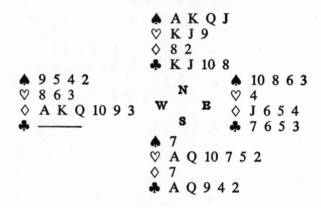

♠ A K Q J
♡ K J 9
◇ 8 2
♣ K J 10 8

♠ 9 5 4 2
♡ 8 6 3
◇ A K Q 10 9 3
♣ ———

♠ 10 8 6 3
♡ 4
◇ J 6 5 4
♣ 7 6 5 3

♠ 7
♡ A Q 10 7 5 2
◇ 7
♣ A Q 9 4 2

North-South vulnerable. West dealer.

West	North	East	South
3 ◇	Double	Pass	4 NT
5 ◇	Pass	Pass	6 ♡
Pass	Pass		

West opened the *three* of diamonds, on the assumption that the only way the slam could be defeated would be if he could get to trump a club. East won the trick with his jack.

Fully realizing that his partner had made the very risky underlead of the A K Q of diamonds *only for a purpose,* East soon found the reason: West had a void in some suit—either clubs or spades—and he wanted a ruff. Reverting to the bidding, East discovered the correct answer.

South had bid the small slam virtually all by himself, holding no high cards in either spades or diamonds and no more than (in theory) the A Q of hearts. So East deduced that South had to have quality in clubs, and probably also length. East therefore returned a club, West ruffing it for the setting trick.

Had Sheinwold made the normal opening lead of the king of diamonds, he would have obtained the normal result: paying the opponents for a small slam bid and made.

Deal 9:

The winners of the National Womens Pair Championship of 1961 were Mrs. A. H. Woods and May Belle Long, both of El Paso, Texas. Here is a deal that contributed to their victory.

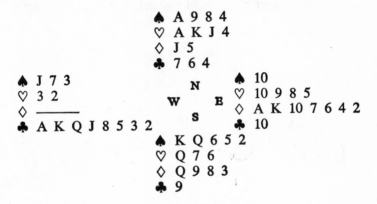

Neither side vulnerable. West dealer.

West	North	East	South
1 ♣	Double	3 ◊	4 ♠
Pass	Pass	Pass	

West led the two of clubs, and the trick was won by East's ten-spot. East then played the king and ace of diamonds, West discarding the three and two of hearts. East then led a heart, which West trumped for the setting trick.

Admittedly, West was lucky to have found East with

the ten of clubs. But, as Mrs. Woods viewed it, she needed luck ʰo defeat South's four-spade contract—and, in a certain sense, she created her own luck.

Deal 10:
This deal was a favorite of the late Dr. Louis Mark. It arose in a "social" (non-expert) bridge game, and the West defender was a neophyte who had learned to play bridge about six months earlier. As will be evidenced, the neophyte's learning was not complete—but, as luck would have it, the incomplete knowledge paid handsome dividends.

```
                    ♠ 10 9 6 4
                    ♡ Q 6 3
                    ◇ K 8 6 2
                    ♣ Q J
   ♠ A                             ♠ 3 2
   ♡ K J 10 9 7 5      N           ♡ 8
   ◇ Q 10 4         W     E        ◇ J 9 7 5
   ♣ A 9 8             S           ♣ 10 7 6 5 4 3
                    ♠ K Q J 8 7 5
                    ♡ A 4 2
                    ◇ A 3
                    ♣ K 2
```

Both sides vulnerable. North dealer.

North	East	South	West
Pass	Pass	1 ♠	2 ♡
2 ♠	Pass	4 ♠	Pass
Pass	Pass		

West opened the king of hearts and thereby produced a most amazing result!

Declarer took the king with the ace and led a trump,

West's ace winning. The jack of hearts was now continued, the board's queen was put up—and East trumped. West subsequently obtained a heart trick that with the ace of clubs, combined to hand declarer a one-trick set.

Had West opened any heart but the king—or had led any other card in her hand—declarer would have fulfilled his contract: whether he led the jack or a low heart, dummy's queen would win. Upon capturing the trump lead at trick two, West would now lead another heart, East ruffing. But declarer would still retain the ace of hearts, for a second heart winner, as contrasted to just the one heart trick that he obtained when the king of hearts was opened.

Deal 11:
This deal presents another "screwball type" opening lead that achieved the optimum result. It should be emphasized that this lead was completely illogical and it was made with no particular objective in mind. The kindest thing we can say about the leader is that in making the lead he just happened to pull the wrong card. But, as happens on occasion, our declarer assumed that a rational defender was making a rational lead, whereas in reality a temporarily irrational leader was making an irrational lead. The deal arose in the Regional Mens Pair Championship held in Pittsburgh in 1959.

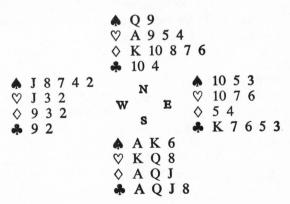

Both sides vulnerable. West dealer.

West	North	East	South
Pass	Pass	Pass	4 NT*
Pass	7 NT	Pass	Pass
Pass			

West opened the *jack of hearts,* which declarer captured with his king. Declarer counted 12 sure winners: three spades, three hearts, five diamonds, and one club. Since West's lead of the jack of hearts *had to be* from a combination headed by the J 10 (could it be anything else?), declarer next played the queen of hearts and then led the eight of hearts. When West followed to the third round of hearts with the three-spot, declarer "naturally" finessed dummy's nine, with the certainty that it would win. His expectation was rudely shattered a split second later, as East pounced on the nine with his ten-spot.

As is readily apparent, had a heart not been led, declarer would have cashed the king, queen, and ace of hearts, hoping that the six adversely held hearts were divided 3-3, in which case the board's fourth heart would become declarer's thirteenth trick. And when it would have been revealed that the adverse hearts were not divided 3-3, declarer would have no recourse but to take the club finesse, which would have yielded declarer his thirteenth trick.

This deal was played thirteen times, and the twelve other declarers all made thirteen tricks. Only our unfortunate declarer made but 12 tricks.

Deal 12:
On this final deal, the victory did not go to the defender, who declined to make the normal lead. But, had he made the normal lead, declarer would have claimed his grand-slam contract *at trick one!* With the "unnatural" lead, declarer had to sweat and strain and eventually, via keen analysis, was able to bring his contract home safely. The deal arose in the final round of the National Team-of-Four

*Showing 28–30 high-card points.

Championships of 1961. The West defender was Marshall Miles, and the South declarer was Harold Ogust.

```
                    ♠ 6 5 4
                    ♡ A K 6 5
                    ◇ K J 10 7 4 3
                    ♣ —
♠ 10 8                              ♠ J 9 7 2
♡ J                  N             ♡ 7 3
◇ Q 9 5          W       E         ◇ 8
♣ A J 10 7 5 4 3     S             ♣ K Q 9 8 6 2
                    ♠ A K Q 3
                    ♡ Q 10 9 8 4 2
                    ◇ A 6 2
                    ♣ —
```

Both sides vulnerable. North dealer.

North	East	South	West
1 ◇	Pass	1 ♡	Pass
2 ♡	Pass	2 ♠	Pass
4 ♡	Pass	5 NT*	Pass
7 ♡	Pass	Pass	Pass

Had West opened the ace of clubs, dummy would have trumped it, while South, on this trick, would have discarded his losing diamond. It would then have become a routine for declarer to draw trumps and ruff his losing spade in dummy.

But Marshall Miles opened the jack of trumps, feeling certain that his expert opponents would not have bid the grand slam unless one of them was void of clubs.

Harold Ogust won the opening lead and played another round of trumps, picking up East's last piece. He then played his three top spades and ruffed his fourth spade in dummy. He now paused for reflection.

He finally concluded that West possessed the queen of diamonds. The ace of diamonds was now led, followed

---

*This is a conventional expert bid that demands that the responder bid a grand slam if he possesses two of the three top trumps: A K, A Q, or K Q.

by another diamond, dummy's jack being finessed—successfully!

Why did Ogust, with nine diamonds in the combined hands, elect to finesse West for the queen, as opposed to playing the ace and king in the hope that the four adverse diamonds were divided 2-2? Ogust knew, by observation, that West had started with two spades and one heart. And, when the ace of diamonds was cashed, both opponents had followed suit. Thus West had, at most, three diamonds and, therefore, at least seven clubs. If West had only two diamonds, Ogust reasoned, he would have had to start with *eight* clubs. And with *eight* clubs, Ogust felt that West would have entered the bidding. Since West had failed to bid clubs, Ogust concluded that West had but seven of them, and, hence, he had to have *three* diamonds. And so it was. Of such stuff are experts made.

chapter 13 Opening Lead: The Deceptive Lead

♠ It was emphasized earlier that deceptive tactics employed by the defenders must not be used promiscuously; and that when they are resorted to, they must be handled with care. The reason behind this is, of course, that in most defensive situations the defenders must cooperate to the maximum extent in order to defeat declarer; and where a deceptive play, or lead, is apt to either misinform or confuse partner, the defense is on the road to collapsing. Thus the danger that lurks when one makes a deceptive opening lead is apparent: it may mislead partner rather than mislead declarer, the intended victim.

But, nevertheless, frequent situations arise when the leader can be reasonably sure that his deceptive lead will tend to lead declarer up the wrong path, while simultaneously having no adverse or detrimental effect on the subsequent actions of partner. In these situations, the deceptive lead can often develop into the only winning lead.

Let us look at some of these deceptive leads as they came into being in top-level bridge games. In analyzing the logic that brought them into being, the reader will then appreciate that these leads have their little niche in the world of opening leads.

Deal 1:
There is nothing deceptive about leading a small trump from, let us say, a K x x combination. If an opening trump lead seems to be called for, one of the low trumps can easily be spared for that purpose. But when one opens a low trump from a doubleton K x combination, he is making a most dangerous lead, for declarer now has it in his power on the second lead of trumps (by *declarer*) to fell the now unsupported king. However, the lead of a low

trump from a doubleton K x combination can have a tremendous deceptive value, for it is usually almost impossible for declarer to diagnose the true situation.

On occasion, the risky opening lead of the low trump away from a doubleton K x sometimes becomes necessary if the best result is to be obtained. As examples of this risky lead, witness this deal and the next one.

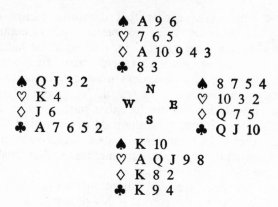

Neither side vulnerable. South dealer.

South	West	North	East
1 ♡	Pass	2 ♡	Pass
4 ♡	Pass	Pass	Pass

Sitting **West** was Albert H. Morehead, bridge editor of the *New York Times,* and one of the world's finest players. No lead seemed worthwhile to him—and he was right: had he led either a spade, a diamond, or a club, declarer would have fulfilled his contract. Morehead chose to open the *four of trumps!*

East, on this trick, put up the ten, which declarer captured with his jack. Convinced that East possessed the king of trumps, declarer entered dummy via the spade ace to take another heart finesse. When Morehead won the trick with his singleton king, he now had a safe exit, the queen of spades, declarer's king winning.

Subsequently South led a low diamond and put in

dummy's nine, hoping that when it lost, East would play back a spade. However, upon taking dummy's nine with his queen, East returned his top club, and declarer lost two club tricks—and his contract.

Had Morehead opened the queen of spades, declarer would have won it with his king and then would have finessed Morehead for the "marked" jack of spades. If, instead, Morehead had elected to open the jack of diamonds, it would have been captured by dummy's ace, after which East would have been finessed for the queen of diamonds. Or, instead, if he had opened any club, he would have given declarer a present of the king of clubs, declarer's game-going trick. But he chose to open a low heart, away from the doubleton K x, and declarer—even as you and I— went down to defeat.

Deal 2:
This deal arose in the Mens Pair Championships of 1956. The West defender Dr. Richard Greene, came up with virtually the identical lead that was made by Albert Morehead in the preceding deal.

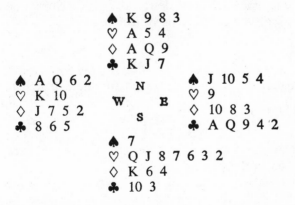

```
                ♠ K 9 8 3
                ♡ A 5 4
                ◇ A Q 9
                ♣ K J 7
  ♠ A Q 6 2        N        ♠ J 10 5 4
  ♡ K 10      W        E    ♡ 9
  ◇ J 7 5 2        S        ◇ 10 8 3
  ♣ 8 6 5                   ♣ A Q 9 4 2
                ♠ 7
                ♡ Q J 8 7 6 3 2
                ◇ K 6 4
                ♣ 10 3
```

North-South vulnerable. North dealer.

North	East	South	West
1 NT	Pass	4 ♡	Pass
Pass	Pass		

West opened the *ten* of trumps on this reasoning:

(1) On the bidding, North figured to have the ace of hearts, and South figured to have a long heart suit.

(2) Even if South had something like the A Q J x x x and dummy the x x x of hearts, West would still make his king, since declarer couldn't possibly diagnose the situation. (Upon winning the opening lead with the jack, declarer would enter dummy and lead a low heart, finessing East for the king.)

What would you, as declarer, have played to the first trick? Probably the same as our actual declarer did: he went up with the board's ace on the assumption (hope) that West was leading from the doubleton 10 9 and that, hence, East held the singleton king.

Had Dr. Greene not opened a heart, declarer, upon obtaining the lead, would undoubtedly have made the standard, percentage play of leading the queen of trumps and finessing. But, as you see, he was "talked out" of finessing and thus went down, losing two clubs, one spade —and, of course, the king of trumps.

Deal 3:
The deceptive value of the lead of the low card from a doubleton K x is not restricted to where this suit is the trump suit. It can also prove effective in a side suit, especially when the dummy-to-be has bid that suit, and the opening lead of the low card can give declarer an immediate problem that the latter would prefer to defer until later on in the play.

Here is an example of the opening lead of a low card from a K x doubleton into a suit that dummy had bid vigorously. The purpose was to scare off declarer from finessing, for on the bidding the dummy figured to come down with a suit headed by the A Q. It didn't turn out as planned, but the lead nevertheless brought about the best possible result for the defenders.

The deal, by the way, arose in the famous Lenz-Culbertson match of 1931. The West defender was Oswald Jacoby, who, even at that time, was already one of the world's top players. Mrs. Josephine Culbertson was the South declarer, and she was partnered by her husband, Ely Culbertson. Sitting East was Sidney Lenz.

```
                ♠ Q J 10 9 5 3
                ♡ —
                ◇ A 2
                ♣ A Q 9 4 3
  ♠ K 6                          ♠ A 8 2
  ♡ J 10 6 5 4 3      N          ♡ 9 8 2
  ◇ J 10          W       E      ◇ 8 6 4
  ♣ 8 5 2             S          ♣ J 10 7 6
                ♠ 7 4
                ♡ A K Q 7
                ◇ K Q 9 7 5 3
                ♣ K
```

North-South vulnerable. South dealer.

South	West	North	East
1 ◇	2 ♡*	3 ♠	Pass
3 NT	Pass	4 ♣	Pass
4 ◇	Pass	4 ♡	Pass
4 NT	Pass	5 ♣	Pass
5 NT	Pass	6 ◇	Pass
Pass	Pass		

Jacoby, on lead, was desperate. No lead seemed to offer any future. So, hoping to talk Mrs. Culbertson out of finessing, he led the six of spades. As is obvious, his partner had the ace and, upon winning the trick with it, returned a spade, Jacoby's king taking the setting trick.

Had any lead except a spade been made, Mrs. Culbertson would have taken all thirteen tricks.

*The weak jump overcall, which went into hibernation for a couple of decades has, during the last few years, emerged again.

Deal 4:
This deal was played in the National Mens Team Championships many years ago. The West defender was the renowned Howard Schenken.

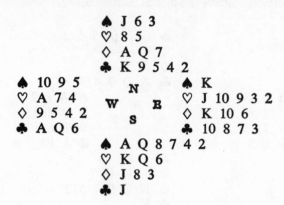

```
                    ♠ J 6 3
                    ♡ 8 5
                    ◇ A Q 7
                    ♣ K 9 5 4 2
    ♠ 10 9 5           N          ♠ K
    ♡ A 7 4     W            E     ♡ J 10 9 3 2
    ◇ 9 5 4 2          S          ◇ K 10 6
    ♣ A Q 6                       ♣ 10 8 7 3
                    ♠ A Q 8 7 4 2
                    ♡ K Q 6
                    ◇ J 8 3
                    ♣ J
```

East-West vulnerable. South dealer.

South	West	North	East
1 ♠	Pass	2 ♣	Pass
2 ♠	Pass	3 ♠	Pass
4 ♠	Pass	Pass	Pass

Schenken opened the *nine* of spades! Declarer undoubtedly assumed that *East* had either the doubleton K 10 or the K 10 5 and, intending to finesse East's presumed tenspot later on, put up dummy's jack. East covered the jack with the king (what else?), and declarer won the trick with his ace. Though declarer didn't know it, he had just loss his contract, for Schenken's ten of spades was now a winner.

If Schenken had chosen to open anything but a spade, declarer would have fulfilled his contract, for the normal finesse in trump would have been to lead a low spade from dummy, intending to finesse the queen. East, of

course, would have had no option but to play the king—
and declarer would have had no losers in the trump suit.

Deal 5:
The deceptive opening lead contained in this deal has
become a standard type of play by the defenders, and all
experts are familiar with it. Obviously, it brings advantageous results more often than not.

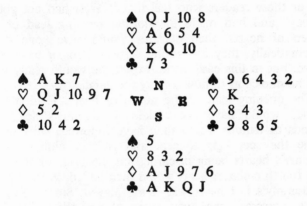

```
              ♠ Q J 10 8
              ♡ A 6 5 4
              ◇ K Q 10
              ♣ 7 3
♠ A K 7              N          ♠ 9 6 4 3 2
♡ Q J 10 9 7    W       B      ♡ K
◇ 5 2                S         ◇ 8 4 3
♣ 10 4 2                       ♣ 9 8 6 5
              ♠ 5
              ♡ 8 3 2
              ◇ A J 9 7 6
              ♣ A K Q J
```

East-West vulnerable. South dealer.

South	West	North	East
1 ◇	Pass	1 ♠	Pass
2 ♣	Pass	3 ◇	Pass
5 ◇	Pass	Pass	Pass

West elected to open the *ace* of spades instead of the
conventional king from an A K x combination, for he
felt it would be advantageous to declarer if the latter
knew that West possessed both the ace and king. At trick
two he shifted to the queen of hearts, dummy's ace winning, with East dropping the king.

If you were the declarer, would you not assume that
East possessed the king of spades? Our declarer did. After

cashing the king and queen of trumps, he then laid down dummy's queen of spades, discarding a heart when East followed with a low spade. West won the trick with his king of spades and cashed the jack of hearts for the setting trick.

Had the king of spades been opened, declarer would undoubtedly have established one of dummy's high spades by ruffing out two spades, thereby felling West's ace. On the established spade, he would then have discarded one of his losing hearts.

For those readers who feel that if West had not gotten "fancy" and had made the normal opening lead of the queen of hearts, then declarer would have gone down automatically, they are wrong. True, he *might* have gone down, but in this case, as an expert, he would really have had no choice as to how to play the hand.

The opening lead of the queen of hearts (had it been made) would have been taken by dummy's ace. Two rounds of trumps would then have followed. Now would come the ace, king, queen, and jack of clubs, two of dummy's hearts being discarded on the leads of the third and fourth clubs. A heart would then be led, West winning as dummy's last heart was being played. Since East, not West, possessed the outstanding trump, West would be unable to remove dummy's last trump. Whatever he chose to lead, declarer could not be prevented from trumping his remaining heart with dummy's last trump. Declarer's only losers would be the ace of spades and one heart trick.

Deal 6:

In making a deceptive opening lead, the leader, in virtually every situation, has his sights set on deceiving declarer as to the true state of affairs. But on occasion, a deceptive lead is made with the expressed purpose of deceiving one's partner! The aim here is, of course, not to sabotage, but rather to get partner to play a suit that, if the normal opening lead had been made, would not (or might not) be played. Here is such a situation.

```
              ♠ K J 7 5
              ♡ A Q 8 2
              ◇ 5 2
              ♣ K Q 8
♠ 6 2                        ♠ 8
♡ ———            N            ♡ J 10 7 6 4 3
◇ K Q 10 9 7 6 4   W   E      ◇ A J 3
♣ 10 5 3 2          S        ♣ 9 7 6
              ♠ A Q 10 9 4 3
              ♡ K 9 5
              ◇ 8
              ♣ A J 4
```

Both sides vulnerable. West dealer.

West	North	East	South
3 ◇	Double	4 ◇	4 NT
Pass	5 ◇	Pass	6 ♠
Pass	Pass	Pass	

West opened the *queen* of diamonds, East taking the trick
with his ace. Since the lead of the queen denied the king
(the king *is* led from a K Q combination), East perceived
the futility of playing back a diamond, since declarer was
marked with the diamond king. So West chose to return
a heart, which West trumped, for the setting trick.

From West's point of view, he was most desirous of having a heart led by East. And from the bidding, it was not
unreasonable to suppose that East might have the ace of
diamonds. But West appreciated that if he led the king of
diamonds, East would probably not overtake the king with
the ace (after all, how many players are there who are
that gifted?). By leading the diamond queen (thereby denying the king), West put East into the position of being
forced to win the trick with the ace, *if* East held that vital
card. And, in addition, having denied the possession of
the king by the lead of the queen, declarer knew that

East would recognize the hopelessness of returning a diamond. In these circumstances, a heart return by a thinking East became a distinct hope—and, as it turned out,
the hope became a most beautiful reality.

Deal 7:
The following deal arose in a high-stake game played at
New York City's Cavendish Club many years ago.

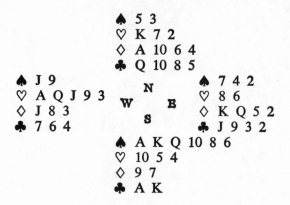

```
                    ♠ 5 3
                    ♡ K 7 2
                    ◊ A 10 6 4
                    ♣ Q 10 8 5
    ♠ J 9              N          ♠ 7 4 2
    ♡ A Q J 9 3                   ♡ 8 6
    ◊ J 8 3        W      E       ◊ K Q 5 2
    ♣ 7 6 4           S           ♣ J 9 3 2
                    ♠ A K Q 10 8 6
                    ♡ 10 5 4
                    ◊ 9 7
                    ♣ A K
```

Neither side vulnerable. South dealer.

South	West	North	East
1 ♠	Pass	1 NT	Pass
3 ♠	Pass	3 NT	Pass
4 ♠	Pass	Pass	Pass

West was not happy about being the leader, for he had
no attractive lead to make. The only thing he was fairly
certain of was that North, for his three no-trump rebid,
had the king of hearts, since otherwise, missing the ace,
king, queen, and jack, North would probably have found
a better rebid than three no-trump. Anticipating what
might develop—namely, the declarer, if left to his own
resources and if necessity so demanded, might later lead a
heart towards dummy's K x or K x x combination to make
a winner out of the king—West decided to open the
queen of hearts!

From declarer's point of view (after the dummy was put down), he correctly concluded that West was leading from some Q J combination and that if he played the board's king, it would be taken by East's (presumed) ace. A heart return would then entrap South's ten-spot, and the defenders would take three heart tricks.

But, if a low heart were played from dummy on the opening lead of the queen, then a heart continuation would create a trick for declarer: if West continued with the jack of hearts, it would be covered by dummy's king and taken by East's ace, thereby establishing South's ten-spot as a winner; if, at trick two, West chose to lead a low heart away from his jack, declarer would play low from dummy, forcing East to win with his ace and promoting dummy's king into the highest remaining heart.

On the opening lead of the queen of hearts, the deuce was played from dummy, and East (probably from force of habit), started a high-low signal by playing the eight. West then laid down the ace of hearts, and East completed the signal by following with the six. A third heart was now led, East trumping away dummy's king.

East then led the king of diamonds—and our poor declarer, after taking the ace, realized that he could never get to dummy again to discard his losing diamond on the board's queen of clubs.

Admittedly, West got off to an inspirational lead, which also embodied an element of deception (any underlead of an ace qualifies automatically as a deceptive lead). Had hearts not been led initially, declarer, after drawing trumps and cashing the A K of clubs, would undoubtedly have led a heart towards dummy's king, hoping that West held the ace. He would then have made eleven tricks instead of only nine.

Deal 8:
This deal arose in a duplicate game, and each of the 13 South declarers who played the hand arrived at a four-spade contract. Twelve of them fulfilled this contract, *each with an overtrick*. But our declarer not only did not make

11 tricks, he did not even make 10 tricks—and all because West got off to a deceptive, illogical lead.

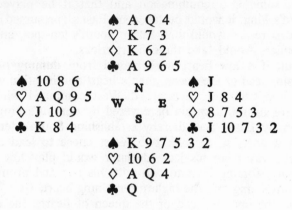

```
                    ♠ A Q 4
                    ♡ K 7 3
                    ◇ K 6 2
                    ♣ A 9 6 5
   ♠ 10 8 6              N            ♠ J
   ♡ A Q 9 5         W       E        ♡ J 8 4
   ◇ J 10 9             S            ◇ 8 7 5 3
   ♣ K 8 4                            ♣ J 10 7 3 2
                    ♠ K 9 7 5 3 2
                    ♡ 10 6 2
                    ◇ A Q 4
                    ♣ Q
```

Neither side vulnerable. North dealer.

North	East	South	West
1 NT	Pass	3 ♠	Pass
4 ♠	Pass	Pass	Pass

Had West made the normal opening of the jack of diamonds, declarer's only losers would have been two heart tricks. But West, being reasonably certain that North held the king of hearts, decided to put declarer to the test immediately: he opened the *queen of hearts!*

As on the preceding deal, declarer assumed that West was leading from some Q J combination and that, if the queen were covered by the king, East's ace would win, after which a heart return would entrap declarer's remaining 10 6 and would enable the defenders to make three heart tricks.

So he played low from dummy, West's queen winning. West, flushed with success, now followed through by leading the five of hearts. Declarer *knowing* that West possessed the jack of hearts, played low from dummy, expecting thereby to force East's (hypothetical) ace. But East won the trick with the jack, to return his remaining heart, West taking the trick with his ace.

West now came through with the crushing lead: he played the thirteenth heart! Dummy discarded a club, East ruffed with his singleton jack, and declarer overruffed with the king. No matter what declarer did from here in, he could not prevent West from making a trump trick out of the 10 8 6.

Here is a declarer for whom I have the greatest sympathy, for "there, but for the grace of God, go I."

Deal 9:

Here is a deal where "the punishment fitted the crime." North-South overbid so much that, had they fulfilled their contract, they would have "gotten away with murder."

```
                    ♠ A 9 5
                    ♡ 7 6
                    ◇ K 10 8 3
                    ♣ A 10 5 2
    ♠ 4 2                        ♠ 10 8 6 3
    ♡ A K 10 5 3 2      N        ♡ J 9
    ◇ Q 9 6          W     E     ◇ 7 5 2
    ♣ 9 3               S        ♣ Q 8 6 4
                    ♠ K Q J 7
                    ♡ Q 8 4
                    ◇ A J 4
                    ♣ K J 7
```

Both sides vulnerable. South dealer.

South	West	North	East
1 ♣	Pass (?)	1 ◇	Pass
2 NT (!)	Pass	4 NT (!)	Pass
Pass	Pass		

The lead of the fourth highest against no-trump contracts is the standard, accepted lead. Hence, whenever a player leads a deuce against a no-trump contract, he is known to have exactly a four-card suit, since he has, by definition, three higher cards, and there exists none that is lower.

So West opened the *deuce* of hearts, and as declarer took East's jack with the queen, he recognized that East and West had started with four hearts apiece. A count of declarer's winners revealed that he had nine of them: four spades, one heart, two diamonds, and two clubs. Not knowing which minor-suit finesse to take, declarer came up with a brilliant (I mean it!) line of play designed to eliminate the necessity of guessing which finesse to take: he cashed four spades (discarding a club from dummy on the fourth spade)—and he then led a heart!

Had the hearts been divided 4-4 originally (as declarer expected they were), the defenders would now have cashed *three* heart tricks, after which they would have had no option but to lead a club or a diamond, either of which would have given declarer a "free" finesse and would have provided him with his tenth trick in whatever minor suit was led.

But when declarer led a heart, West grabbed it with his ten and rattled off five heart tricks. Is there anybody in the world who could have known that West's lead of the deuce of hearts was his sixth highest?

Deal 10:
While it is not considered proper etiquette for an author to blow his own horn, I trust the reader will forgive me on this occasion. I am quite proud of this deal, for it arose under the stress and strain of top flight competitive play. I quote:

Thursday, April 22, 1948.
THE SAN FRANCISCO CHRONICLE
Contract Contacts:
Brilliant Opening Lead by Karpin
by Maureen Bailey

Charles Solomon, one of the top-ranking life masters of the country and widely read bridge author and columnist, told us about the following hand which stars a brilliant opening lead by Fred Karpin, another luminary of the contract world. It is based on a theory which we first heard expounded by the late Charles

Schwartz a wizard on defense. This was the bidding sequence:

North	East	South	West
1 ♡	Pass	3 ♣	Pass
3 ◊	Pass	4 NT	Pass
5 ♡	Pass	7 NT	Pass
Pass	Pass		

The five-heart call was the Blackwood response to show two aces. You are West on opening lead with the following:

    ♠ J 10 9 7
    ♡ 6 2
    ◊ K 9 8
    ♣ J 7 5 3

What do you lead?

Well, here was Mr. Karpin's reasoning before he made that choice, as Mr. Solomon related it to us:

South's three-club bid, followed by his subsequent jump to seven no-trump seems to indicate that he holds a very good club suit. The fact that South, after finding that North held two aces, plunged right into the seven–no-trump contract without inquiring about kings, seems to substantiate my suspicion that South's club suit is pretty solid. In fact, I'm just about sure that South expects to make that grand slam on the basis of bringing home his clubs. But—South doesn't know, as I do, that the club suit is not going to break. I could, of course, make the perfectly safe opening lead of the spade jack. However, if I do that, declarer may be forced to take a diamond finesse after finding out about the club situation, and that diamond finesse may be all he needs to make his contract. So— I'll lead a diamond on the reasonably sound assumption that declarer will surely not risk a finesse on the very first trick unless no better line of play is available. Here goes with the nine of diamonds.

And as you will see by looking the hand over, this

is the only opening which will defeat the contract.
Here is the complete deal:

```
                  ♠ 3
                  ♡ A J 10 9
                  ◇ A Q J 10 2
                  ♣ 8 6 4
 ♠ J 10 9 7            N            ♠ 8 6 5 4 2
 ♡ 6 2        W              E      ♡ 8 7 5 4 3
 ◇ K 9 8                    S       ◇ 7 4 3
 ♣ J 7 5 3                          ♣ ———
                  ♠ A K Q
                  ♡ K Q
                  ◇ 6 5
                  ♣ A K Q 10 9 2
```

No declarer in his right mind will take that diamond
finesse on the opening lead with what looks like six
sure club tricks, four sure heart tricks, three sure
spade tricks, and the ace of diamonds for frosting.
Whereas, if West makes any other opening, declarer
will try out his club suit, find it doesn't break, and be
forced to finesse the diamonds whether he likes to or
not.

chapter 14 The Play by the Leader's Partner:* An Ear to the Bidding

♠ As has been stated, the opening lead is frequently nothing more than a wishful-thinking shot in the dark, based on hearsay evidence: the bidding of the opponents. Thus, the first blow struck by the defenders is an action that does not generally fall into the realm of scientific selection.

But *after* the opening lead has been made, science comes to the fore and begins to take over. From the viewpoint of the leader's partner (third hand), he comes into possession of much meaningful knowledge when the dummy is put down. First, the proper interpretation of partner's opening lead conveys significant information as to the leader's holding in that suit (the top of a sequence lead, the fourth highest, etc.). Secondly, dummy's strong points and weak points become visible. Thirdly, declarer's bidding presents clues as to which are his strong suits and which are presumably his vulnerable spots. All of these data not only become evident but, with the application of reason, can be brought into sharp focus.

It is at this point—after the exposure of the dummy—that the defenders can really start coordinating their attack intelligently and get rolling. And it is at this point that *the leader's partner* rises to command and assumes the responsibility for directing his side's attack. He is the one who must give a positive or a negative signal with respect to the continuation or discontinuation of the leader's suit; he must at times make apparently unorthodox plays if the defenders are to triumph; he must determine whether it

---

*All bridge authorities, both past and present, have referred to *the partner* of the opening leader as "third hand," so we shall do likewise in the chapters that follow. Technically, "third hand" is the *defender*, who plays in third position to *any* given trick.

is worthwhile to deceive declarer and his partner simultaneously. In brief, he must continue in *active* fashion the attack on declarer that has been initiated by his partner, the opening leader. He must bring into play not only his ear and his eye, but also the most important sense of all: his judgment.

Let us now take a look at the play by third hand, as it developed in expert games.

Deal 1:
This deal arose in the Vanderbilt Championships of 1957. The East defender was the late Ralph Hirschberg.

```
                    ♠ 6 2
                    ♡ Q 10 9 6 3
                    ◇ A 5
                    ♣ A K 6 5
   ♠ 8 7 3                         ♠ Q J 5
   ♡ K             N               ♡ A J 8 5 2
   ◇ 10 6 2    W       E           ◇ 7 4
   ♣ Q J 9 8 4 2     S             ♣ 10 7 3
                    ♠ A K 10 9 4
                    ♡ 7 4
                    ◇ K Q J 9 8 3
                    ♣ ——————
```

Both sides vulnerable. North dealer.

North	East	South	West
1 ♡	Pass	1 ♠	Pass
1 NT	Pass	3 ◇	Pass
3 NT	Pass	4 ◇	Pass
4 ♠	Pass	4 NT	Pass
5 ♡	Double	6 ◇	Pass
Pass	Pass		

East, having doubled North's five-heart (Blackwood) bid, commanded a heart lead, so West dutifully opened the king of hearts. After a few moments' deliberation, Ralph overtook the king with the ace and returned a heart, which West trumped for the setting trick.

How did Ralph know his partner's king was a singleton? Frankly, he didn't. But from the bidding, South was known to possess a minimum of five spades and a minimum of five diamonds. Hence, he had at most three cards in the ᴏᴛʜᴇʀ minor suits. If South had two clubs and a singleton heart, Hirschberg concluded, then the slam could not be defeated. So he assumed that South had a doubleton heart, in which case West's king was a singleton.

Deal 2:
Third hand's play at trick one on this deal would have been labeled "highly imaginative" years ago. However, through its frequent recurrence, it is now accepted as a standard defensive play.

```
                    ♠ A Q 5
                    ♡ Q 10 6
                    ◇ A Q J 8 2
                    ♣ 10 7
    ♠ 10 7 6 3           N           ♠ J 8 2
    ♡ 9 5 4                          ♡ J 8 3 2
    ◇ 7            W         E        ◇ K 5 4
    ♣ J 9 8 3 2         S            ♣ A Q 4
                    ♠ K 9 4
                    ♡ A K 7
                    ◇ 10 9 6 3
                    ♣ K 6 5
```

Both sides vulnerable. North dealer.

North	East	South	West
1 ◇	Pass	2 NT	Pass
3 NT	Pass	Pass	Pass

On West's opening lead of the three of clubs, East, without any deliberation, played the queen, South taking the trick with his king. South now tried the diamond finesse, unsuccessfully, East's king winning. The ace of clubs was then laid down, and this was followed by the four of clubs, enabling West to cash his club suit.

From East's point of view, the "finesse against partner" at trick one could never be a losing play: if West happened to have the king of clubs, then East's queen would win, after which East would lead the ace of clubs and then the four of clubs for West to obtain the lead to cash his club suit. There was no danger, incidentally, that South might possess a singleton king of clubs. West's opening lead of the three-spot denoted a five-card club suit, at most.

In conclusion, declarer had no choice but to take the queen with the king at trick one. And East's correct play was to put up the queen, not the ace, at trick one, to compel declarer to take his king. The only other card that West could have below the three-spot was the deuce, in which case he would have a five-card suit. So South had to have a minimum of three clubs (and, possibly, four clubs).

The main point of East's play of the queen of clubs rather than the ace was *to force* South to play the king, if the latter held that card. Then when East later obtained the lead—as he surely figured to do via the king of diamonds—he would have full communication with his partner; and East, by then leading the ace of clubs, after which he would follow up by leading the four-spot, would enable West to cash the now established club suit.

Had East won the opening lead with the ace of clubs and then played the queen of clubs to trick two, declarer would have declined to take his king, employing the holdup play. East would then have returned his remaining club, South's king winning. But when East subsequently obtained the lead via the king of diamonds, he would have no club to return—and whatever else he returned, declarer would romp in with his contract.

From declarer's point of view, he could have made his contract by declining to capture the queen of clubs at trick one. But this would have been a horrible play for declarer to make. Just image the screams by North if South had declined to take the queen with the king and this had been the situation:

♣ 10 7

N

♣ A J 9 3 2   W   E   ♣ Q 8 4

S

♣ K 6 5

East, upon being permitted to win the first trick with the queen, would now play back a club, and the defenders would take the first five club tricks.

Deal 3:
This is another good hand on which to test some of your non-expert friends. Have them sit in the East seat.

♠ K 8 6 5
♡ 7 5 4
◇ K Q 9 2
♣ J 7

♠ ———
♡ K Q 10 3
◇ 8 7 6 4
♣ Q 9 5 4 2

N

W   E

S

♠ A 3
♡ A J 9 8 6
◇ 5 3
♣ K 10 8 6

♠ Q J 10 9 7 4 2
♡ 2
◇ A J 10
♣ A 3

North-South vulnerable. East dealer.

East	South	West	North
1 ♡	1 ♠	4 ♡	4 ♠
Pass	Pass	5 ♡	Pass
Pass	5 ♠	Pass	Pass
Double	Pass	Pass	Pass

West opened the king of hearts, which East overtook with the ace. To trick two, East led a low club—and South now couldn't avoid the loss of a club trick. Of course, he also lost a trick to East's ace of trumps.

Had West been permitted to win the opening lead, in all probability he would have continued the heart suit. Declarer would then have ruffed the second heart lead and would have knocked out East's ace of spades. East's shift to a club would now come too late, for declarer would win this lead, pick up East's remaining trump, and then cash his diamonds, discarding his losing club on dummy's fourth diamond.

From the East seat, South had, at most one heart, since West's leap to four hearts indicated that West had a minimum of four hearts. Hence, it became imperative for East to overtake his partner's king of hearts in order to shift to clubs. After all, how many West players are there who could be that clairvoyant to know that they had to shift to clubs at trick two?

Deal 4:
This deal arose in the 1958 San Francisco Championships.

```
                    ♠ 9 5
                    ♡ Q 10 6 4 2
                    ◇ J 6
                    ♣ J 10 8 6
    ♠ 7 4 2                         ♠ J 8
    ♡ A J 9 5         N             ♡ K 8 7 3
    ◇ K 8 7 5 3    W     E          ◇ 2
    ♣ 4               S             ♣ K Q 9 7 3 2
                    ♠ A K Q 10 6 3
                    ♡ ———
                    ◇ A Q 10 9 4
                    ♣ A 5
```

South	West	North	East
2 ♠	Pass	2 NT	Pass
3 ◇	Pass	3 NT	Pass
4 ♠	Pass	Pass	Pass

West led the four of clubs, the jack was put up from dummy—and East played *the deuce!!*

Dummy's jack of diamonds was now led, and the finesse taken when East followed with the deuce, West's king winning. Hoping declarer had started with a five-card diamond suit, West now returned a diamond, which East trumped. East then played back a club, South followed with the ace, and West trumped. West next played another diamond, dummy ruffed with the nine, and East overruffed with the jack, for the setting trick.

What was East's logic in not covering the jack of clubs with the queen at trick one? After all, in not covering, he knew that he was giving away a club trick—West's lead of the club four was an obvious singleton, since West would not have led the four from a 5-4 combination; and West assuredly would not be underleading the club ace on the strong spade-diamond bidding by South. Hence, South was known to have started with, specifically, the A 5 of clubs.

Very simply, East felt that if he covered the jack with the queen, declarer would win the trick with the ace, after which he would draw trumps. On South's vigorous bidding in spades (he had bid the game in spades all by himself), South figured, to have no spade losers. And, with the appearance of the diamond jack in dummy, that card certainly figured to consolidate declarer's diamond suit. The only sure trick that East could see for the defense was a club trick—and to defeat the contract four tricks were needed, a virtual impossibility as East viewed it.

Hence, the only hope was deception: to give the declarer the opportunity to get to dummy, which opportunity he would not have if the jack of clubs were covered by the queen. And from this, the wishful thinking that declarer would have a diamond finesse to take, and would take if he were given the chance to do so. East knew that the diamond finesse would lose if declarer took a finesse. The defenders would now have a cross-ruff going, in diamonds and clubs. And, as it came to pass, it developed precisely in the fashion that an imaginative East had foreseen that it might.

Regarding declarer's play, all I can say is that he was greedy. Having obtained a "present" of a trick on the opening club lead, he should have drawn trumps and then conceded a diamond trick. But he just couldn't overcome the lure of a finesse; and, as a consequence, he made nine tricks instead of twelve.

Deal 5:
Here is another illustration of a defender who, having had an ear to the bidding, had no hesitancy in making the correct play of overtaking his partner's king with his own ace in order to shift to another suit. The deal came up in a top flight game a few years ago.

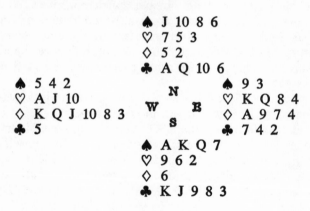

<pre>
                    ♠ J 10 8 6
                    ♡ 7 5 3
                    ◇ 5 2
                    ♣ A Q 10 6
    ♠ 5 4 2   ♠ 9 3
    ♡ A J 10   N   ♡ K Q 8 4
    ◇ K Q J 10 8 3 W   E   ◇ A 9 7 4
    ♣ 5   S   ♣ 7 4 2
                    ♠ A K Q 7
                    ♡ 9 6 2
                    ◇ 6
                    ♣ K J 9 8 3
</pre>

North-South vulnerable. South dealer.

South	West	North	East
1 ♣	1 ◇	2 ♣	2 ◇
2 ♠	3 ◇	3 ♠	Pass
Pass	4 ◇	Pass	Pass
4 ♠	Pass	Pass	Double
Pass	Pass	Pass	

West opened the king of diamonds, the dummy came into view, and East paused for reflection. Mentally reviewing the bidding, East concluded that West surely had a six-card diamond suit to justify his repeated overcalls in diamonds. And he also figured to have something on the outside.

So East overtook his partner's king of diamonds and shifted to the king of hearts, winning the trick as West followed with the ten-spot. Had he now played a low heart, there is no telling what might have happened: West, upon winning, might then have attempted to cash the queen of diamonds, with dire consequences. But East, at trick three, played the queen of hearts, felling West's jack. He then led a third heart to West's ace, for the setting trick.

Deal 6:
In this deal, our expert East defender was partnered by a non-expert West defender. As happens on occasion in such circumstances, East erroneously gave his partner credit for being a man of complete clairvoyancy. As a result the opponents fulfilled an "unmakable" small slam.

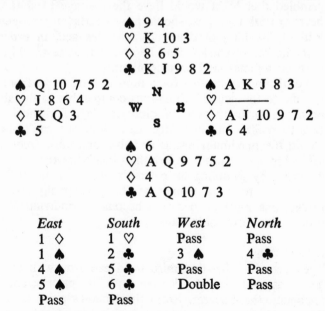

```
                    ♠ 9 4
                    ♡ K 10 3
                    ◇ 8 6 5
                    ♣ K J 9 8 2
  ♠ Q 10 7 5 2         N         ♠ A K J 8 3
  ♡ J 8 6 4       W         E    ♡ ─────
  ◇ K Q 3             S           ◇ A J 10 9 7 2
  ♣ 5                             ♣ 6 4
                    ♠ 6
                    ♡ A Q 9 7 5 2
                    ◇ 4
                    ♣ A Q 10 7 3
```

East	*South*	*West*	*North*
1 ◇	1 ♡	Pass	Pass
1 ♠	2 ♣	3 ♠	4 ♣
4 ♠	5 ♣	Pass	Pass
5 ♠	6 ♣	Double	Pass
Pass	Pass		

West opened the king of diamonds and, despite East's

discouraging deuce on this trick, continued with the queen of diamonds, declarer ruffing.

It now became a routine proposition for declarer. He drew the adverse trumps in two rounds, after which he laid down the ace of hearts, East failing to follow suit. West was then finessed for the "marked" jack of hearts, and declarer brought home the heart suit, discarding dummy's two spades. He subsequently ruffed his losing spade, and that was that. His only loser was to West's diamond king at trick one.

When East played the deuce of diamonds at trick one, West should not have continued the diamond suit. This is rather obvious, both in retrospect and at the table in actual play. Nevertheless, I think East is more guilty than West.

Being void of hearts, East naturally wanted a shift to that suit—but how could West have possibly have guessed it? There was simply too much at stake for East to have gambled that West would have the courage to shift to a heart at trick two. East should have overtaken the opening lead of the king of diamonds with his ace, in order to cash the ace of spades. Had he done so, there would have been no regrets—and no recriminations.

Permit me to disgress for a moment and to go from the specific to the general. Situations comparable to the above occur in virtually every session of play. Somehow, one fails to realize that in bridge, as in life, one can't always obtain the maximum result; and that one must frequently settle for a sure profit rather than incur the risk of going bankrupt by gambling on partner's judgment or intuition.

And so, to be a winner at the partnership game of bridge, one must on occasion become an individualist, to protect the partnership interests.

Deal 7:
The deceptive play that third hand came up with on this deal was calculated to deceive both his partner and his opponent, the declarer. From third hand's point of view, the gamble was worth taking—and it turned out to be a very profitable gamble.

```
                    ♠ 8 3
                    ♡ A Q 6 4
                    ◇ K 10 3
                    ♣ K Q 9 5
    ♠ J 9 7 4              N        ♠ A K 6 2
    ♡ J 8 2          W         E    ♡ 10 9 5 3
    ◇ A 7 6 5                       ◇ 8 4
    ♣ 8 2                S          ♣ 7 6 3
                    ♠ Q 10 5
                    ♡ K 7
                    ◇ Q J 9 2
                    ♣ A J 10 4
```

Neither side vulnerable. North dealer.

North	East	South	West
1 ♣	Pass	2 NT	Pass
3 NT	Pass	Pass	Pass

West opened the four of spades, which East captured with the *ace*. East returned the deuce of spades, South misguessed and played the ten, West's jack winning. For want of a better return, West exited with a spade, which East won with the "concealed" king, after which he played back a spade to West's nine. West then cashed the ace of diamonds, for the setting trick.

Had East made the normal play at trick one of winning with the king of spades, and then cashing the ace of spades, declarer would have fulfilled his contract, losing just *three* spades and the ace of diamonds. But when East chose to capture the opening lead with the ace, to return a low spade, declarer assumed that West held the king of spades —and hoped that East possessed the jack. If the top spades had been so divided, declarer's ten would have forced the king, thereby promoting South's queen into a winner.

From East's point of view, he was quite certain—based on South's jump to two no-trump—that South held the queen of spades. But, even more important, he was also certain that South did not have the Q x doubleton: East

knew that West had led from a four-card suit, for the
three of spades was in dummy, and East himself held the
deuce. Hence West's lead of the four-spot denoted precisely a four-card suit—and South was therefore marked
with the Q x x. So when East returned a low spade at
trick two, there was no danger that South had just a
singleton queen remaining.

Deal 8:
I imagine that at least half of our nation's bridge players,
had they been sitting in the East seat, would have played
the incorrect card at trick one on this deal. Our actual
East declarer, having an ear to the bidding, came up with
the correct play.

```
                      ♠ Q 10
                      ♡ A 3 2
                      ◇ K 10 4
                      ♣ Q 10 9 5 3
        ♠ 7 4                         ♠ 8 5 3
        ♡ K 9 7 6         N           ♡ Q J 4
        ◇ Q 9 6 3     W       E       ◇ J 8 5 2
        ♣ A J 4           S           ♣ K 8 7
                      ♠ A K J 9 6 2
                      ♡ 10 8 5
                      ◇ A 7
                      ♣ 6 2
```

Neither side vulnerable. South dealer.

South	West	North	East
1 ♠	Pass	2 ♣	Pass
2 ♠	Pass	3 ♠	Pass
4 ♠	Pass	Pass	Pass

West opened the three of diamonds, the four was played
from dummy, and East properly put up the eight-spot,
South's ace winning. After drawing trumps, South led a
low club, putting in dummy's nine, East's king taking the

trick. East then shifted to the queen of hearts, and South now had to lose two hearts and two clubs.

Had East played the jack of diamonds at trick one, declarer would have fulfilled his contract. He would have won the trick with the ace, drawn trumps, and then would have led his remaining seven of diamonds, successfully finessing the board's ten-spot. On the king of diamonds, he would then have discarded one of his four losers.

From East's point of view, the play of the eight of diamonds (rather than the jack) had to be proper. Surely, on the given bidding, West was not underleading the diamond ace. Hence, South was marked as the possessor of the ace of diamonds and would capture the jack with the ace. He would then be able to finesse West for the queen, resulting in his making three diamond tricks. If South happened to also have the nine-spot in addition to the ace, no matter what East put up on the opening lead, South would have it in his power to make three diamond tricks.

Incidentally, as was stated, certainly no "modern" player would have underled his ace of diamonds (on the given bidding) at trick one. But suppose, for the sake of discussion, that he had done so. That is, suppose that West held the A 9 6 3 of diamonds, and that South held the Q 7. What would East gain by putting up the jack of diamonds, which would be captured by declarer's (presumed) queen? As is apparent, nothing could be gained.

Of course, if West were underleading some combination of the A Q, then the play of the jack would be the winning play. But (we hope) such West players do not exist.

As East saw it, his play of the eight-spot at trick one couldn't ever cost his side anything, but it could bring in a profit—as it did.

Deal 9:
At tricks one and two on this deal, the East defender indulged in a bit of deceptive razzle-dazzle; and, as a result, obtained a triumph that, in theory, did not belong to him. The deal was played in the National Mens Pair Championship of 1955.

```
                  ♠ 9 3
                  ♡ A Q
                  ◇ A Q 10 7 6 4
                  ♣ 10 9 8
♠ 10 4 2                        ♠ A K 8 6 5
♡ J 10 8 5 3 2      N           ♡ 7 4
◇ J 3            W     E         ◇ 9 5
♣ A 5              S            ♣ K J 7 4
                  ♠ Q J 7
                  ♡ K 9 6
                  ◇ K 8 2
                  ♣ Q 6 3 2
```

Neither side vulnerable. North dealer.

North	East	South	West
1 ◇	1 ♠	1 NT	2 ♡
3 ◇	Pass	3 NT	Pass
Pass	Pass		

West led the deuce of spades and East won the trick with his ace! It seemed to East that West, for his two heart bid, might have a top club, so at trick two East led king of clubs, which won the trick. He next played with the four of clubs—and declarer went into a huddle with himself.

From declarer's point of view, it appeared that West had the king of spades (deduced from East's play of the spade ace at trick one). And East's lead of the king of clubs seemed to indicate that East had the club ace and was underleading it at trick two. So South put up the queen of clubs, which West's ace captured.

After much deliberation (he, too, didn't know what was going on), West returned a spade, East taking it with his king. East now cashed the jack of clubs, after which he took the high seven of clubs (dummy's eight, nine, and ten having been played to the three previous club leads). Declarer thus lost four clubs and two spades, for a two-trick set.

Had West—who, as was stated, was also deceived by East's plays—not returned a spade at trick four, declarer would have made his contract. But, then, such are the risks inherent in deceptive plays: partner might go astray as well as declarer, the intended victim. On this deal, as luck, or fate, would have it, deception paid dividends.

Deal 10:

This final deal illustrates the heights to which the imagination of the expert can soar. The East defender was Morrie Elis, one of our all-time great players. The hand was played in the Vanderbilt Championships of 1947.

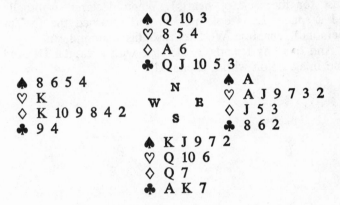

```
                    ♠ Q 10 3
                    ♡ 8 5 4
                    ◇ A 6
                    ♣ Q J 10 5 3
   ♠ 8 6 5 4          N          ♠ A
   ♡ K                           ♡ A J 9 7 3 2
   ◇ K 10 9 8 4 2   W   E        ◇ J 5 3
   ♣ 9 4               S         ♣ 8 6 2
                    ♠ K J 9 7 2
                    ♡ Q 10 6
                    ◇ Q 7
                    ♣ A K 7
```

North-South vulnerable. East dealer.

East	South	West	North
1 ♡	1 ♠	Pass	2 ♠
Pass	2 NT	Pass	3 ♣
Pass	3 ♠	Pass	3 NT
Pass	Pass	Pass	

West dutifully opened the king of hearts, and Morrie, sitting East, stopped to take inventory. On the bidding, he was reasonably sure that South held the protected queen of hearts (the Q 10 6 specifically). Hence, if West's king were permitted to win, West would have no heart to return. Thus Morrie concluded that he could not establish the heart suit.

If the defenders had any future, it had to be in the diamond suit. So Morrie overtook his partner's king of hearts with his ace and led the three of diamonds, upon which South played the queen, and West covered with the king. Declarer permitted the king to win, but West continued with a diamond, forcing the board's ace. On this trick, Morrie "unblocked" by throwing the jack of diamonds.

All declarer could now make were eight tricks: five clubs, one diamond, and two hearts (the latter by finessing East for the jack of hearts). When declarer eventually led a spade, East took his ace and returned the five of diamonds, enabling West to cash his diamond suit.

And this, my friends, is Defense with a capital D! And also Imagination with a capital I!!

chapter 15 The Play by the Leader's Partner: The Application of Imagination

♠ One of the dominant characteristics of the expert player is his ability to look ahead at the outset of play (when the dummy is put down) and to envision what the future holds in store for him. And if it appears that nature is operating to his detriment, he makes every possible effort to alter the course of nature. In brief, at the bridge table the expert does not subscribe to the passive tenet, "They also serve who only stand and wait." Instead, the expert adopts as an active guiding principle the philosophy: to envision, to plan, and to create.

A good illustration of visualizing the future—and molding it to his advantage—was evidenced in the last deal of the preceding chapter, in which Morrie Elis, at trick one, overtook his partner's opening lead of the king of hearts and shifted to the diamond suit. Admittedly, these first two plays are imaginative and brilliant to the nth degree; and certainly most bridge players have not as yet reached this stage of development where they can, on the spur of the moment, bring into action the faculty of producing ideal creations consistent with reality.

However, many situations arise during the course of an evening's play where virtually every bridge player, by employing "normal" imagination, can transform impending defeat into victory. Unfortunately, either inertia or laziness (or lack of training) usually deprives him of the victory that could be his, for he tends to play mechanically, without vision and without the application of imagination.

In this chapter there are presented some real-life deals in which the imagination of the third-hand defender either came into play, or it failed to come into play when it should have. Where the imagination actively projected itself into the picture, the end result proved to be most satis-factory. And when it failed to do so, the offender suffered a defeat that could have been avoided.

A few of the deals are tough ones, for they depict the "superimagination" that only our very best players are capable of invoking. Nevertheless, the reader can learn much from these deals, for, in retrospect, they are easily understandable, and they serve to demonstrate the func-tioning of the expert mind, which we mortals are contin-ually striving to emulate.

Deal 1:

In horse racing, they pay off on speed. In bridge, speed does not enter into consideration. Our East defender on this deal played too quickly to the first trick, after which there was no recovery.

South	West	North	East
1 ♡	Pass	1 ♠	Pass
2 ◇	Pass	2 ♠	Pass
3 NT	Pass	Pass	Pass

West opened the deuce of clubs, the queen was played from dummy, and East unhesitatingly covered with the king, declarer's ace winning. It now became a routine prop-osition for declarer to establish dummy's spade suit and to use the jack of clubs as an entry to cash that suit.

East's unhesitating play of the king of clubs at trick one must be classed as an error of the first magnitude and as a mechanical play made without thought and without imagination. East should have realized that declarer was going to develop the spade suit and that the only entry to dummy to cash that suit had to be in clubs. Of course, it was rather apparent that declarer did not have the spade ace, there being only one spade ace in the deck.

All East had to do was to play the six of clubs on dummy's queen at trick one—and declarer could never again get to dummy to cash the to-be-established spade suit, for East would retain the K 10 of clubs over dummy's remaining J 3. But East, from force of habit in all probability, "covered an honor with an honor."

Deal 2:
The come-on high-low signal given by a defender is probably the most powerful practical weapon possessed by the defensive side. But situations arise in which the mechanical employment of this signal can result in a most unhappy ending for the user. Here is a case in point. The deal arose in the Vanderbilt Championships of 1962.

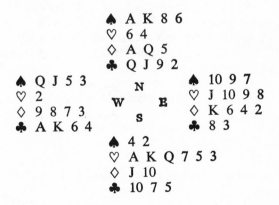

North-South vulnerable. North dealer.

North	East	South	West
1 ♣	Pass	1 ♡	Pass
1 ♠	Pass	3 ♡	Pass
3 NT	Pass	4 ♡	Pass
Pass	Pass		

On the opening lead of the king of clubs, East played the eight-spot. West then continued with the club ace, upon which East dropped the three. Properly interpreting East's high-low play as a come-on signal, West led a third round of clubs, East ruffing dummy's jack.

From here in declarer had smooth sailing. He drew the adverse trumps in three rounds, and on the board's established queen of clubs he discarded his losing diamond.

On the opening lead of the king of clubs, East should have played the discouraging three of clubs. What did East have to gain by ruffing a third round of clubs? Not a thing. East had a natural trump trick in the J 10 9 8, which could never be taken away from him. Certainly East wanted West, at trick two, to lead a diamond, not the club ace.

Had East played the three of clubs on the opening lead, West, looking at the dummy, would undoubtedly have shifted to a diamond; and there would now have been no way for declarer to prevent the defenders from winning two club tricks, one diamond trick, and one trump trick.

East's play of the club eight at trick one must surely be classified as a most unimaginative play—and, from the viewpoint of justice, East's defeat was no more and no less than what he deserved.

Deal 3:
There was nothing especially brilliant in East's play to the first trick on this deal. But it did necessitate looking ahead in order to create a happy future for the defenders. The East defender was Olive Peterson, one of the world's greatest women players.

```
                    ♠ 9 8 6 3
                    ♡ Q J 9
                    ◇ A J 10 2
                    ♣ 9 3
   ♠ 2                          ♠ A 7 4
   ♡ 10 7 3           N         ♡ 8 6 5 4 2
   ◇ K 9 8 7 5    W     E       ◇ 4
   ♣ K Q J 4         S          ♣ A 8 6 5
                    ♠ K Q J 10 5
                    ♡ A K
                    ◇ Q 6 3
                    ♣ 10 7 2
```

Both sides vulnerable. South dealer.

South	West	North	East
1 ♠	Pass	2 ♠	Pass
3 ♠	Pass	4 ♠	Pass
Pass	Pass		

West's opening lead of the king of clubs was overtaken by Olive's ace, after which she led her singleton diamond, dummy's ace capturing East's king. A trump was then led off the board, and Olive climbed right up with her ace. She now returned a club, West's jack winning. West then came back a diamond, which Olive trumped, for the setting trick.

How simple (and how unimaginative) it would have been for East to have given a come-on signal with the eight of clubs on the opening lead of the club king. West dutifully would then have played another club—and the defense would have been ruined, for East would now never get to trump a diamond.

If there is a moral to this deal, it is that the defenders can't sit back and wait for tricks to come their way. They have to create them—and usually in a hurry.

Deal 4:
In this deal, as in the preceding one, it became mandatory for the self-preservation of the defenders that East over-

take his partner's king at trick one. And East rose to the occasion.

```
                    ♠ 6 5 2
                    ♡ A Q
                    ◇ K J 10 9 6
                    ♣ 5 3 2
  ♠ K 10 4                         ♠ 9
  ♡ J 7 6 5 3 2       N            ♡ 10 8
  ◇ 7 4 2          W     E         ◇ 8 5 3
  ♣ K                  S           ♣ A Q 10 9 8 6 4
                    ♠ A Q J 8 7 3
                    ♡ K 9 4
                    ◇ A Q
                    ♣ J 7
```

North-South vulnerable. East dealer.

East	South	West	North
3 ♣	3 ♠	Pass	4 ♠
Pass	Pass	Pass	

West opened the king of clubs, which East overtook with the ace. East then played the queen of clubs, felling South's jack, after which the ten of clubs was led. Whichever card South now trumped with, he could not prevent West from making two trump tricks.

Actually, declarer ruffed with the queen of spades, but West did not make the mistake of overruffing. West simply discarded the deuce of hearts, thus retaining his K 10 4 over declarer's remaining A J 8 7 3. He thereby guaranteed himself two trump tricks.

From East's point of view, the overtaking of the king of clubs at trick one could never be a losing play. If West's king were a singleton, then it became a necessity to overtake. If the king were the top of a doubleton (K J or K 7), then the defense could never make more than one club trick, for in this case declarer would possess just a singleton club. The overtaking could never be costly—but the failure to overtake could be costly, as it would have been.

As is apparent, had East failed to overtake his partner's king of clubs at trick one, West would have been unable to continue clubs. Declarer would then have made 11 tricks, the defenders only additional winner being West's king of spades. (After drawing trumps, declarer would have discarded his club jack on one of dummy's diamonds.)

Deal 5:
This deal illustrates how the proper interpretation of opener's lead, plus the imagination of the leader's partner, combined to defeat declarer.

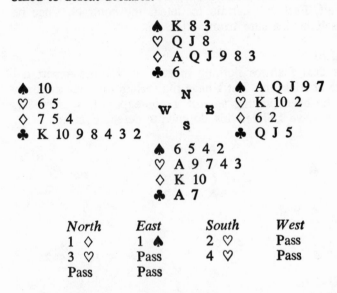

```
                    ♠ K 8 3
                    ♡ Q J 8
                    ◇ A Q J 9 8 3
                    ♣ 6
  ♠ 10                  N          ♠ A Q J 9 7
  ♡ 6 5                            ♡ K 10 2
  ◇ 7 5 4           W     E        ◇ 6 2
  ♣ K 10 9 8 4 3 2      S          ♣ Q J 5
                    ♠ 6 5 4 2
                    ♡ A 9 7 4 3
                    ◇ K 10
                    ♣ A 7
```

North	East	South	West
1 ◇	1 ♠	2 ♡	Pass
3 ♡	Pass	4 ♡	Pass
Pass	Pass		

West opened the ten of spades, the three was played from dummy, and East overtook the ten with the jack. The ace of spades was now cashed, after which a third spade was led, West ruffing. Eventually East obtained a trump trick—which he could not be done out of—to defeat declarer.

Had East played mechanically and permitted West's ten-spot to win the opening lead, declarer would have fulfilled his contract. Whatever West would then have led to trick two, declarer would have captured. Declarer would

next have drawn trumps—losing a trick to East's king or
ten—and all East could make after that would have been
the spade ace.

East's overtaking of the ten of spades with the jack at
trick one had to be the only proper play. West was *known*
to have started with either a singleton or a doubleton
spade (had West held the 10 x x in his partner's suit, he
would have made the conventional lead of the third highest). Hence, declarer had to have either three or four
spades. By overtaking the ten with the jack, then cashing
the ace, and next leading a third round of spades for West
to ruff, East was certain to defeat the contract, since he
himself held a sure trump trick.

Deal 6:
This deal features nothing more than routine expert defense at trick one. Yet I have the feeling that our declarer,
had he been playing against a non-expert East defender,
would have fulfilled his doomed-to-defeat contract.

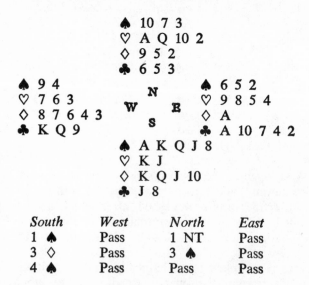

| ♠ 10 7 3 |
| ♡ A Q 10 2 |
| ◇ 9 5 2 |
| ♣ 6 5 3 |

South	West	North	East
1 ♠	Pass	1 NT	Pass
3 ◇	Pass	3 ♠	Pass
4 ♠	Pass	Pass	Pass

West made the normal lead of the king of clubs, which

East overtook with the ace. The ace of diamonds was then cashed, after which East led the deuce of clubs to West's known queen. West now returned a diamond, which East trumped. The defenders thus took the first four tricks, and declarer was down owing to circumstances beyond his control.

From East's position, he knew that the opening lead of the club king was being made from a K Q combination. Hence, he could afford to overtake the king with the ace, lay down his singleton ace of diamonds, and then return a club to his partner's marked queen, trusting that his partner would employ some imagination and recognize that the diamond ace was a singleton. As is obvious, West did not let East down.

Deal 7:

Third hand displayed fine imagination at trick one on this deal, and his partner subsequently cooperated nicely, but, unfortunately for them, they were playing against a declarer who knew enough not to panic and was able to counterattack successfully.

	♠ 9 6 3 2	
	♡ A 7 5 4	
	◇ K 6 2	
	♣ J 6	
♠ 8	**N**	♠ J 5 4
♡ Q 9 2	**W** **E**	♡ J 10 6 3
◇ Q 10 4	**S**	◇ J 9 7 5
♣ K Q 10 9 5 3		♣ A 2
	♠ A K Q 10 7	
	♡ K 8	
	◇ A 8 3	
	♣ 8 7 4	

South	West	North	Pass
1 ♠	Pass	2 ♠	*East*
3 ♠	Pass	4 ♠	Pass
Pass	Pass		

West's opening lead of the club king was promptly overtaken by East's ace, after which East returned his remaining club, West's queen winning. West then laid down the high ten of clubs.

It was obvious to declarer that East was prepared to trump this lead. Had he attempted to prevent this by ruffing with dummy's nine-spot (as most declarers would have attempted), East would have overruffed with the jack; and eventually the defenders would have obtained a diamond trick, to inflict a one-trick set on declarer.

But, on the lead of the third club from West, declarer calmly discarded dummy's deuce of diamonds, West's ten of clubs winning the trick. West now switched to a heart, declarer taking it with his king. It now became a routine proposition for declarer to pull the adverse trumps in three rounds, cash the king and ace of diamonds, and then ruff his eight of diamonds with dummy's remaining trump.

From declarer's point of view, when West led the high ten of clubs at trick three, instead of fighting for the trick by ruffing with the board's nine of trumps, he exchanged a trick for a trick: he conceded his inevitable diamond loser now rather than later. And, as a result, he was able to trump a diamond later, when it was safe, instead of trying to trump a club at trick three, when it was obviously highly dangerous.

From East's point of view, had he not overtaken West's opening lead, declarer would never have had a problem, for in this case *East* would have been forced to win the second club lead—and East would not have arrived at the trick three position where he would be able to overtrump dummy on the third club lead.

Deal 8:
It is difficult to criticize East for his trick-one play on this deal, for the proper play is a tough one to find at the table. In retrospect, after it's all over, the justification for the correct action becomes visible to the naked, untrained eye. At the table, the correct play requires "superimagination."

```
                        ♠ 8 5 2
                        ♡ K 2
                        ◇ A K Q
                        ♣ J 10 8 4 3
        ♠ 7 3                          ♠ K Q 10 9 6
        ♡ 10 8 5 4 3      N            ♡ J 9
        ◇ 7 5 4 2      W     E         ◇ J 10 9
        ♣ K 6            S             ♣ A 7 2
                        ♠ A J 4
                        ♡ A Q 7 6
                        ◇ 8 6 3
                        ♣ Q 9 5
```

North	East	South	West
1 ♣	1 ♠	2 NT	Pass
3 NT	Pass	Pass	Pass

West opened the seven of spades, East played the queen, and declarer permitted the queen to win the trick. East returned the ten of spades (no other return could have changed the outcome), South taking the trick with his jack.

Declarer now led the queen of clubs, and it matters not which of the defenders elected to win it. If West did, he would have no spade to return. And if East took the queen of clubs, he could lead a spade, knocking out declarer's last stopper in that suit—but East would be unable to ever regain the lead to cash his established spade suit.

Proper play by East was to put up the nine (or ten) of spades at trick one! From East's point of view, he should have been absolutely certain that South, for his jump to two no-trump, had either the A J x or the A J x x of spades; and that South would know that East, for his overcall, had a spade suit headed by the K Q. Also, East knew that South was a good player and that South, if it were to his advantage, would permit East's queen of spades to win the opening lead and thus retain the A J over East's king.

As an expert East should have viewed it, his only hope of establishing and cashing his spade suit was for West to have started with a doubleton spade; and for declarer to have started with the A J x of spades. The play of the nine would, in this case, *compel* declarer to win the trick with the jack at trick one. (If declarer didn't, he would win but one spade trick.)

Now if West obtained the lead—as he would have via the king of clubs—West would still possess a spade to return, and East would be able to establish his spade suit while still retaining the ace of clubs.

Putting it another way, East knew from the opening lead (which had to be the "top-of-nothing" since it couldn't be either the fourth best or the third best) that declarer had *two* sure spade tricks. By putting up the nine rather than the queen, East would not be losing a thing; and his gain would be that he would be maintaining communication with his partner within the spade suit.

Deal 9:
The proper third-hand play on this deal would be a simple one for the expert. Many players would do the wrong thing, however, as did our actual defender.

```
                    ♠ Q 10 4
                    ♡ K 8 2
                    ◇ A J 9 7 4
                    ♣ Q 8
     ♠ 7 5              N          ♠ 9 6 3
     ♡ 10 6 4 3                    ♡ J 9 7
     ◇ Q 2         W        E      ◇ K 8 5
     ♣ A 9 7 5 3         S         ♣ K 10 6 2
                    ♠ A K J 8 2
                    ♡ A Q 5
                    ◇ 10 6 3
                    ♣ J 4
```

South	West	North	East
1 ♠	Pass	2 ◇	Pass
2 ♠	Pass	3 ♠	Pass
3 NT	Pass	Pass	Pass

West opened the five of clubs, the eight was played

from dummy, and East put up—the ten-spot! Declarer breathed a sigh of relief, took the ten with the jack, and spread his cards, claiming ten tricks: one club, one diamond, three hearts, and five spades.

On the face of it, East had a serious problem on the opening club lead: if West were leading from the jack of clubs, then the ten-spot would force declarer's ace, holding declarer to just one club trick, whereas the alternative play of the king, taken by declarer's ace, would promote the queen of clubs into a winner. But East did not go far enough in his thinking, for he did not look at the situation through the eyes of the declarer.

Suppose you were the declarer and had held in your hand either the A x or the A x x of clubs. What would you have played from dummy on the opening lead? Would it not have been the *queen* of clubs, in the hope that West was leading away from the king? Surely every declarer would have put up dummy's queen. Hence, did not declarer's play of the eight of clubs from dummy at trick one indicate *that he did not possess the ace?*

Of course, had East properly played the club king at trick one, the defenders would have made the first five tricks in that suit—and South would have regretted his failure to have bid four spades.

Deal 10:
As we all know, the urge to grab an opponent's king with one's ace is sometimes an impulse that is difficult to resist. This grabbing attitude, unfortunately, has been developed through years of training, years in which one was taught that aces were created only for the lofty purpose of capturing kings and queens.

From past experiences, we all agree that it is quite a problem to break a habit that has been cultivated and nurtured throughout one's lifetime. But we all appreciate that there are times when it must be done.

On this deal, our East defender resisted the urge to capture a king with an ace, thus gaining the victory.

```
                        ♠ 8 7
                        ♡ K 10 2
                        ◇ K J 10 7 3
                        ♣ K 7 4
        ♠ 9 5 3 2          N        ♠ Q 10 6 4
        ♡ 8 6 5 4      W       E    ♡ J 9 3
        ◇ A 9 2            S        ◇ 4
        ♣ 10 6                      ♣ A Q 8 5 3
                        ♠ A K J
                        ♡ A Q 7
                        ◇ Q 8 6 5
                        ♣ J 9 2
```

South	*West*	*North*	*East*
1 NT	Pass	3 NT	Pass
Pass	Pass		

West got off to the terrific lead of the ten of clubs. Had he led any other suit, declarer would have waltzed in with his contract.

Declarer recognized that West was making a short suit lead, for it was impossible for the ten-spot to be West's fourth highest. East, therefore, figured to have both the ace and queen of clubs. So declarer put up dummy's king of clubs on the lead of the ten.

Had East captured the king with the ace, he would have been a dead duck, for declarer's jack of clubs would effectively have prevented East from establishing and cashing his club suit. On this trick, East gave a come-on signal by playing the encouraging eight of clubs, dummy's king winning. When declarer now attacked the diamond suit, West took the ace and returned his remaining club enabling East to cash four club tricks. Let's see what motivated East to decline winning the opening lead.

It was perfectly apparent to East—as it was to declarer —that West's opening lead of the ten of clubs was a "top-of-nothing" lead. Going farther, East knew that West didn't have three clubs, for with the 10 x x of clubs, the third highest is led, even in an "off-suit." Also, the lead was not a singleton, since singletons "just ain't led" against no-trump contracts. So West was known to have started with the 10 x or 10 9 doubleton of clubs—and South therefore was marked with the J x x or the J 9 x of clubs. In this situation, to take the king with the ace at trick one would leave South with a stopper in clubs. And whatever club East elected to lead at trick two, West would then become void of clubs, and he would become unable to lead another club should he subsequently obtain the lead.

Thus, to maintain communication with his partner, East allowed the board's king of clubs to win the opening lead. The result was most gratifying to East-West.

Deal 11:
This is another deal about an iconoclast who did not play "third-hand high." The East defender was my good friend and frequent partner, Mike Michaels, of Miami, Florida. I was sitting West, minding my own business.

```
              ♠ K Q 6 3
              ♡ K 7
              ◇ A Q J 10
              ♣ K 5 4
  ♠ A 8 4          N        ♠ 9 7 2
  ♡ A 5 2      W       E    ♡ Q 10 8 6 3
  ◇ 9 6                     ◇ 7 5 4 3
  ♣ Q J 8 7 3      S        ♣ 2
              ♠ J 10 5
              ♡ J 9 4
              ◇ K 8 2
              ♣ A 10 9 6
```

North-South vulnerable. South dealer.

South	West	North	East
Pass	1 ♣	Double	1 ♡
1 NT	Pass	3 NT	Pass
Pass	Pass		

I opened the deuce of hearts, the seven was played from dummy, and, after about a ten-second hesitation, Mike put up the ten-spot! Declarer, upon taking the trick with his jack, led a spade, which I won with the ace. I then cashed the ace of hearts, dropping dummy's king, after which I led my remaining heart, and Mike took three more heart tricks, thus defeating declarer. Declarer now claimed the balance of the tricks. We conceded him his claim.

From Mike's position, here was his reasoning: If declarer had the ace and jack of hearts, whether the A J was a doubleton or part of an A J x or A J x x holding, it didn't matter whether he played the queen or the ten, for declarer would get no more and no less than he was entitled to. If declarer had the A x, the A x x, or the A x x x, then again it didn't matter whether Mike played the queen or the ten, for with either play declarer would make exactly two heart tricks. The only remaining possibilities were that declarer had the J x or the J x x of hearts. Mike promptly dismissed the possibility that declarer had the doubleton J x, for surely if he (a *good* player) had just the J x, he would have put up dummy's king on the opening lead, assuming that I, the opening bidder, would possess the ace of hearts. So Mike gave consideration to the possibility that declarer had the J x x.

If such were the situation, then Mike could win the opening heart lead with the queen, return a heart to my ace—to fell dummy's king—and then I would return my remaining heart, which declarer would win with his jack. Mike's heart suit would now be established—but he could never regain the lead to cash it. Thus, logically, Mike dismissed the play of the queen.

But if, Mike reasoned, he put up the ten-spot, then declarer, holding the J x x, would have no option but to win the trick. Now when (if) I obtained the lead, I could cash the ace of hearts, decapitating dummy's king, and then another heart lead by me would enable Mike to bring home the rest of the heart suit.

And so Mike "created" the situation that had to exist if we were to gain the victory—and he then proceeded to play on the assumption that his creation was a reality.

Deal 12:
Here is another deal where successful third-hand defense hinged on the application of "superimagination." But this

time our East defender, Ivan Erdos, came through with flying colors, as one would expect of a topflight expert.

♠ J 10 8
♡ Q 7 2
◇ K 10 9 5
♣ J 9 3

♠ K 7
♡ 8 5 4 3
◇ 7 6 2
♣ A 7 5 2

♠ 6 5 3 2
♡ J 10 9
◇ A 4
♣ Q 8 6 4

♠ A Q 9 4
♡ A K 6
◇ Q J 8 3
♣ K 10

North	East	South	West
Pass	Pass	1 ◇	Pass
2 ◇	Pass	3 NT	Pass
Pass	Pass		

When West opened his fourth highest club, the deuce, the three was played from dummy, and Ivan studied the situation. Since West was known to have started with exactly four clubs, declarer obviously had started with two clubs. If declarer's two clubs were the ace and king, then if East put up the queen, he would create a winner out of dummy's jack. If declarer had started with either the A 10 or A x of clubs, then the play of the queen or a low club would be immaterial, for declarer would, in either of these cases, always be able to make two club tricks. But if the declarer had started with the doubleton K x of clubs—?

Seizing the hope that South possessed the doubleton K x of clubs, Ivan played the eight on the opening lead, South's ten winning. South then led the jack of diamonds, East taking the trick with his ace. The four of clubs was now returned, declarer's king falling to West's ace, after which West returned another club, Ivan's queen taking dummy's jack. Then came the six of clubs, West's seven overtaking. Later West's king of spades took the setting trick.

Had Ivan mechanically played the queen of clubs on the opening lead, declarer would have made two club tricks, and his contract. With the play of the low club at trick one by East, declarer was restricted to just one club trick. And there was the difference between victory and defeat.

Deal 13:
This final deal has become a classic in the tournament world. About two decades ago, the National Open Pair Championship was lost because third hand played automatically to trick one and really "fixed" himself as a result. This is not a simple hand—except in retrospect. Let's see how you fare on it, as the East defender.

```
            ♠ A K Q 2
            ♡ A Q 8 3
            ◇ Q 10 8
            ♣ 7 5
                    N        ♠ J 9 6
                             ♡ K 2
               W        E    ◇ 7 6 4 2
                    S        ♣ K J 9 4
```

North	East	South	West
1 ♠	Pass	2 ♡	Pass
4 ♡	Pass	6 ♡	Pass
Pass	Pass		

Your partner, West, opens the three of clubs against South's six-heart contract, the five is played from dummy, you put up your king, and declarer takes it with his ace. Declarer then tries the heart finesse, losing to your king. What do you now return, a club or a diamond?

Permit me to make an attempt to delve into the thoughts that may be running through your mind. Your immediate reaction would probably be to return a club on the very sound assumption that your partner may hold the queen of clubs. You remember, of course, that partner had opened the three of clubs, which was either from a five-card suit, or possibly from a four-card suit, or from a three-card suit. In any case, declarer had to have started with at least two clubs. Then you probably give at least a passing thought to leading a diamond, but an echo haunts you: "Partner, why didn't you return *the suit I opened?* Why do you always make decisions that turn out to be wrong?" So, not wishing to incur (or perpetuate) the ever-lasting enmity of partner—and not really having anything intelligent to guide you—you dutifully play back a club. You have just lost the National Open Pair Championship!!

Did you defend badly when you returned a club? Actually not. The club return could easily have been the winning play. Your mistake did not come at trick three when you played back a club. It came at trick one, *when you incorrectly put up the king of clubs!*

Let's go back. Is it conceivable that on the given bidding, your partner would have opened a low club, *away from the ace?* This is an impossible lead, unless partner had a screw loose. Why then not put up your jack of clubs? If declarer has both the ace and queen of clubs, what difference which club you play? But if you play your jack and declarer wins it with the queen, you will realize that he still retains the ace of clubs—and when you obtain the lead you will automatically switch to a diamond, not because it is right, *but because a club return must be wrong.* You have just won the National Open Pairs Championships.

Of course, when you put up your jack on the opening lead, should declarer win it with the ace, you would know that your partner had the queen. So, upon winning trick two with the king of hearts, you would in this latter case return a club.

You would have done nothing brilliant or spectacular, but you would have achieved the optimum result—and the plaudits of the world would have echoed in your ears.

The complete deal was:

```
              ♠ A K Q 2
              ♡ A Q 8 3
              ◇ Q 10 8
              ♣ 7 5
♠ 10 8 7 5 3         N          ♠ J 9 6
♡ 5                             ♡ K 2
◇ A J 5        W       E        ◇ 7 6 4 2
♣ 10 8 6 3          S           ♣ K J 9 4
              ♠ 4
              ♡ J 10 9 7 6 4
              ◇ K 9 3
              ♣ A Q 2
```

If East returns a club at trick three, declarer wins it with the queen (assuming the king and ace have been played to the first trick). He then trumps his remaining club, after which he plays all of the trumps. This would be the situation just prior to declarer playing his last trump:

```
              ♠ A K Q 2
              ♡
              ◇ Q
              ♣
♠ 10 8 7 5           N          ♠ J 9 6
♡                               ♡
◇ A            W       E        ◇ 7 6
♣                   S           ♣
              ♠ 4
              ♡ 4
              ◇ K 9 3
              ♣
```

South now leads his last trump—and poor West has become the victim of a squeeze. If he discards a spade, dummy's deuce of spades will be promoted into a winner (dummy discarding the queen of diamonds); if West elects to discard the ace of diamonds instead, then declarer's king of diamonds will become a winner, after which dummy's A K Q of spades will yield declarer his slam.

chapter 16 The Play by the Leader's Partner: Deception

♠ Throughout this text, whenever the subject of deception has been discussed, it has been emphasized that the employment of deceptive tactics by the defenders can be bad business. Although the purpose of trying to fool declarer is a most praiseworthy one, there is all too often the attendant risk that instead, partner may wind up as the one who has been fooled.

However, many situations do arise in which a defender can afford to deceive his partner because the deception figures to do no physical harm, and it might do a lot of good. Also, occasional situations arise in which a defender deliberately misleads partner while he simultaneously misleads declarer, the objective being to get both declarer and your partner to think as you want them to think. Of course, when this "universal" deception is undertaken, the deceiver has an ulterior purpose in mind, which he hopes will work out to his complete satisfaction. On rare occasions, a defender will deliberately mislead partner without intending to deceive declarer at all. In these cases, the purpose is to paint a different picture for partner than the one that actually exists, and thus induce him to adopt a line of defense he would not ordinarily follow without the deception. Illustrations of each of these various cases of deception are presented in this chapter.

Deal 1:
This deal arose in the National Team-of-Four Championships of 1961. The East defender was Robert Reynolds, of Miami Beach, Florida.

```
              ♠ K Q 8 5 4 2
              ♡ Q J 9 5 4
              ◇ 4
              ♣ K
♠ 10 6              N              ♠ J 9 7
♡ 10 6                            ♡ 3 2
◇ Q 10 8 5    W         E         ◇ A 9 6 3
♣ Q 10 9 5 4       S              ♣ J 8 3 2
              ♠ A 3
              ♡ A K 8 7
              ◇ K J 7 2
              ♣ A 7 6
```

North	East	South	West
Pass	Pass	1 ◇	Pass
2 ♠	Pass	3 ♣	Pass
3 ♡	Pass	4 NT	Pass
5 ♣	Pass	6 NT	Pass
Pass	Pass		

West led the ten of spades, the deuce was played from dummy, Bob put up the jack, and declarer won the trick with the ace.

Would you not assume that East's jack of spades had been a singleton and that, hence, West had started with an original spade holding of 10 9 7 6? Our declarer so assumed—and at trick two he led his remaining three of spades and put in dummy's eight-spot. Bob took this trick with the nine and cashed the ace of diamonds for the setting trick.

Had East played normally to trick one—following suit with the "economical" seven—declarer would have won the trick with the ace. He would then have cashed the king and queen of spades and would thus have made six spade tricks, five hearts, and two clubs.

Deal 2:
An identical type of false card is the following. The deal arose in a rubber-bridge game a few years ago.

```
            ♠ K 8 6 3
            ♡ 8 4 3
            ◇ A K 4
            ♣ A J 10
♠ J 5                 N           ♠ Q 10
♡ 9 7 6 2       W         E       ♡ A 10 5
◇ 10 8 7 5          S             ◇ 9 6 3 2
♣ 9 7 4                           ♣ 8 6 5 2
            ♠ A 9 7 4 2
            ♡ K Q J
            ◇ Q J
            ♣ K Q 3
```

North	*East*	*South*	*West*
1 ♣	Pass	1 ♠	Pass
2 ♠	Pass	4 NT	Pass
5 ♡	Pass	6 ♠	Pass
Pass	Pass		

West opened the jack of spades, dummy's three was played, and East followed with the *queen!* Declarer, of course, took the trick with his ace. And who could blame him (except his partner) for deducing that East's queen was a singleton and that West's original trump holding had been the J 10 5? At trick two, South led a low spade, West followed with the five, and dummy's eight-spot was inserted. As is obvious, East produced the ten of spades, after which he cashed the ace of hearts.

And, once again, had the East defender played normally, by following with the ten-spot at trick one, declarer would have won the trick with the ace, after which he would have cashed the board's king, felling East's known queen. (No West defender, against a slam contract, would have led the jack—or any spade—from a Q J 5 combination. Thus, if East had not put up the spade queen at trick one, declarer would have known that he still possessed that card.)

Deal 3:
A timely false card by East on this deal convinced declarer that a certain situation existed. Belatedly, declarer realized that he had been tricked.

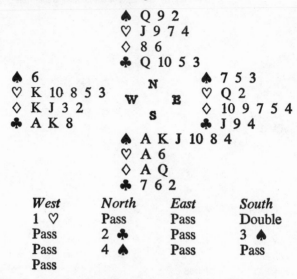

West	North	East	South
1 ♡	Pass	Pass	Double
Pass	2 ♣	Pass	3 ♠
Pass	4 ♠	Pass	Pass
Pass			

West's opening lead was the king of clubs, dummy followed with the three, and East played the *nine-spot!* The ace of clubs was cashed next, East completing his high-low signal by dropping the four. West then led the eight of clubs. As is apparent when one looks at all four hands, declarer should have played dummy's queen. But he didn't— and neither would you or I at the table.

Surely East figured to have started with the doubleton 9 4 of clubs, and West figured to still possess the club jack. And declarer desperately needed to get rid of a loser (either a heart or a diamond) from his hand. So, at trick three, he put up dummy's ten of clubs—preserving the queen—and East won the trick with the jack.

Later on South was able to discard his six of hearts on the queen of clubs, but when the diamond finesse lost, he was defeated. Of course, had he put up dummy's queen of clubs at trick three, he would have made his contract.

Deal 4:
The defensive false card by East on this deal is virtually identical to that employed on the preceding deal. And, once again, it accomplished its objective of leading declarer astray.

```
                    ♠ J 10 7
                    ♡ A J 10 7 3
                    ◇ A 9 3
                    ♣ Q 8
   ♠ 2                 N              ♠ K 9 8 6
   ♡ 8 6 4         W       E         ♡ 9 5 2
   ◇ Q 7 5 4 2         S             ◇ J 10 8
   ♣ A K 9 6                         ♣ J 10 2
                    ♠ A Q 5 4 3
                    ♡ K Q
                    ◇ K 6
                    ♣ 7 5 4 3
```

North-South vulnerable. South dealer.

South	West	North	East
1 ♠	Pass	2 ♡	Pass
2 ♠	Pass	4 ♠	Pass
Pass	Pass		

On the opening lead of the king of clubs, East promptly dropped the *jack*. West then continued with the ace, and East played the deuce. West, properly assuming that his partner had held a doubleton club, now led the six of clubs.

Declarer quite naturally feared that East was going to trump this trick, so he ruffed with dummy's jack, not caring much if East (in theory) overruffed with the king, since the king of trumps figured to be lost to the defenders half the time anyway. But on this trick, East nonchalantly followed suit with the club ten. Although declarer didn't know it, his contract had just become unmakable, for East now had two sure trump tricks.

To trick four, the seven of trumps was led, East covered with the eight, and South successfully finessed his queen. He then reentered dummy via the ace of diamonds, to play the ten of trumps. This was covered by East's king, South's ace winning. East's remaining 9 6 of trumps had just become the highest ranking trumps.

Deal 5:
If the reader will look at all four hands below, he will perceive that there is no way of defeating declarer's *six-*

spade contract. Nevertheless, by virtue of a brilliant defensive false card, the East defender succeeded in creating a trend of thought in declarer's mind that led to the latter's defeat. This deal, which arose in the National Masters Pairs Championship of 1955, has become accepted as a classic illustration of the role of deceptive tactics by the defenders. The East defender was Jack Ehrlenbach.

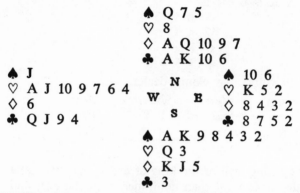

```
                    ♠ Q 7 5
                    ♡ 8
                    ◊ A Q 10 9 7
                    ♣ A K 10 6
  ♠ J                            ♠ 10 6
  ♡ A J 10 9 7 6 4      N        ♡ K 5 2
  ◊ 6                 W     E     ◊ 8 4 3 2
  ♣ Q J 9 4             S        ♣ 8 7 5 2
                    ♠ A K 9 8 4 3 2
                    ♡ Q 3
                    ◊ K J 5
                    ♣ 3
```

Neither side vulnerable. West dealer.

West	North	East	South
4 ♡	Pass	Pass	4 ♠
Pass	6 ♠	Pass	Pass
Pass			

West opened the ace of hearts, upon which Mr. Ehrlenbach dropped *the king!* West, of course, continued with another heart, which was ruffed by dummy's queen (to prevent the "obvious" overruff). When East followed to the second round of hearts, declarer was certain that the only plausible justification for East's false card was that East possessed the J 10 6 of trumps. Having the courage of his convictions, declarer now led the seven of spades from dummy and finessed when East followed suit with the six-spot. West's jack took this trick—and gloom descended upon declarer.

Before you criticize declarer, remember one thing: East would also have made the identical false card if he *had held* the J 10 6 of trumps—and declarer would then have become a temporary genius instead of—as his partner called him—a gullible victim.

Deal 6:

Through the years, one of Canada's top-ranking experts has been Mrs. Jackie Begin. Here is an example of her defensive ability.

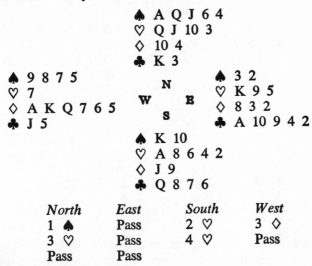

```
                    ♠ A Q J 6 4
                    ♡ Q J 10 3
                    ◇ 10 4
                    ♣ K 3
  ♠ 9 8 7 5                        ♠ 3 2
  ♡ 7              N               ♡ K 9 5
  ◇ A K Q 7 6 5   W   B            ◇ 8 3 2
  ♣ J 5              S             ♣ A 10 9 4 2
                    ♠ K 10
                    ♡ A 8 6 4 2
                    ◇ J 9
                    ♣ Q 8 7 6
```

North	East	South	West
1 ♠	Pass	2 ♡	3 ◇
3 ♡	Pass	4 ♡	Pass
Pass	Pass		

The king of diamonds was opened, upon which "Jackie" played the eight. Then followed the ace of diamonds, upon which the deuce was played, completing the come-on signal. West now led the diamond queen.

You, I, and the rest of the world would now all make the same play: we would trump with the queen of hearts (or the jack or ten). And all of us, including our actual South declarer, have just lost our contract.

In the actual play, when declarer ruffed the third diamond lead with the queen, East followed suit in diamonds. Declarer then led the jack of trumps, which won the trick, after which the ten of trumps was led. Jackie covered this with her king, declarer won the trick with his ace—and East's nine of trumps had just become the highest ranking trump left in the deck. This nine-spot, combined with the club ace, resulted in declarer's defeat.

Deal 7:

Here is another "swindle" perpetrated by a third-hand defender, who just happened to be Helen Sobel.

```
                    ♠ A 6 3
                    ♡ K Q J 10
                    ◇ A K Q 2
                    ♣ 7 5
♠ ———                             ♠ 10 9 8 5
♡ 7 6 5 2          N              ♡ A 4
◇ 10 8 7 4      W     E           ◇ J 9 5 3
♣ K Q 10 9 2       S             ♣ A 6 4
                    ♠ K Q J 7 4 2
                    ♡ 9 8 3
                    ◇ 6
                    ♣ J 8 3
```

North	East	South	West
1 ♡	Pass	1 ♠	Pass
3 ◇	Pass	3 ♠	Pass
4 ♠	Pass	Pass	Pass

West opened the king of clubs, which Helen overtook with her ace, and returned the four of clubs, West's nine taking South's eight. West then laid down the queen of clubs.

Certainly everybody at the table (except East) "knew" that East had started with the doubleton A 4 of clubs. Quite naturally, declarer ruffed West's queen of clubs with dummy's ace of spades—and thereby created a positive trump winner for East.

Although it turned out to be the losing play, South did the right thing. The only thing that could then defeat South was for either of the opponents to have started with all four of the outstanding spades. Unfortunately for declarer, it happened to be one of those days.

Deal 8:

The type of false card that East made on this deal is a dangerous one to employ in that it is certain to have an adverse effect on partner should the latter regain the lead. But when it accomplishes its objective—the misleading of the declarer—the deceiver becomes a hero.

```
                    ♠ A J
                    ♡ K 10 9
                    ◇ A Q 10 8 4
                    ♣ J 9 7
    ♠ K 10 6 5 3         N           ♠ 8 7 4
    ♡ 7 4          W         E        ♡ 6 5 3 2
    ◇ 7 2                             ◇ 9 5 3
    ♣ 6 5 3 2           S             ♣ K Q 10
                    ♠ Q 9 2
                    ♡ A Q J 8
                    ◇ K J 6
                    ♣ A 8 4
```

South	West	North	East
1 NT	Pass	3 ◇	Pass
3 NT	Pass	5 NT	Pass
6 NT	Pass	Pass	Pass

West elected to open the deuce of clubs, the seven was played from dummy, and East put up *the queen.* As declarer won the trick with his ace, there was no doubt in his mind that West possessed the ten of clubs, for what "sane" East player, possessing a Q 10 combination, would have played the queen on the opening lead?

Declarer had 11 sure winners, and rather than risk the 50-50 spade finesse for his twelfth trick, he led a club right back, inserting the board's nine-spot. To his amazement, East won the trick with the ten-spot, after which East cashed the king of clubs, for the setting trick.

Had East made the technically proper play of putting up the ten of clubs at trick one—forcing declarer's ace—declarer would have had no option but to resort to the spade finesse for his slam-going trick. As is evident, the finesse would have been successful.

Deal 9:
This deal features the defensive holdup of an ace. The

play is a most logical one and has become a standby in the experts' arsenal of defensive weapons.

```
                    ♠ 8 6 4
                    ♡ Q 5 2
                    ◇ A J 7 3
                    ♣ K Q 10
    ♠ J 9 5 3                      ♠ Q 10 7
    ♡ 8 7 6 4         N            ♡ J 10 3
    ◇ 5          W         E       ◇ Q 10 9 8
    ♣ J 9 6 3         S            ♣ A 8 4
                    ♠ A K 2
                    ♡ A K 9
                    ◇ K 6 4 2
                    ♣ 7 5 2
```

South	West	North	East
1 NT	Pass	3 NT	Pass
Pass	Pass		

West decided to open the three of clubs (the club suit being *stronger* than the spade suit!), dummy's king was put up, and East, without undue haste or undue deliberation, followed with the four of clubs. A diamond was then led to declarer's king, after which another diamond was played from the closed hand, with the intention of finessing the board's jack. But when West failed to follow suit—discarding a heart—it became obvious that declarer could not obtain his ninth trick in the diamond suit. On this trick dummy's seven of diamonds was put up, East's nine winning.

East now shifted to a spade, declarer taking this lead with his ace. Declarer's sole hope of making his ninth trick now rested in the club suit, so he led a low club, West following with the six-spot.

Assuming from East's play of the four of clubs at trick one that West held the ace of clubs, declarer put up dummy's queen. East, of course, took the trick with his ace and returned his remaining club, West cashing two more club tricks. It was now impossible for declarer to make his ninth, and game-going, trick. He struggled quietly for a few more moments and then went down.

Had East captured dummy's king of clubs with his ace at trick one, declarer would have fulfilled his contract. Upon attacking the diamond suit and discovering the bad division, declarer would have had no choice but to finesse West for the missing jack of clubs, thereby making a winner out of the board's ten-spot. But when East declined to win the opening lead, he put declarer into a guessing position—and, as happens quite often, when one is forced to guess, he sometimes misguesses.

Deal 10:
In many situations, a thinking partner will be able to determine for himself (and by himself) what the right play should be. Nevertheless, even if the proper course of action *should be* apparent to him, he (as all of us) occasionally will develop a blind spot and fail to see the perfectly obvious line of play. Whenever possible, one should help his partner out, even in seemingly clear-cut situations, thereby eliminating or minimizing the chances of partner making a mistake.

In this final deal, the East defender deliberately misled his partner at trick one, the aim being to make sure that partner *would not* continue the suit that the latter had opened. Even without the deception, partner *probably* would have made the right decision at trick two (he was an *expert* partner). But then again, he *might not have*.

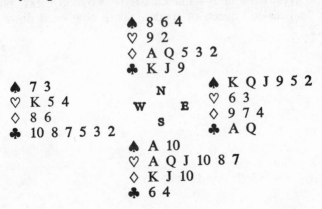

North-South vulnerable. East dealer.

East	South	West	North
1 ♠	Double	Pass	3 ◊
Pass	4 ♡	Pass	Pass
Pass			

West opened the seven of spades, the suit East had bid. Technically, East's proper play should have been the jack, the lower of adjacent high cards. But instead, East put up the king, declarer winning it with his ace.

The king of diamonds was then led and overtaken by the board's ace, after which the nine of trumps was laid down, and the finesse taken, losing to West's king. Had West now returned his remaining spade, declarer would have made his contract. In this case, East would have won the trick, and the best he then could have done would have been to cash the ace of clubs. Declarer's second club would have been discarded on one of dummy's high diamonds.

But when West won the king of trumps (at trick three), he did not play back a spade, for a most obvious reason: on the opening lead, East had put up the *king* of spades, which denied possession of the queen, since with the king and queen East would have played the queen. From West's point of view, therefore, it was futile to lead a spade, since declarer was "marked" with the high queen.

So West led a club—and East took two club tricks, plus his "concealed" queen of spades. South now went down a trick.

chapter 17 The Play by the Leader's Partner: Standard "Book" Plays

♠ When contract bridge was in its infancy a little more than three decades ago, there were many spur-of-the-moment plays that were considered to be either brilliantly imaginative or just plain fancy. But with the impact of experience, it became apparent that the occasions for the appropriate utilization of these plays were frequent and repetitive. Thus, with the passage of time, they became known as stock, standard plays, and were included as integral components in the experts' storehouse of useful weapons.

And so, just as there were evolved conventional, accepted, standard opening leads (the top of a sequence, the fourth best, etc.), there were evolved conventional, accepted, standard plays by the leader's partner (third hand) at trick one. The presentation of these latter types of plays comprises this final chapter.

It should be emphasized that the play that will be introduced are all frequently recurring plays, and the reader will do himself a service if he analyzes them and earmarks them for future employment.

The Play of the Queen on the Opening Lead of a King Against a Suit Contract (Deals 1, 2 and 3)

It is an established convention that when your partner opens a king against a suit contract and you play the queen on his king, the play of the queen *demands* that he underlead his ace at trick two. Hence, it should be obvious that when you give this most drastic signal, you will have the queen *and jack* in your possession:

♡ 9 8 2

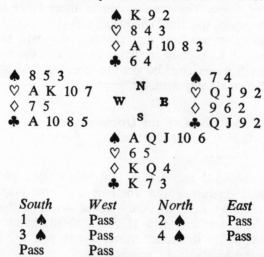

♡ A K 6 5   W   E   ♡ Q J 3

♡ 10 7 4

Your partner opens the king, upon which you play your queen. Partner then leads a low heart, which you capture with the jack, after which a third round of the suit is taken by West's ace.

Do not, therefore, go playing the queen in the following type of situation:

♡ 9 8 2

♡ A K 6 5   W   E   ♡ Q 3

♡ J 10 7 4

Deal 1:

Here is a deal in which, without the use of the convention of playing the queen on the king to show the jack, declarer would almost certainly have fulfilled his contract.

♠ K 9 2
♡ 8 4 3
◇ A J 10 8 3
♣ 6 4

♠ 8 5 3   ♠ 7 4
♡ A K 10 7   ♡ Q J 9 2
◇ 7 5   W   E   ◇ 9 6 2
♣ A 10 8 5   ♣ Q J 9 2

♠ A Q J 10 6
♡ 6 5
◇ K Q 4
♣ K 7 3

South	West	North	East
1 ♠	Pass	2 ♠	Pass
3 ♠	Pass	4 ♠	Pass
Pass	Pass		

The opening lead was the king of hearts, upon which East played the queen. A low heart was then led to East's known jack, after which East shifted to the queen of clubs. The defenders now took two clubs, to defeat South's contract.

If, on the lead of the king of hearts, East had mechanically played his nine-spot as a come-on signal, West might then have cashed the ace of hearts at trick two. And, if this had been done, South would then have fulfilled his contract, for he would have avoided the loss of two club tricks by discarding them on dummy's diamonds.

Deal 2:
The East player on this deal is one of the greatest players in the world, Terence Reese, of England. The deal arose in a high-stakes rubber-bridge game.

```
                    ♠ Q 3
                    ♡ K 10 8 6 5
                    ◇ 7 4
                    ♣ 10 8 5 2
      ♠ J 9 5 4         N          ♠ K 10 8 7
      ♡ J 4 3                      ♡ Q 9 7
      ◇ Q 9 6     W        E       ◇ 8 2
      ♣ A K 6         S            ♣ Q J 9 3
                    ♠ A 6 2
                    ♡ A 2
                    ◇ A K J 10 5 3
                    ♣ 7 4
```

South	West	North	East
1 ◇	Pass	1 ♡	Pass
3 ◇	Pass	Pass	Pass

When West opened the king of ~~hearts~~ *CLUBS*, Mr. Reese, sitting East, came to the proper conclusion that the defenders' best chance of defeating South's contract was by getting a couple of spade tricks. This could be accomplished only if dummy were prevented from ruffing spades.

On the lead of the club king, Mr. Reese dropped the queen, commanding West to underlead his ace, which West dutifully did at trick two. Upon winning this trick with the club nine, East switched to a trump, declarer taking the trick with his king.

Declarer, hoping that West possessed the king of spades, now led the deuce of spades towards the board's queen, West following with the four-spot, with dummy's queen being captured by Mr. Reese's king. East now led his remaining trump—and declarer's cause was lost. When the smoke had cleared, declarer had lost two clubs, two spades, and a trump trick (to West's queen).

Had East not played the club queen on the opening lead, West would probably have cashed the club ace. Whatever he led next—to trick three—he could not now prevent declarer from making his contract: if he led a diamond, away from his queen, he would never make a trump trick. And, whatever else he led, declarer would win, after which he would play the ace of spades and then give up the queen of spades to East's king. East's trump shift would now be belated, for South would win that lead and then trump his losing spade with the board's last trump.

Unfortunately for declarer, he had the misfortune to be playing against Terence Reese, who visualized that his partner might not be able to lead a trump at trick two without sacrificing a trick. And so Reese took control of the situation by playing the queen of clubs on the opening lead, which enabled him to obtain the lead at trick two. He could now make the desired trump lead without sacrificing a trick—and he did so, causing declarer's downfall.

Deal 3:
This deal presents a final example of an East defender guiding and controlling the defense by playing his queen on the opening lead of partner's king.

```
              ♠ 7 4
              ♥ 8 4
              ♦ A Q J 9 3
              ♣ K Q J 4
♠ 9 5              N          ♠ K 8 3
♥ A K 7 5 2   W       E      ♥ Q J 9
♦ 7 6 2                      ♦ 10 5
♣ 7 5 3           S          ♣ A 10 8 6 2
              ♠ A Q J 10 6 2
              ♥ 10 6 3
              ♦ K 8 4
              ♣ 9
```

East-West vulnerable. North dealer.

North	East	South	West
1 ♦	Pass	1 ♠	Pass
2 ♣	Pass	4 ♠	Pass
Pass	Pass		

West led the king of hearts, East putting up the queen. To trick two, West led the deuce of hearts, East's jack winning. To trick three, East cashed the ace of clubs. To trick four, East led his nine of hearts, declarer followed with the ten, West covered with the ace, and dummy trumped.

Dummy's remaining trump was now led, and declarer put up his queen when East played the three of spades. The finesse won, of course, but eventually declarer had to concede a trump trick to East's king of trumps.

East planned the defense gorgeously. He perceived that if declarer were able to lead trumps twice from dummy, he would be able to take two successful finesses against East's twice-guarded king. But if dummy were forced to expend one of its two trumps by trumping, then declarer would be able to finesse against East's king but once; and thus the king would remain guarded, resulting in its eventually becoming a winner. So East made sure of first cashing the defenders' three top tricks (two in hearts plus the ace of clubs) and then leading a third heart, forcing dummy to trump.

If East had played the nine-spot (instead of the queen) on West's opening lead of the heart king, West would probably have cashed the ace of hearts at trick two. And if West then led a diamond (rather than a club), declarer would have won it with dummy's jack, to take a successful trump finesse. The board would then have been reentered via the diamond queen, and declarer would again have finessed successfully against East's king of trumps. The ace of trumps lead would then have felled East's king, after which the diamond king would have been overtaken by the board's ace of diamonds. On the two high diamonds, declarer would now have discarded his ten of hearts and nine of clubs, thereby making eleven tricks.

Unfortunately for declarer, East's play of the heart queen on the opening lead doomed declarer to defeat.

Playing a Picture Card on Partner's Ace or King (Deals 4 and 5)

The three preceding deals have illustrated the convention that when your partner opens a king against a suit contract and you possess a Q J combination *plus the desire to have the suit continued,* you play *the queen,* asking for the underlead of the ace at trick two. Extending this point (signalling with a picture card), whenever your partner opens the ace or king of a suit and you have touching (adjacent) honor cards in his suit, play the *higher* honor to inform him that you also have the honor card directly below the one that you have just played. That is, if your partner leads the king against a suit contract and you hold the J 10 9, *play the jack,* not the ten or the nine. The jack play will inform him not only that you have the ten, but will also specifically deny possession of the queen, since with the Q J you would have played the queen. This information, thus coneveyed, is bound to serve as an invaluable aid to him in conducting the defense. As examples, witness Deals 4 and 5, which follow.

Deal 4:

```
            ♠ K Q 9 7
            ♡ 7 3
            ◇ K J 7
            ♣ K 8 4 3
♠ 8 6                      ♠ 5
♡ A 8          N          ♡ Q J 10 9 5 4 2
◇ 10 9 6 5 4  W   E       ◇ A Q 3
♣ 10 9 7 5      S         ♣ 6 2
            ♠ A J 10 4 3 2
            ♡ K 6
            ◇ 8 2
            ♣ A Q J
```

Both sides vulnerable. East dealer.

East	South	West	North
3 ♡	3 ♠	Pass	4 NT*
Pass	5 ♡*	Pass	5 ♠
Pass	Pass	Pass	

West opens the ace of hearts, and you, sitting East, play the queen, thereby denying possession of the king. Whatever your partner now leads to trick two, it will *not* be a heart. If he gets his finger on a diamond, the five-spade contract will be defeated.

The reader might say: "Well, why not play the deuce of hearts on the opening lead? In this case, since I have played the lowest possible heart, my partner will know that I don't want hearts continued and he still will have to make the identical guess that he would have had to make if I had played the queen."

All well and good on this particular deal: the end result would have been the same whether the queen or the deuce of hearts had been played. But suppose the situation had been the one contained in Deal 5?

*The Blackwood Slam Convention.

Deal 5:

```
                  ♠ A K 9 3
                  ♡ Q J 9 4
                  ◊ 7 5
                  ♣ Q 10 7
    ♠ 8 6 4 2        N        ♠ 7 5
    ♡ 6 5                     ♡ K 3 2
    ◊ A 8 4 2    W     E      ◊ Q J 10 9
    ♣ 9 8 3          S        ♣ A K J 4
                  ♠ Q J 10
                  ♡ A 10 8 7
                  ◊ K 6 3
                  ♣ 6 5 2
```

East	South	West	North
1 ◊	Pass	Pass	Double
Pass	2 ♡	Pass	3 ♡
Pass	4 ♡	Pass	Pass
Pass			

West dutifully (and unfortunately) opens the ace of diamonds, and if you play the nine-spot, your partner *may well* interpret it as a come-on signal. True, the nine is your lowest diamond, but, as your partner views it, it is *to him* an unusually high card. If he then continues diamonds, declarer will fulfill his contract.

But if, on your partner's lead of the ace, you properly play the queen of diamonds, no misunderstanding can develop, for your partner will know that you don't have the king. He will then almost certainly shift to clubs, since by looking at dummy he will realize that you figure to possess club strength for your opening bid. You will now take three club tricks, to defeat the contract.

The Suit-Preference Signal
(Deals 6–10)

This is a conventional signal that is put to excellent use by the better players but is misapplied by the majority of bridge players. Before introducing it, let us take another look at the come-on signal *(See* Chapter 10) in its normal, frequently recurring application.

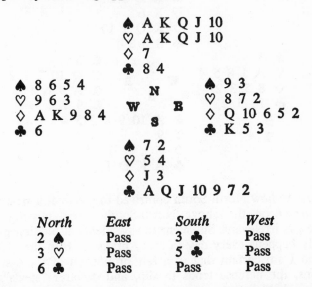

	North	East	South	West
	2 ♠	Pass	3 ♣	Pass
	3 ♡	Pass	5 ♣	Pass
	6 ♣	Pass	Pass	Pass

Your partner opens the king of diamonds against the six-club contract. Glancing at the dummy, you may feel quite pessimistic, for at the moment your king of trumps looks as if it will be trapped. But on closer examination, if you can get your partner to continue diamonds, dummy will ruff and thus be reduced to one trump. Your king of clubs will then become untrappable. So, on partner's lead of the diamond king, you play the "unnecessarily high" ten of diamonds—urging the continuation—and when partner continues diamonds, forcing dummy to ruff, declarer can no longer take two finesses through your king of trumps; and you eventually make your trump king, for the setting trick.

Deal 6:
We now come to the suit-preference signal, which at first glance may appear to be related to East's come-on signal of the ten-spot of diamonds on the preceding deal. Actually, *there is no relationship whatsoever.*

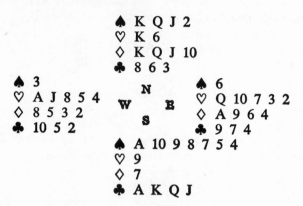

```
                    ♠ K Q J 2
                    ♡ K 6
                    ◇ K Q J 10
                    ♣ 8 6 3
  ♠ 3                      N          ♠ 6
  ♡ A J 8 5 4       W            E    ♡ Q 10 7 3 2
  ◇ 8 5 3 2                S          ◇ A 9 6 4
  ♣ 10 5 2                           ♣ 9 7 4
                    ♠ A 10 9 8 7 5 4
                    ♡ 9
                    ◇ 7
                    ♣ A K Q J
```

As to how North-South contrived to arrive at a *six-spade contract* on the above North-South cards, missing two aces, is irrelevant. Sufficient to say, identical bidding probably happens every day in every bridge club in the U.S.A. And I am certain that in a fair proportion of these situations, the defense tends to slip, and declarer "steals" his "unmakable" contract.

Against South's six-spade contract, West opened the ace of hearts, which won the trick. At a loss as to what to play next, West decided to switch to a club, and declarer waltzed home with his contract, discarding his singleton diamond on dummy's king of hearts. Had West shifted to a diamond at trick two, East would have cashed his ace. How could the defenders have gotten together to direct their defense—specifically to have gotten West to lead a diamond at trick two? Answer: THE SUIT-PREFERENCE SIGNAL.

The purpose of this signal is to eliminate the guesswork as to which of *two suits* partner should lead in situations analogous to the one just presented. The reference to "two suits" may appear to be a typographical error. Actually, it is not. Of the four suits, the trump suit is eliminated automatically, for when partner gives any signal whatsoever, it is never to direct the lead of the trump suit. Also, the suit that is being led, on which the suit-preference signal is given, is excluded. That leaves the leader with a choice of two "obvious" suits. In the above deal, after West cashed the heart ace at trick one, either a heart continuation or a trump lead was illogical. So it became a choice of diamonds or clubs, the two obvious suits.

On the lead of the ace of hearts, had East-West been employing the suit-preference signal, East would have played the *ten* of hearts, which, upon West's examination of the dummy, could not have been construed as asking for a heart continuation. The ten-spot would have said to West: "Play the *higher ranking* of the two obvious suits!" Obeying the signal, West would now have led a diamond (the higher ranking suit) instead of clubs (the lower ranking suit), thereby enabling East to cash the ace of diamonds.

Stating the suit-preference signal as a principle, it comes to this:

> Whenever partner plays an unnecessarily high card that is *obviously* not a come-on signal, it commands partner to lead the *higher* of the two self-evident suits; whenever partner plays a very low card that is obviously not a discouraging "no interest in this suit" signal, that low card asks partner to shift to the lower of the two obvious suits. If the leader's partner has no interest in either of the two obvious suits, he should play some intermediate card in the suit being led.

When correctly used, the play of either an unnecessarily high card or an obviously low card will be unmistakable. Partner will invariably make the right shift when you direct him properly.

Deal 7:
I mentioned a few pages back that this suit-preference convention is often misapplied by the majority of bridge players. The reason behind this abuse is that the offenders attempt to apply it indiscriminately. For instance, take a look at this deal, which I saw arise in an average bridge game a few years ago:

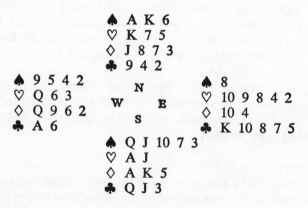

```
              ♠ A K 6
              ♡ K 7 5
              ◇ J 8 7 3
              ♣ 9 4 2
♠ 9 5 4 2          N
♡ Q 6 3
◇ Q 9 6 2    W         E
♣ A 6              S
```

Against South's *four-spade* contract, West elects to open the ace of clubs, East plays *the ten*, and South the three-spot. West, having recently discovered that there is a new toy called the "suit-preference signal," now demonstrates his learning by banging down the queen of hearts, saying to himself: "My partner's ten of clubs was a signal to me to lead the higher of the two obvious suits." Utter nonsense!! Partner wanted clubs continued, and so he, conventional fashion, played the unnecessarily high ten-spot. The suit-preference signal is used only when it MUST BE OBVIOUS that partner wants another suit to be led. The actual deal was:

```
              ♠ A K 6
              ♡ K 7 5
              ◇ J 8 7 3
              ♣ 9 4 2
♠ 9 5 4 2          N          ♠ 8
♡ Q 6 3                       ♡ 10 9 8 4 2
◇ Q 9 6 2    W         E      ◇ 10 4
♣ A 6              S          ♣ K 10 8 7 5
              ♠ Q J 10 7 3
              ♡ A J
              ◇ A K 5
              ♣ Q J 3
```

Deal 8:
On this deal, the suit-preference signal was quite obvious to the West defender, and he made the directed play at

trick two, to defeat South's slam contract. The East defender was Sam Fry, Jr.

	♠ A J 3		
	♡ 9		
	◇ K Q 9 5 2		
	♣ Q J 8 5		

♠ 8
♡ A K Q J 6
◇ J 10 8 4
♣ 10 9 7

♠ 4
♡ 10 8 7 5 4 2
◇ A 3
♣ 6 4 3 2

♠ K Q 10 9 7 6 5 2
♡ 3
◇ 7 6
♣ A K

West	North	East	South
1 ♡	Double	4 ♡	6 ♠
Pass	Pass	Pass	

West opened the king of hearts, upon which East played the ten-spot. West now shifted to a diamond, and East's ace captured the setting trick. Had West led anything but a diamond at trick two, South would have fulfilled his contract by discarding his two diamonds on dummy's Q J of clubs.

From West's point of view, East's ten of hearts play *had to be* a suit-preference signal. On South's leap to six spades, he was marked with a long, solid spade suit. Assuredly East, by playing the unusually high ten of hearts (the highest that East could have held, as West could see by looking at his own hand), could not be asking for a heart coninuation, since nothing could ever be gained by forcing dummy to ruff with the three of trumps. Hence, the ten of hearts was a signal to West to play the higher ranking of the two *obvious* suits: diamonds versus clubs.

Deal 9:
This deal depicts a most imaginative application of the

suit-preference signal. The deal arose in the National Women's Pairs Championships of 1950.

```
              ♠ 10 6 5 2
              ♡ A K 10 9 8
              ◇ Q 7
              ♣ 10 9
♠ A J 8 7                      ♠ K Q
♡ Q J 7          N             ♡ 6 4 2
◇ A 10 9 6   W      E          ◇ J 8 5 4 3 2
♣ 7 5            S             ♣ J 4
              ♠ 9 4 3
              ♡ 5 3
              ◇ K
              ♣ A K Q 8 6 3 2
```

South	West	North	East
1 ♣	Double	1 ♡	2 ◇
3 ♣	3 ◇	4 ♣	Pass
Pass	Pass		

West opened the ace of diamonds, and East paused for consideration. As East viewed the situation, West figured to have four diamonds for her raise to three diamonds. Had West held the A K x x of diamonds, she would have opened the king. Hence, West was assumed (by East) to hold the A 10 9 6 of diamonds, which left the South declarer with an original holding of the singleton king.

Anticipating the fall of South's king of diamonds at trick one, East played *the jack* of diamonds on West's lead of the ace. And, as expected by East, South's king fell. From West's point of view, it was quite apparent that East did not want diamonds continued, with dummy's queen of diamonds being the highest ranking diamond remaining. So West properly interpreted East's jack of diamonds as a suit-preference signal, demanding the lead of the higher ranking of the obvious suits (spades versus hearts).

West, at trick two, led a low spade, which East won with the king. When East returned the queen of spades, West knew that East had started with doubleton K Q of spades, for conventionally, if East had held the K Q x, or the K Q x x x, etc., she would have captured the initial spade lead with the queen, the lower of adjacent picture cards. So West overtook partner's queen of spades and cashed the spade jack, for the setting trick.

I do not know the names of the East-West defenders, but when they apply for membership to Bridgedom's Hall of Fame, I suggest to them that they use this deal as a reference.

Deal 10:
Probably the most frequent situation in which the suit-preference signal is applied is when you are returning a suit that your partner is obviously going to trump, and you want to direct him to then play back a specific suit so that you can quickly reobtain the lead and give him another ruff. The denomination of the card that you lead when you give him his first ruff becomes the clear-cut signal: if you play an unnecessarily high card, he is to return the higher ranking of the two obvious suits (the trump suit and the suit being ruffed are eliminated); if you play an obviously low card instead, he is to return the lower ranking of the two obvious suits. To illustrate:

```
                 ♠ J 7 2
                 ♡ Q J 4
                 ◇ 5 4 3
                 ♣ K Q J 2
  ♠ 9 6 5              N        ♠ 8 3
  ♡ 10 8 6                      ♡ A 7 5 3
  ◇ Q 10 9 8 6 2   W       E    ◇ J 7
  ♣ 3               S           ♣ A 9 8 5 4
                 ♠ A K Q 10 4
                 ♡ K 9 2
                 ◇ A K
                 ♣ 10 7 6
```

Against South's *four-spade* contract, West opens the three of clubs, dummy plays low, and East's ace captures the trick as South follows with the six-spot. It is, of course,

perfectly apparent to East that the three-spot was a singleton, for it could not have been the fourth best, nor could
it have been the top card of a worthless doubleton or
tripleton. So East is going to return a club for West to
trump—and employing the suit-preference signal, he returns the *nine-spot*. When West trumps this trick, he recognizes the nine-spot as being unnecessarily high, and he
now plays back a heart (as opposed to a diamond), which
East captures with his ace. East then returns another club
for West to trump, for the setting trick. It is apparent that
if West had not played back a heart, declarer would have
captured any other return, drawn trumps, and fulfilled his
contract.

Suppose this had been the set-up:

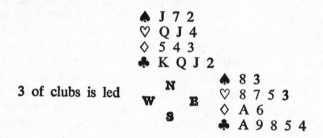

```
            ♠ J 7 2
            ♡ Q J 4
            ◊ 5 4 3
            ♣ K Q J 2
                            ♠ 8 3
3 of clubs is led     N     ♡ 8 7 5 3
                 W     E    ◊ A 6
                    S       ♣ A 9 8 5 4
```

East, upon capturing the three of clubs with his ace,
would now lead back the *four* of clubs—obviously the lowest possible club, since the three and four are in evidence—
directing West to return the lower of the two obvious suits
(*diamonds* versus hearts); and, upon its being done, East
would win with the ace and return another club for East to
ruff.

As is apparent, the suit-preference signal is a most useful weapon for the defending side to possess.

What to Play When Partner Opens an
Ace Against a No-Trump Contract
(Deals 11 and 12)

It is a relatively rare case when an ace is the opening lead against a no-trump contract. When this lead is made, it denotes a specific type of suit in the leader's hand: long and almost solid (A K J 10 x x; A K Q x x x, etc.)

It is accepted as standard procedure that, when your partner opens an ace against declarer's no-trump contract, you follow with *your highest card in that suit* regardless of its denomination. In so doing, you will very often convey most important information to him.

Let us look at two illustrations, as contained in Deals 11 and 12.

Deal 11:

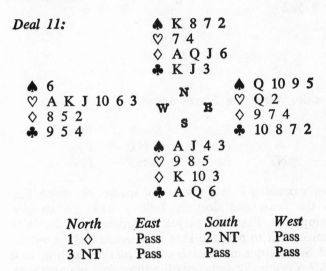

```
                    ♠ K 8 7 2
                    ♡ 7 4
                    ♢ A Q J 6
                    ♣ K J 3
    ♠ 6                             ♠ Q 10 9 5
    ♡ A K J 10 6 3      N           ♡ Q 2
    ♢ 8 5 2         W       E       ♢ 9 7 4
    ♣ 9 5 4             S           ♣ 10 8 7 2
                    ♠ A J 4 3
                    ♡ 9 8 5
                    ♢ K 10 3
                    ♣ A Q 6
```

North	East	South	West
1 ◇	Pass	2 NT	Pass
3 NT	Pass	Pass	Pass

If you do not approve of South's jump to two no-trump, you are part of the majority. All too often, unfortunately, bids like this are made, and the maximum result is obtained.

West opens the ace of hearts, and, if East plays the discouraging deuce, West will undoubtedly shift to some other suit for fear that if, instead, he next leads the king of hearts, he will establish declarer's (hypothetical) queen.

But following convention, on West's lead of the heart ace East plays the queen—and declarer has plenty of time to reflect about his jump to two no-trump as West cashes six heart tricks.

Deal 12:

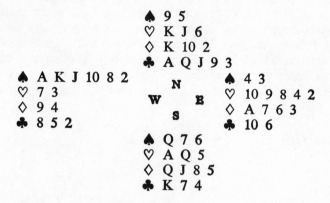

```
                    ♠ 9 5
                    ♡ K J 6
                    ◇ K 10 2
                    ♣ A Q J 9 3
♠ A K J 10 8 2           N            ♠ 4 3
♡ 7 3                                 ♡ 10 9 8 4 2
◇ 9 4              W         E         ◇ A 7 6 3
♣ 8 5 2                   S            ♣ 10 6
                    ♠ Q 7 6
                    ♡ A Q 5
                    ◇ Q J 8 5
                    ♣ K 7 4
```

Both sides vulnerable. North dealer.

North	East	South	West
1 ♣	Pass	2 NT	Pass
3 NT	Pass	Pass	Pass

West's opening lead is the ace of spades, on which East plays the *four,* and declarer follows with the six-spot. Knowing that East has played his highest spade, West recognizes that to play the king now would make a winner out of South's queen, since South is marked with at least the Q 7 6 originally (who has the three-spot is unknown). West therefore discontinues the spade suit—and no matter what other suit he elects to lead at trick two, South will go down, for sooner or later East will obtain the lead via the ace of diamonds and will then return his remaining spade, trapping South's queen.

If West cashes the king of spades at trick two, he will establish South's queen of spades as declarer's ninth, and game-going, trick.

A CATALOGUE OF
SELECTED DOVER BOOKS
IN ALL FIELDS OF INTEREST

A CATALOGUE OF SELECTED DOVER
BOOKS IN ALL FIELDS OF INTEREST

RACKHAM'S COLOR ILLUSTRATIONS FOR WAGNER'S RING. Rackham's finest mature work—all 64 full-color watercolors in a faithful and lush interpretation of the *Ring*. Full-sized plates on coated stock of the paintings used by opera companies for authentic staging of Wagner. Captions aid in following complete Ring cycle. Introduction. 64 illustrations plus vignettes. 72pp. 8⅝ x 11¼.   23779-6 Pa. $6.00

CONTEMPORARY POLISH POSTERS IN FULL COLOR, edited by Joseph Czestochowski. 46 full-color examples of brilliant school of Polish graphic design, selected from world's first museum (near Warsaw) dedicated to poster art. Posters on circuses, films, plays, concerts all show cosmopolitan influences, free imagination. Introduction. 48pp. 9⅜ x 12¼.
23780-X Pa. $6.00

GRAPHIC WORKS OF EDVARD MUNCH, Edvard Munch. 90 haunting, evocative prints by first major Expressionist artist and one of the greatest graphic artists of his time: *The Scream, Anxiety, Death Chamber, The Kiss, Madonna,* etc. Introduction by Alfred Werner. 90pp. 9 x 12.
23765-6 Pa. $5.00

THE GOLDEN AGE OF THE POSTER, Hayward and Blanche Cirker. 70 extraordinary posters in full colors, from Maitres de l'Affiche, Mucha, Lautrec, Bradley, Cheret, Beardsley, many others. Total of 78pp. 9⅜ x 12¼.   22753-7 Pa. $5.95

THE NOTEBOOKS OF LEONARDO DA VINCI, edited by J. P. Richter. Extracts from manuscripts reveal great genius; on painting, sculpture, anatomy, sciences, geography, etc. Both Italian and English. 186 ms. pages reproduced, plus 500 additional drawings, including studies for *Last Supper*, Sforza monument, etc. 860pp. 7⅞ x 10¾. (Available in U.S. only)
22572-0, 22573-9 Pa., Two-vol. set $15.90

THE CODEX NUTTALL, as first edited by Zelia Nuttall. Only inexpensive edition, in full color, of a pre-Columbian Mexican (Mixtec) book. 88 color plates show kings, gods, heroes, temples, sacrifices. New explanatory, historical introduction by Arthur G. Miller. 96pp. 11⅜ x 8½. (Available in U.S. only)   23168-2 Pa. $7.95

UNE SEMAINE DE BONTÉ, A SURREALISTIC NOVEL IN COLLAGE, Max Ernst. Masterpiece created out of 19th-century periodical illustrations, explores worlds of terror and surprise. Some consider this Ernst's greatest work. 208pp. 8⅛ x 11.   23252-2 Pa. $5.00

DRAWINGS OF WILLIAM BLAKE, William Blake. 92 plates from Book of Job, *Divine Comedy, Paradise Lost*, visionary heads, mythological figures, Laocoon, etc. Selection, introduction, commentary by Sir Geoffrey Keynes. 178pp. 8⅛ x 11.   22303-5 Pa. $4.00

ENGRAVINGS OF HOGARTH, William Hogarth. 101 of Hogarth's greatest works: *Rake's Progress, Harlot's Progress, Illustrations for Hudibras, Before and After, Beer Street and Gin Lane*, many more. Full commentary. 256pp. 11 x 13¾.   22479-1 Pa. $12.95

DAUMIER: 120 GREAT LITHOGRAPHS, Honore Daumier. Wide-ranging collection of lithographs by the greatest caricaturist of the 19th century. Concentrates on eternally popular series on lawyers, on married life, on liberated women, etc. Selection, introduction, and notes on plates by Charles F. Ramus. Total of 158pp. 9⅜ x 12¼.   23512-2 Pa. $5.50

DRAWINGS OF MUCHA, Alphonse Maria Mucha. Work reveals draftsman of highest caliber: studies for famous posters and paintings, renderings for book illustrations and ads, etc. 70 works, 9 in color; including 6 items not drawings. Introduction. List of illustrations. 72pp. 9⅜ x 12¼. (Available in U.S. only)   23672-2 Pa. $4.00

GIOVANNI BATTISTA PIRANESI: DRAWINGS IN THE PIERPONT MORGAN LIBRARY, Giovanni Battista Piranesi. For first time ever all of Morgan Library's collection, world's largest. 167 illustrations of rare Piranesi drawings—archeological, architectural, decorative and visionary. Essay, detailed list of drawings, chronology, captions. Edited by Felice Stampfle. 144pp. 9⅜ x 12¼.   23714-1 Pa. $7.50

NEW YORK ETCHINGS (1905-1949), John Sloan. All of important American artist's N.Y. life etchings. 67 works include some of his best art; also lively historical record—Greenwich Village, tenement scenes. Edited by Sloan's widow. Introduction and captions. 79pp. 8⅜ x 11¼.   23651-X Pa. $4.00

CHINESE PAINTING AND CALLIGRAPHY: A PICTORIAL SURVEY, Wan-go Weng. 69 fine examples from John M. Crawford's matchless private collection: landscapes, birds, flowers, human figures, etc., plus calligraphy. Every basic form included: hanging scrolls, handscrolls, album leaves, fans, etc. 109 illustrations. Introduction. Captions. 192pp. 8⅞ x 11¾.   23707-9 Pa. $7.95

DRAWINGS OF REMBRANDT, edited by Seymour Slive. Updated Lippmann, Hofstede de Groot edition, with definitive scholarly apparatus. All portraits, biblical sketches, landscapes, nudes, Oriental figures, classical studies, together with selection of work by followers. 550 illustrations. Total of 630pp. 9⅛ x 12¼.   21485-0, 21486-9 Pa., Two-vol. set $15.00

THE DISASTERS OF WAR, Francisco Goya. 83 etchings record horrors of Napoleonic wars in Spain and war in general. Reprint of 1st edition, plus 3 additional plates. Introduction by Philip Hofer. 97pp. 9⅜ x 8¼.   21872-4 Pa. $3.75

THE EARLY WORK OF AUBREY BEARDSLEY, Aubrey Beardsley. 157 plates, 2 in color: *Manon Lescaut, Madame Bovary, Morte Darthur, Salome,* other. Introduction by H. Marillier. 182pp. 8⅛ x 11. 21816-3 Pa. $4.50

THE LATER WORK OF AUBREY BEARDSLEY, Aubrey Beardsley. Exotic masterpieces of full maturity: *Venus and Tannhauser, Lysistrata, Rape of the Lock, Volpone,* Savoy material, etc. 174 plates, 2 in color. 186pp. 8⅛ x 11. 21817-1 Pa. $4.50

THOMAS NAST'S CHRISTMAS DRAWINGS, Thomas Nast. Almost all Christmas drawings by creator of image of Santa Claus as we know it, and one of America's foremost illustrators and political cartoonists. 66 illustrations. 3 illustrations in color on covers. 96pp. 8⅜ x 11¼.
23660-9 Pa. $3.50

THE DORÉ ILLUSTRATIONS FOR DANTE'S DIVINE COMEDY, Gustave Doré. All 135 plates from Inferno, Purgatory, Paradise; fantastic tortures, infernal landscapes, celestial wonders. Each plate with appropriate (translated) verses. 141pp. 9 x 12. 23231-X Pa. $4.50

DORÉ'S ILLUSTRATIONS FOR RABELAIS, Gustave Doré. 252 striking illustrations of *Gargantua and Pantagruel* books by foremost 19th-century illustrator. Including 60 plates, 192 delightful smaller illustrations. 153pp. **9 x 12.** 23656-0 Pa. $5.00

LONDON: A PILGRIMAGE, Gustave Doré, Blanchard Jerrold. Squalor, riches, misery, beauty of mid-Victorian metropolis; 55 wonderful plates, 125 other illustrations, full social, cultural text by Jerrold. 191pp. of text. 9⅜ x 12¼. 22306-X Pa. $7.00

THE RIME OF THE ANCIENT MARINER, Gustave Doré, S. T. Coleridge. Dore's finest work, 34 plates capture moods, subtleties of poem. Full text. Introduction by Millicent Rose. 77pp. 9¼ x 12. 22305-1 Pa. $3.50

THE DORE BIBLE ILLUSTRATIONS, Gustave Doré. All wonderful, detailed plates: Adam and Eve, Flood, Babylon, Life of Jesus, etc. Brief King James text with each plate. Introduction by Millicent Rose. 241 plates. 241pp. 9 x 12. 23004-X Pa. $6.00

THE COMPLETE ENGRAVINGS, ETCHINGS AND DRYPOINTS OF ALBRECHT DURER. "Knight, Death and Devil"; "Melencolia," and more—all Dürer's known works in all three media, including 6 works formerly attributed to him. 120 plates. 235pp. 8⅜ x 11¼.
22851-7 Pa. $6.50

MAXIMILIAN'S TRIUMPHAL ARCH, Albrecht Dürer and others. Incredible monument of woodcut art: 8 foot high elaborate arch—heraldic figures, humans, battle scenes, fantastic elements—that you can assemble yourself. Printed on one side, layout for assembly. 143pp. 11 x 16.
21451-6 Pa. $5.00

THE COMPLETE WOODCUTS OF ALBRECHT DURER, edited by Dr. W. Kurth. 346 in all: "Old Testament," "St. Jerome," "Passion," "Life of Virgin," Apocalypse," many others. Introduction by Campbell Dodgson. 285pp. 8½ x 12¼. 21097-9 Pa. $7.50

DRAWINGS OF ALBRECHT DURER, edited by Heinrich Wolfflin. 81 plates show development from youth to full style. Many favorites; many new. Introduction by Alfred Werner. 96pp. 8⅛ x 11. 22352-3 Pa. $5.00

THE HUMAN FIGURE, Albrecht Dürer. Experiments in various techniques—stereometric, progressive proportional, and others. Also life studies that rank among finest ever done. Complete reprinting of *Dresden Sketchbook*. 170 plates. 355pp. 8⅜ x 11¼. 21042-1 Pa. $7.95

OF THE JUST SHAPING OF LETTERS, Albrecht Dürer. Renaissance artist explains design of Roman majuscules by geometry, also Gothic lower and capitals. Grolier Club edition. 43pp. 7⅞ x 10¾ 21306-4 Pa. $3.00

TEN BOOKS ON ARCHITECTURE, Vitruvius. The most important book ever written on architecture. Early Roman aesthetics, technology, classical orders, site selection, all other aspects. Stands behind everything since. Morgan translation. 331pp. 5⅜ x 8½. 20645-9 Pa. $4.50

THE FOUR BOOKS OF ARCHITECTURE, Andrea Palladio. 16th-century classic responsible for Palladian movement and style. Covers classical architectural remains, Renaissance revivals, classical orders, etc. 1738 Ware English edition. Introduction by A. Placzek. 216 plates. 110pp. of text. 9½ x 12¾. 21308-0 Pa. $10.00

HORIZONS, Norman Bel Geddes. Great industrialist stage designer, "father of streamlining," on application of aesthetics to transportation, amusement, architecture, etc. 1932 prophetic account; function, theory, specific projects. 222 illustrations. 312pp. 7⅞ x 10¾. 23514-9 Pa. $6.95

FRANK LLOYD WRIGHT'S FALLINGWATER, Donald Hoffmann. Full, illustrated story of conception and building of Wright's masterwork at Bear Run, Pa. 100 photographs of site, construction, and details of completed structure. 112pp. 9¼ x 10. 23671-4 Pa. $5.50

THE ELEMENTS OF DRAWING, John Ruskin. Timeless classic by great Viltorian; starts with basic ideas, works through more difficult. Many practical exercises. 48 illustrations. Introduction by Lawrence Campbell. 228pp. 5⅜ x 8½. 22730-8 Pa. $3.75

GIST OF ART, John Sloan. Greatest modern American teacher, Art Students League, offers innumerable hints, instructions, guided comments to help you in painting. Not a formal course. 46 illustrations. Introduction by Helen Sloan. 200pp. 5⅜ x 8½. 23435-5 Pa. $4.00

THE ANATOMY OF THE HORSE, George Stubbs. Often considered the great masterpiece of animal anatomy. Full reproduction of 1766 edition, plus prospectus; original text and modernized text. 36 plates. Introduction by Eleanor Garvey. 121pp. 11 x 14¾. 23402-9 Pa. $6.00

BRIDGMAN'S LIFE DRAWING, George B. Bridgman. More than 500 illustrative drawings and text teach you to abstract the body into its major masses, use light and shade, proportion; as well as specific areas of anatomy, of which Bridgman is master. 192pp. 6½ x 9¼. (Available in U.S. only) 22710-3 Pa. $3.50

ART NOUVEAU DESIGNS IN COLOR, Alphonse Mucha, Maurice Verneuil, Georges Auriol. Full-color reproduction of *Combinaisons ornementales* (c. 1900) by Art Nouveau masters. Floral, animal, geometric, interlacings, swashes—borders, frames, spots—all incredibly beautiful. 60 plates, hundreds of designs. 9⅜ x 8-1/16. 22885-1 Pa. $4.00

FULL-COLOR FLORAL DESIGNS IN THE ART NOUVEAU STYLE, E. A. Seguy. 166 motifs, on 40 plates, from *Les fleurs et leurs applications decoratives* (1902): borders, circular designs, repeats, allovers, "spots." All in authentic Art Nouveau colors. 48pp. 9⅜ x 12¼.
23439-8 Pa. $5.00

A DIDEROT PICTORIAL ENCYCLOPEDIA OF TRADES AND IN-DUSTRY, edited by Charles C. Gillispie. 485 most interesting plates from the great French Encyclopedia of the 18th century show hundreds of working figures, artifacts, process, land and cityscapes; glassmaking, paper-making, metal extraction, construction, weaving, making furniture, clothing, wigs, dozens of other activities. Plates fully explained. 920pp. 9 x 12.
22284-5, 22285-3 Clothbd., Two-vol. set $40.00

HANDBOOK OF EARLY ADVERTISING ART, Clarence P. Hornung. Largest collection of copyright-free early and antique advertising art ever compiled. Over 6,000 illustrations, from Franklin's time to the 1890's for special effects, novelty. Valuable source, almost inexhaustible.
Pictorial Volume. Agriculture, the zodiac, animals, autos, birds, Christmas, fire engines, flowers, trees, musical instruments, ships, games and sports, much more. Arranged by subject matter and use. 237 plates. 288pp. 9 x 12.
20122-8 Clothbd. $14..50

Typographical Volume. Roman and Gothic faces ranging from 10 point to 300 point, "Barnum," German and Old English faces, script, logotypes, scrolls and flourishes, 1115 ornamental initials, 67 complete alphabets, more. 310 plates. 320pp. 9 x 12. 20123-6 Clothbd. $15.00

CALLIGRAPHY (CALLIGRAPHIA LATINA), J. G. Schwandner. High point of 18th-century ornamental calligraphy. Very ornate initials, scrolls, borders, cherubs, birds, lettered examples. 172pp. 9 x 13.
20475-8 Pa. $7.00

ART FORMS IN NATURE, Ernst Haeckel. Multitude of strangely beautiful natural forms: Radiolaria, Foraminifera, jellyfishes, fungi, turtles, bats, etc. All 100 plates of the 19th-century evolutionist's *Kunstformen der Natur* (1904). 100pp. 9⅜ x 12¼.   22987-4 Pa. $5.00

CHILDREN: A PICTORIAL ARCHIVE FROM NINETEENTH-CENTURY SOURCES, edited by Carol Belanger Grafton. 242 rare, copyright-free wood engravings for artists and designers. Widest such selection available. All illustrations in line. 119pp. 8⅜ x 11¼.
23694-3 Pa. $3.50

WOMEN: A PICTORIAL ARCHIVE FROM NINETEENTH-CENTURY SOURCES, edited by Jim Harter. 391 copyright-free wood engravings for artists and designers selected from rare periodicals. Most extensive such collection available. All illustrations in line. 128pp. 9 x 12.
23703-6 Pa. $4.50

ARABIC ART IN COLOR, Prisse d'Avennes. From the greatest ornamentalists of all time—50 plates in color, rarely seen outside the Near East, rich in suggestion and stimulus. Includes 4 plates on covers. 46pp. 9⅜ x 12¼.   23658-7 Pa. $6.00

AUTHENTIC ALGERIAN CARPET DESIGNS AND MOTIFS, edited by June Beveridge. Algerian carpets are world famous. Dozens of geometrical motifs are charted on grids, color-coded, for weavers, needleworkers, craftsmen, designers. 53 illustrations plus 4 in color. 48pp. 8¼ x 11. (Available in U.S. only)   23650-1 Pa. $1.75

DICTIONARY OF AMERICAN PORTRAITS, edited by Hayward and Blanche Cirker. 4000 important Americans, earliest times to 1905, mostly in clear line. Politicians, writers, soldiers, scientists, inventors, industrialists, Indians, Blacks, women, outlaws, etc. Identificatory information. 756pp. 9¼ x 12¾.   21823-6 Clothbd. $40.00

HOW THE OTHER HALF LIVES, Jacob A. Riis. Journalistic record of filth, degradation, upward drive in New York immigrant slums, shops, around 1900. New edition includes 100 original Riis photos, monuments of early photography. 233pp. 10 x 7⅞.   22012-5 Pa. $7.00

NEW YORK IN THE THIRTIES, Berenice Abbott. Noted photographer's fascinating study of city shows new buildings that have become famous and old sights that have disappeared forever. Insightful commentary. 97 photographs. 97pp. 11⅜ x 10.   22967-X Pa. $5.00

MEN AT WORK, Lewis W. Hine. Famous photographic studies of construction workers, railroad men, factory workers and coal miners. New supplement of 18 photos on Empire State building construction. New introduction by Jonathan L. Doherty. Total of 69 photos. 63pp. 8 x 10¾.
23475-4 Pa. $3.00

THE DEPRESSION YEARS AS PHOTOGRAPHED BY ARTHUR ROTH-STEIN, Arthur Rothstein. First collection devoted entirely to the work of outstanding 1930s photographer: famous dust storm photo, ragged children, unemployed, etc. 120 photographs. Captions. 119pp. 9¼ x 10¾.
23590-4 Pa. $5.00

CAMERA WORK: A PICTORIAL GUIDE, Alfred Stieglitz. All 559 illustrations and plates from the most important periodical in the history of art photography, Camera Work (1903-17). Presented four to a page, reduced in size but still clear, in strict chronological order, with complete captions. Three indexes. Glossary. Bibliography. 176pp. 8⅜ x 11¼.
23591-2 Pa. $6.95

ALVIN LANGDON COBURN, PHOTOGRAPHER, Alvin L. Coburn. Revealing autobiography by one of greatest photographers of 20th century gives insider's version of Photo-Secession, plus comments on his own work. 77 photographs by Coburn. Edited by Helmut and Alison Gernsheim. 160pp. 8⅛ x 11.
23685-4 Pa. $6.00

NEW YORK IN THE FORTIES, Andreas Feininger. 162 brilliant photographs by the well-known photographer, formerly with Life magazine, show commuters, shoppers, Times Square at night, Harlem nightclub, Lower East Side, etc. Introduction and full captions by John von Hartz. 181pp. 9¼ x 10¾.
23585-8 Pa. $6.00

GREAT NEWS PHOTOS AND THE STORIES BEHIND THEM, John Faber. Dramatic volume of 140 great news photos, 1855 through 1976, and revealing stories behind them, with both historical and technical information. Hindenburg disaster, shooting of Oswald, nomination of Jimmy Carter, etc. 160pp. 8¼ x 11.
23667-6 Pa. $5.00

THE ART OF THE CINEMATOGRAPHER, Leonard Maltin. Survey of American cinematography history and anecdotal interviews with 5 masters—Arthur Miller, Hal Mohr, Hal Rosson, Lucien Ballard, and Conrad Hall. Very large selection of behind-the-scenes production photos. 105 photographs. Filmographies. Index. Originally Behind the Camera. 144pp. 8¼ x 11.
23686-2 Pa. $5.00

DESIGNS FOR THE THREE-CORNERED HAT (LE TRICORNE), Pablo Picasso. 32 fabulously rare drawings—including 31 color illustrations of costumes and accessories—for 1919 production of famous ballet. Edited by Parmenia Migel, who has written new introduction. 48pp. 9⅜ x 12¼. (Available in U.S. only)
23709-5 Pa. $5.00

NOTES OF A FILM DIRECTOR, Sergei Eisenstein. Greatest Russian filmmaker explains montage, making of Alexander Nevsky, aesthetics; comments on self, associates, great rivals (Chaplin), similar material. 78 illustrations. 240pp. 5⅜ x 8½.
22392-2 Pa. $4.50

HOLLYWOOD GLAMOUR PORTRAITS, edited by John Kobal. 145 photos capture the stars from 1926-49, the high point in portrait photography. Gable, Harlow, Bogart, Bacall, Hedy Lamarr, Marlene Dietrich, Robert Montgomery, Marlon Brando, Veronica Lake; 94 stars in all. Full background on photographers, technical aspects, much more. Total of 160pp. 8⅜ x 11¼. 23352-9 Pa. **$6.00**

THE NEW YORK STAGE: FAMOUS PRODUCTIONS IN PHOTO-GRAPHS, edited by Stanley Appelbaum. 148 photographs from Museum of City of New York show 142 plays, 1883-1939. *Peter Pan, The Front Page, Dead End, Our Town,* O'Neill, hundreds of actors and actresses, etc. Full indexes. 154pp. 9½ x 10. 23241-7 Pa. **$6.00**

DIALOGUES CONCERNING TWO NEW SCIENCES, Galileo Galilei. Encompassing 30 years of experiment and thought, these dialogues deal with geometric demonstrations of fracture of solid bodies, cohesion, leverage, speed of light and sound, pendulums, falling bodies, accelerated motion, etc. 300pp. 5⅜ x 8½. 60099-8 Pa. **$4.00**

THE GREAT OPERA STARS IN HISTORIC PHOTOGRAPHS, edited by James Camner. 343 portraits from the 1850s to the 1940s: Tamburini, Mario, Caliapin, Jeritza, Melchior, Melba, Patti, Pinza, Schipa, Caruso, Farrar, Steber, Gobbi, and many more—270 performers in all. Index. 199pp. 8⅜ x 11¼. 23575-0 Pa. **$6.50**

J. S. BACH, Albert Schweitzer. Great full-length study of Bach, life, background to music, music, by foremost modern scholar. Ernest Newman translation. 650 musical examples. Total of 928pp. 5⅜ x 8½. (Available in U.S. only) 21631-4, 21632-2 Pa., Two-vol. set **$11.00**

COMPLETE PIANO SONATAS, Ludwig van Beethoven. All sonatas in the fine Schenker edition, with fingering, analytical material. One of best modern editions. Total of 615pp. 9 x 12. (Available in U.S. only) 23134-8, 23135-6 Pa., Two-vol. set **$15.00**

KEYBOARD MUSIC, J. S. Bach. Bach-Gesellschaft edition. For harpsichord, piano, other keyboard instruments. English Suites, French Suites, Six Partitas, Goldberg Variations, Two-Part Inventions, Three-Part Sinfonias. 312pp. 8⅛ x 11. (Available in U.S. only) 22360-4 Pa. **$6.95**

FOUR SYMPHONIES IN FULL SCORE, Franz Schubert. Schubert's four most popular symphonies: No. 4 in C Minor ("Tragic"); No. 5 in B-flat Major; No. 8 in B Minor ("Unfinished"); No. 9 in C Major ("Great"). Breitkopf & Hartel edition. Study score. 261pp. 9⅜ x 12¼. 23681-1 Pa. **$6.50**

THE AUTHENTIC GILBERT & SULLIVAN SONGBOOK, W. S. Gilbert, A. S. Sullivan. Largest selection available; 92 songs, uncut, original keys, in piano rendering approved by Sullivan. Favorites and lesser-known fine numbers. Edited with plot synopses by James Spero. 3 illustrations. 399pp. 9 x 12. 23482-7 Pa. **$9.95**

PRINCIPLES OF ORCHESTRATION, Nikolay Rimsky-Korsakov. Great classical orchestrator provides fundamentals of tonal resonance, progression of parts, voice and orchestra, tutti effects, much else in major document. 330pp. of musical excerpts. 489pp. 6½ x 9¼. 21266-1 Pa. **$7.50**

TRISTAN UND ISOLDE, Richard Wagner. Full orchestral score with complete instrumentation. Do not confuse with piano reduction. Commentary by Felix Mottl, great Wagnerian conductor and scholar. Study score. 655pp. 8⅛ x 11. 22915-7 Pa. $13.95

REQUIEM IN FULL SCORE, Giuseppe Verdi. Immensely popular with choral groups and music lovers. Republication of edition published by C. F. Peters, Leipzig, n. d. German frontmaker in English translation. Glossary. Text in Latin. Study score. 204pp. 9⅜ x 12¼.
23682-X Pa. $6.00

COMPLETE CHAMBER MUSIC FOR STRINGS, Felix Mendelssohn. All of Mendelssohn's chamber music: Octet, 2 Quintets, 6 Quartets, and Four Pieces for String Quartet. (Nothing with piano is included). Complete works edition (1874-7). Study score. 283 pp. 9⅜ x 12¼.
23679-X Pa. **$7.50**

POPULAR SONGS OF NINETEENTH-CENTURY AMERICA, edited by Richard Jackson. 64 most important songs: "Old Oaken Bucket," "Arkansas Traveler," "Yellow Rose of Texas," etc. Authentic original sheet music, full introduction and commentaries. 290pp. 9 x 12. 23270-0 Pa. **$7.95**

COLLECTED PIANO WORKS, Scott Joplin. Edited by Vera Brodsky Lawrence. Practically all of Joplin's piano works—rags, two-steps, marches, waltzes, etc., 51 works in all. Extensive introduction by Rudi Blesh. Total of 345pp. 9 x 12. 23106-2 Pa. $14.95

BASIC PRINCIPLES OF CLASSICAL BALLET, Agrippina Vaganova. Great Russian theoretician, teacher explains methods for teaching classical ballet; incorporates best from French, Italian, Russian schools. 118 illustrations. 175pp. 5⅜ x 8½. 22036-2 Pa. $2.50

CHINESE CHARACTERS, L. Wieger. Rich analysis of 2300 characters according to traditional systems into primitives. Historical-semantic analysis to phonetics (Classical Mandarin) and radicals. 820pp. 6⅛ x 9¼.
21321-8 Pa. $10.00

EGYPTIAN LANGUAGE: EASY LESSONS IN EGYPTIAN HIERO-GLYPHICS, E. A. Wallis Budge. Foremost Egyptologist offers Egyptian grammar, explanation of hieroglyphics, many reading texts, dictionary of symbols. 246pp. 5 x 7½. (Available in U.S. only)
21394-3 Clothbd. $7.50

AN ETYMOLOGICAL DICTIONARY OF MODERN ENGLISH, Ernest Weekley. Richest, fullest work, by foremost British lexicographer. Detailed word histories. Inexhaustible. Do not confuse this with *Concise Etymological Dictionary*, which is abridged. Total of 856pp. 6½ x 9¼.
21873-2, 21874-0 Pa., Two-vol. set $12.00

A MAYA GRAMMAR, Alfred M. Tozzer. Practical, useful English-language grammar by the Harvard anthropologist who was one of the three greatest American scholars in the area of Maya culture. Phonetics, grammatical processes, syntax, more. 301pp. 5⅜ x 8½.   23465-7 Pa. $4.00

THE JOURNAL OF HENRY D. THOREAU, edited by Bradford Torrey, F. H. Allen. Complete reprinting of 14 volumes, 1837-61, over two million words; the sourcebooks for *Walden*, etc. Definitive. All original sketches, plus 75 photographs. Introduction by Walter Harding. Total of 1804pp. 8½ x 12¼.   20312-3, 20313-1 Clothbd., Two-vol. set $50.00

CLASSIC GHOST STORIES, Charles Dickens and others. 18 wonderful stories you've wanted to reread: "The Monkey's Paw," "The House and the Brain," "The Upper Berth," "The Signalman," "Dracula's Guest," "The Tapestried Chamber," etc. Dickens, Scott, Mary Shelley, Stoker, etc. 330pp. 5⅜ x 8½.   20735-8 Pa. **$4.50**

SEVEN SCIENCE FICTION NOVELS, H. G. Wells. Full novels. *First Men in the Moon, Island of Dr. Moreau, War of the Worlds, Food of the Gods, Invisible Man, Time Machine, In the Days of the Comet.* A basic science-fiction library. 1015pp. 5⅜ x 8½. (Available in U.S. only)
20264-X Clothbd. $8.95

ARMADALE, Wilkie Collins. Third great mystery novel by the author of *The Woman in White* and *The Moonstone.* Ingeniously plotted narrative shows an exceptional command of character, incident and mood. Original magazine version with 40 illustrations. 597pp. 5⅜ x 8½.
23429-0 Pa. $6.00

MASTERS OF MYSTERY, H. Douglas Thomson. The first book in English (1931) devoted to history and aesthetics of detective story. Poe, Doyle, LeFanu, Dickens, many others, up to 1930. New introduction and notes by E. F. Bleiler. 288pp. 5⅜ x 8½. (Available in U.S. only)
23606-4 Pa. $4.00

FLATLAND, E. A. Abbott. Science-fiction classic explores life of 2-D being in 3-D world. Read also as introduction to thought about hyperspace. Introduction by Banesh Hoffmann. 16 illustrations. 103pp. 5⅜ x 8½.
20001-9 Pa. $2.00

THREE SUPERNATURAL NOVELS OF THE VICTORIAN PERIOD, edited, with an introduction, by E. F. Bleiler. Reprinted complete and unabridged, three great classics of the supernatural: *The Haunted Hotel* by Wilkie Collins, *The Haunted House at Latchford* by Mrs. J. H. Riddell, and *The Lost Stradivarius* by J. Meade Falkner. 325pp. 5⅜ x 8½.
22571-2 Pa. $4.00

AYESHA: THE RETURN OF "SHE," H. Rider Haggard. Virtuoso sequel featuring the great mythic creation, Ayesha, in an adventure that is fully as good as the first book, *She.* Original magazine version, with 47 original illustrations by Maurice Greiffenhagen. 189pp. 6½ x 9¼.
23649-8 Pa. $3.50

UNCLE SILAS, J. Sheridan LeFanu. Victorian Gothic mystery novel, considered by many best of period, even better than Collins or Dickens. Wonderful psychological terror. Introduction by Frederick Shroyer. 436pp. 5⅜ x 8½.   21715-9 Pa. $6.00

JURGEN, James Branch Cabell. The great erotic fantasy of the 1920's that delighted thousands, shocked thousands more. Full final text, Lane edition with 13 plates by Frank Pape. 346pp. 5⅜ x 8½.
23507-6 Pa. $4.50

THE CLAVERINGS, Anthony Trollope. Major novel, chronicling aspects of British Victorian society, personalities. Reprint of Cornhill serialization, 16 plates by M. Edwards; first reprint of full text. Introduction by Norman Donaldson. 412pp. 5⅜ x 8½.   23464-9 Pa. $5.00

KEPT IN THE DARK, Anthony Trollope. Unusual short novel about Victorian morality and abnormal psychology by the great English author. Probably the first American publication. Frontispiece by Sir John Millais. 92pp. 6½ x 9¼.   23609-9 Pa. $2.50

RALPH THE HEIR, Anthony Trollope. Forgotten tale of illegitimacy, inheritance. Master novel of Trollope's later years. Victorian country estates, clubs, Parliament, fox hunting, world of fully realized characters. Reprint of 1871 edition. 12 illustrations by F. A. Faser. 434pp. of text. 5⅜ x 8½.   23642-0 Pa. $5.00

YEKL and THE IMPORTED BRIDEGROOM AND OTHER STORIES OF THE NEW YORK GHETTO, Abraham Cahan. Film *Hester Street* based on *Yekl* (1896). Novel, other stories among first about Jewish immigrants of N.Y.'s East Side. Highly praised by W. D. Howells—Cahan "a new star of realism." New introduction by Bernard G. Richards. 240pp. 5⅜ x 8½.   22427-9 Pa. $3.50

THE HIGH PLACE, James Branch Cabell. Great fantasy writer's enchanting comedy of disenchantment set in 18th-century France. Considered by some critics to be even better than his famous *Jurgen*. 10 illustrations and numerous vignettes by noted fantasy artist Frank C. Pape. 320pp. 5⅜ x 8½.   23670-6 Pa. $4.00

ALICE'S ADVENTURES UNDER GROUND, Lewis Carroll. Facsimile of ms. Carroll gave Alice Liddell in 1864. Different in many ways from final Alice. Handlettered, illustrated by Carroll. Introduction by Martin Gardner. 128pp. 5⅜ x 8½.   21482-6 Pa. $2.00

FAVORITE ANDREW LANG FAIRY TALE BOOKS IN MANY COLORS, Andrew Lang. The four Lang favorites in a boxed set—the complete *Red, Green, Yellow* and *Blue* Fairy Books. 164 stories; 439 illustrations by Lancelot Speed, Henry Ford and G. P. Jacomb Hood. Total of about 1500pp. 5⅜ x 8½.   23407-X Boxed set, Pa. $14.95

HOUSEHOLD STORIES BY THE BROTHERS GRIMM. All the great Grimm stories: "Rumpelstiltskin," "Snow White," "Hansel and Gretel," etc., with 114 illustrations by Walter Crane. 269pp. 5⅜ x 8½.
21080-4 Pa. $3.50

SLEEPING BEAUTY, illustrated by Arthur Rackham. Perhaps the fullest, most delightful version ever, told by C. S. Evans. Rackham's best work. 49 illustrations. 110pp. 7⅞ x 10¾. 22756-1 Pa. $2.50

AMERICAN FAIRY TALES, L. Frank Baum. Young cowboy lassoes Father Time; dummy in Mr. Floman's department store window comes to life; and 10 other fairy tales. 41 illustrations by N. P. Hall, Harry Kennedy, Ike Morgan, and Ralph Gardner. 209pp. 5⅜ x 8½. 23643-9 Pa. $3.00

THE WONDERFUL WIZARD OF OZ, L. Frank Baum. Facsimile in full color of America's finest children's classic. Introduction by Martin Gardner. 143 illustrations by W. W. Denslow. 267pp. 5⅜ x 8½.
20691-2 Pa. $3.50

THE TALE OF PETER RABBIT, Beatrix Potter. The inimitable Peter's terrifying adventure in Mr. McGregor's garden, with all 27 wonderful, full-color Potter illustrations. 55pp. 4¼ x 5½. (Available in U.S. only)
22827-4 Pa. $1.25

THE STORY OF KING ARTHUR AND HIS KNIGHTS, Howard Pyle. Finest children's version of life of King Arthur. 48 illustrations by Pyle. 131pp. 6⅛ x 9¼. 21445-1 Pa. $4.95

CARUSO'S CARICATURES, Enrico Caruso. Great tenor's remarkable caricatures of self, fellow musicians, composers, others. Toscanini, Puccini, Farrar, etc. Impish, cutting, insightful. 473 illustrations. Preface by M. Sisca. 217pp. 8⅜ x 11¼. 23528-9 Pa. $6.95

PERSONAL NARRATIVE OF A PILGRIMAGE TO ALMADINAH AND MECCAH, Richard Burton. Great travel classic by remarkably colorful personality. Burton, disguised as a Moroccan, visited sacred shrines of Islam, narrowly escaping death. Wonderful observations of Islamic life, customs, personalities. 47 illustrations. Total of 959pp. 5⅜ x 8½.
21217-3, 21218-1 Pa., Two-vol. set $12.00

INCIDENTS OF TRAVEL IN YUCATAN, John L. Stephens. Classic (1843) exploration of jungles of Yucatan, looking for evidences of Maya civilization. Travel adventures, Mexican and Indian culture, etc. Total of 669pp. 5⅜ x 8½. 20926-1, 20927-X Pa., Two-vol. set $7.90

AMERICAN LITERARY AUTOGRAPHS FROM WASHINGTON IRVING TO HENRY JAMES, Herbert Cahoon, et al. Letters, poems, manuscripts of Hawthorne, Thoreau, Twain, Alcott, Whitman, 67 other prominent American authors. Reproductions, full transcripts and commentary. Plus checklist of all American Literary Autographs in The Pierpont Morgan Library. Printed on exceptionally high-quality paper. 136 illustrations. 212pp. 9⅛ x 12¼. 23548-3 Pa. $12.50

AN AUTOBIOGRAPHY, Margaret Sanger. Exciting personal account of hard-fought battle for woman's right to birth control, against prejudice, church, law. Foremost feminist document. 504pp. 5⅜ x 8½.
20470-7 Pa. $5.50

MY BONDAGE AND MY FREEDOM, Frederick Douglass. Born as a slave, Douglass became outspoken force in antislavery movement. The best of Douglass's autobiographies. Graphic description of slave life. Introduction by P. Foner. 464pp. 5⅜ x 8½. 22457-0 Pa. $5.50

LIVING MY LIFE, Emma Goldman. Candid, no holds barred account by foremost American anarchist: her own life, anarchist movement, famous contemporaries, ideas and their impact. Struggles and confrontations in America, plus deportation to U.S.S.R. Shocking inside account of persecution of anarchists under Lenin. 13 plates. Total of 944pp. 5⅜ x 8½.
22543-7, 22544-5 Pa., Two-vol. set $12.00

LETTERS AND NOTES ON THE MANNERS, CUSTOMS AND CONDITIONS OF THE NORTH AMERICAN INDIANS, George Catlin. Classic account of life among Plains Indians: ceremonies, hunt, warfare, etc. Dover edition reproduces for first time all original paintings. 312 plates. 572pp. of text. 6⅛ x 9¼. 22118-0, 22119-9 Pa.. Two-vol. set $12.00

THE MAYA AND THEIR NEIGHBORS, edited by Clarence L. Hay, others. Synoptic view of Maya civilization in broadest sense, together with Northern, Southern neighbors. Integrates much background, valuable detail not elsewhere. Prepared by greatest scholars: Kroeber, Morley, Thompson, Spinden, Vaillant, many others. Sometimes called Tozzer Memorial Volume. 60 illustrations, linguistic map. 634pp. 5⅜ x 8½.
23510-6 Pa. $7.50

HANDBOOK OF THE INDIANS OF CALIFORNIA, A. L. Kroeber. Foremost American anthropologist offers complete ethnographic study of each group. Monumental classic. 459 illustrations, maps. 995pp. 5⅜ x 8½.
23368-5 Pa. $13.00

SHAKTI AND SHAKTA, Arthur Avalon. First book to give clear, cohesive analysis of Shakta doctrine, Shakta ritual and Kundalini Shakti (yoga). Important work by one of world's foremost students of Shaktic and Tantric thought. 732pp. 5⅜ x 8½. (Available in U.S. only)
23645-5 Pa. $7.95

AN INTRODUCTION TO THE STUDY OF THE MAYA HIEROGLYPHS, Syvanus Griswold Morley. Classic study by one of the truly great figures in hieroglyph research. Still the best introduction for the student for reading Maya hieroglyphs. New introduction by J. Eric S. Thompson. 117 illustrations. 284pp. 5⅜ x 8½. 23108-9 Pa. $4.00

A STUDY OF MAYA ART, Herbert J. Spinden. Landmark classic interprets Maya symbolism, estimates styles, covers ceramics, architecture, murals, stone carvings as artforms. Still a basic book in area. New introduction by J. Eric Thompson. Over 750 illustrations. 341pp. 8⅜ x 11¼.
21235-1 Pa. $6.95

GEOMETRY, RELATIVITY AND THE FOURTH DIMENSION, Rudolf Rucker. Exposition of fourth dimension, means of visualization, concepts of relativity as Flatland characters continue adventures. Popular, easily followed yet accurate, profound. 141 illustrations. 133pp. 5⅜ x 8½.
23400-2 Pa. $2.75

THE ORIGIN OF LIFE, A. I. Oparin. Modern classic in biochemistry, the first rigorous examination of possible evolution of life from nitrocarbon compounds. Non-technical, easily followed. Total of 295pp. 5⅜ x 8½.
60213-3 Pa. $4.00

PLANETS, STARS AND GALAXIES, A. E. Fanning. Comprehensive introductory survey: the sun, solar system, stars, galaxies, universe, cosmology; quasars, radio stars, etc. 24pp. of photographs. 189pp. 5⅜ x 8½. (Available in U.S. only)
21680-2 Pa. $3.75

THE THIRTEEN BOOKS OF EUCLID'S ELEMENTS, translated with introduction and commentary by Sir Thomas L. Heath. Definitive edition. Textual and linguistic notes, mathematical analysis, 2500 years of critical commentary. Do not confuse with abridged school editions. Total of 1414pp. 5⅜ x 8½.
60088-2, 60089-0, 60090-4 Pa., Three-vol. set $18.50

Prices subject to change without notice.

Available at your book dealer or write for free catalogue to Dept. GI, Dover Publications, Inc., 180 Varick St., N.Y., N.Y. 10014. Dover publishes more than 175 books each year on science, elementary and advanced mathematics, biology, music, art, literary history, social sciences and other areas.